THE UPPER ROOM

Disciplines

2016

UPPER
ROOM BOOKS®
NASHVILLE

An Outline for Small-Group Use of Disciplines

Here is a simple plan for a one-hour, weekly group meeting based on reading *Disciplines*. One person may act as convener every week, or the role can rotate among group members. You may choose to light a white Christ candle each week to signal the beginning of your time together.

Opening

Convener: Let us come into the presence of God.

Others: Lord Jesus Christ, thank you for being with us. Let us hear your word to us as we speak to one another.

Scripture

Convener reads the scripture suggested for that day in *Disciplines*. After a one- or two-minute silence, convener asks: What did you hear God saying to you in this passage? What response does this call for? (Group members respond in turn or as led.)

Reflection

- What scripture passage(s) and meditation(s) from this week was (were) particularly meaningful for you? Why? (Group members respond in turn or as led.)
- What actions were you nudged to take in response to the week's meditations? (Group members respond in turn or as led.)
- Where were you challenged in your discipleship this week? How did you respond to the challenge? (Group members respond in turn or as led.)

Praying Together

Convener says: Based on today's discussion, what people and situations do you want us to pray for now and in the coming week? Convener or other volunteer then prays about the concerns named.

Departing

Convener says: Let us go in peace to serve God and our neighbors in all that we do.

Adapted from *The Upper Room* daily devotional guide, January–February 2001. © 2000 The Upper Room. Used by permission.

THE UPPER ROOM DISCIPLINES 2016
© 2015 by Upper Room Books®. All rights reserved.

The Upper Room Books website: books.upperroom.org

Cover design: Left Coast Design, Portland, Oregon

Cover photo: Steve Terrill, SteveTerrillphoto.com

At the time of publication all websites referenced in this book were valid. However, due to the fluid nature of the internet some addresses may have changed, or the content may no longer be relevant.

Revised Common Lectionary copyright © 1992 Consultation on Common Texts. Used by permission.

Scripture quotations not otherwise identified are from the New Revised Standard Version Bible © 1989, Division of Christian Education of the National Council of the Churches of Christ in the United States of America. Used by permission. All rights reserved.

Scripture quotations marked AP are the author's paraphrase.

Quotations marked BCP are taken from The Book of Common Prayer (New York: The Church Hymnal Corporation, 1979)..

Scripture quotations marked CEB are from the Common English Bible. Copyright © 2010 Common English Bible. Used by permission.

Scripture quotations marked KJV are from the King James Version of the Bible.

Scripture quotations marked THE MESSAGE are taken from THE MESSAGE. Copyright © by Eugene H. Peterson 1993, 1994, 1995, 1996, 2000, 2001, 2002. Used by permission of Nav-Press Publishing Group.

Scripture quotations marked (NIV) are taken from the Holy Bible, New International Version®, NIV®. Copyright © 1973, 1978, 1984, 2011 by Biblica, Inc.™ Used by permission of Zondervan. All rights reserved worldwide. www.zondervan.com.

Quotations marked UMH are taken from The United Methodist Hymnal (Nashville, TN: The United Methodist Publishing House, 1989).

Scripture Overview commentary is taken from the CD-ROM Texts for Preaching: A Lectionary Commentary Based on the NRSV—Years A, B, and C (Louisville, KY: Westminster John Knox Press, 2007) Used by permission.

The week of October 24–30 first appeared in The Upper Room Disciplines 2004. Reprinted and used by permission.

Writers of various books of the Bible may be disputed in certain circles; this volume uses the names of the biblically attributed authors.

ISBN: 978-0-8358-1329-7

Printed in the United States of America

CONTENTS

FOREWORD

Discipline —the word evokes many responses that can create a riot of feelings. The term can arouse a sense of dread or excitement, anxiety or anticipation. Yet, the word itself merely suggests regular activity that schools us in behaviors that bring about perfection of skills or practices.

We all engage in disciplines that over time become routine. When awakening, most of us participate in rituals that include the normal activities of drinking coffee, eating breakfast, reading or watching the news, exercising, and brushing our teeth. These customs function as readily as breathing and stretching. Additionally, many of us include some regular practice of reading scripture, attending to meditative words, praying, and spending time alone with God. Others of us have decided not to practice these daily rhythms of life.

The Upper Room Disciplines 2016 invites us—whether we are longtime practitioners or are pondering beginning the habit of spiritual practice—to engage in daily periods of prayer, attention to scripture, and consideration of God's activity in our lives. I find *Disciplines* to be an indispensable and essential aid in delving even more deeply into these daily devotional practices.

The writers of *Disciplines* assist us as we consider and imagine profound understandings of who God is and how we respond to God's daily invitations. These materials take us into deeper engagement with scripture and reflection than do some other daily devotional materials. Writing for a week at a time on the scripture texts from the Revised Common Lectionary, the authors offer insights and ideas that invite us to engage in contemplation and consideration, giving us ways to think about commitments and behaviors that correspond to the daily summons of God.

As I type these words, I recognize the powerful importance of spending time alone each day with God. Yet, I also feel the pull of temptations that lure me into putting off this daily habit. Discipline calls forth intentionality and daily decisions. When I find myself in the place of deciding whether to commit to the daily time required for these spiritual practices, I remember three important quotations:

"The chains of habit are too weak to be felt until they are too strong to be broken." (Samuel Johnson, eighteenth-century English poet and writer)

"Prayer is the key of the morning and the bolt of the evening." (Mahatma Gandhi)

"Take the first step in faith. You don't have to see the whole staircase, just take the first step." (Rev. Dr. Martin Luther King Jr.)

These quotations convict me yet again of the crucial need to practice daily spiritual disciplines.

Upper Room Disciplines 2016 offers the annual gift of deciding to be disciplined—to schedule and to practice the rhythms of daily attention to God through reading scripture, praying, and reflecting. When we say yes to this invitation, we encounter the living presence of God who speaks to us yet again through words offered by these writers and practitioners of the Christian faith. Our engagement through use of this volume grants us the powerful opportunity to meet the living presence of the triune God—Father, Son, and Holy Spirit—the One who creates, redeems, and sustains us across the seasons of our lives.

—REV. KAREN A. GREENWALDT

Rev. Greenwaldt retired in 2013 from her work as the General Secretary, General Board of Discipleship, The United Methodist Church. She and her husband, Russell Harris, live in Waynesville, North Carolina, where she volunteers in hunger advocacy efforts and works as a fabric artist making tiny one-of-a-kind dolls, woven baskets, and other works of art.

Bring Us Home

JANUARY 1–3, 2016 • KENNETH M. LOCKE

Scripture Overview: These scriptures chosen to mark the new year give us a panorama of perspectives, from Ecclesiastes as a poetic musing on how life is measured out in seasons, to the vision in Revelation of what we commonly consider the end of time itself. Psalm 8 asks what the role is for humans in God's magnificent creation, and Matthew 25 gives us a sobering criterion for how that role might be judged. At the core of all these scriptures is a strong sense of God's presence and loving steadfastness in which we can rest.

Questions and Thoughts for Reflection

- Read Ecclesiastes 3:1-13. How often do you find yourself dwelling on the more "sober" aspects of opposites listed? When have you realized that this focus has caused you to miss the joy in your life?
- Read Psalm 8. In what ways can you recognize God's sovereign love in your life and how will this recognition change the way you live?
- Read Revelation 21:1-6a. God comes to be with mortals. In what ways does that understanding give you hope in your daily living?
- Read Matthew 25:31-46. What distinction do you make between career and vocation? How are you living out each?

Interim minister, Presbyterian Church (USA)

NEW YEAR'S DAY

Ecclesiastes can depress us with its time to mourn, to weep, to die. The writer lists fourteen "opposites" in a few short verses. All in all, they reflect twenty-eight facets of human life. So if we focus only on the sobering aspects, we'll overlook God's joyful imperative. Beyond our birth, choices and actions lie within human grasp, and wise is the person who recognizes the appropriate time for each. Life comes to us in an ordered fashion. Yes, there is a time for everything, even sorrow; but there is also a time to laugh and sing and dance. While life has its horrible moments, clearly God yearns for our happiness, and we play a role in discerning the right time for the right action.

As Psalm 8 points out, God has made us a little lower than the divine. God has crowned us with glory and honor and given us power over the earth and all that lives. But we cannot fail to notice that the psalm both opens and closes with emphasis on God's sovereignty. Our glory and honor falls within the parameters of God's oversight. Yes, the coming year will bring its share of hardship and sorrow. After all, there *is* a time for everything. But God has given us all creation, love, laughter, and meaningful work to fill our days. We "eat and drink and take pleasure in all [our] toil." God desires that the tenor of our lives be that of joy.

God of our past and future, your glory and majesty lie beyond our comprehension. However, we know you love us and want us to savor lives of love and happiness. So when inevitable difficulties and sorrows come our way, help us remember the fullness of your blessings. May our lives point toward Jesus, who suffered greatly yet enjoyed your goodness and love. Amen.

Is your career progressing as you'd like, or are you sensing a need for a change? *Career*, from the French word for racetrack, can serve us usefully. Wise career choices guide us from school to retirement in a meaningful and sometimes lucrative fashion. Poor career choices can leave us racing in circles.

Yet, more important than our career is our *vocation*. From the Latin verb meaning "to summon," our vocation is what we are summoned, or called out, to do with our lives.

Yesterday we acknowledged that God wants us to enjoy our work. Today we find that our work—what God calls us to do—involves feeding the hungry, clothing the naked, and visiting the prisoner. The labor God wants us to enjoy is caring for those at the bottom of the social and economic ladder, those who cannot care for themselves.

People who hear God's call and act on it vocationally, regardless of chosen careers, will know the joy of doing God's will and the peace of living in the kingdom, the state of grace and love, that God has prepared for us. Those of us who refuse to hear God's call and take action (perhaps because we concentrate *too much* on our careers) will find life a lot less fun.

The words of today's scripture follow six parables related to living in readiness for the coming of the Son of Man. Perhaps most surprising of all, the judgment does not hinge on confession of faith in Christ but on our vocation of loving care for the least and the lost. The fate of individuals depends on their choices. And those choices carry consequences: "These will go away into eternal punishment, but the righteous into eternal life." May we embrace our call to kingdom living in this new year.

Dear God, in this new year, help us avoid becoming careerist goats. Guide us in our common vocation of caring for the powerless so that we may know the pleasure of your gracious kingdom. Amen.

*I*s *that it?* As you reflect on the past year and look ahead to this new year, is this the question you raise? *Is that it?* Is that all there is? Will next year be any different or just more of the same?

We might ask the same question of this week's scriptures. We have affirmed that God loves us (Ps. 8). We know life has ups and downs, but God calls us to meaningful work and enjoyment of life (Eccles. 3:1-13). We know God calls us to labor on behalf of the powerless (Matt. 25:31-46). But is that it? Does every human life entail a few years of all of us doing the same thing— trying to enjoy God's gifts while caring for those who aren't so blessed? Is there nothing more? What's the point? It's enough to drive a person from existential angst to nihilistic despair.

The good news is that God *does* have greater plans for us than an eternity of human generations struggling to love and provide succor to others. Today's scripture offers a vision of hope.

God comes to be with us. These verses confirm that hope three times: "the home of God is among mortals"; "[God] will dwell with them"; and "God himself will be with them." God joins us and makes provision for God's people. Our hope resides in our relationship to God and to one another. These verses describe a time when there are no more powerless ones to help, a time when weeping and mourning and death are gone forever. The one "seated on the throne" gives water to the thirsty. The time will come when we can stop struggling and simply live in God's loving presence forever.

How can this year become a year of moving ourselves and the world a little closer to God's vision? What can you undertake this year to move the world closer to the reality of God's new heaven and new earth?

Starting the Year with God

JANUARY 4–10, 2016 • DAVID WIGGS

Scripture Overview: Baptism for most Christian communities is the sacrament by which new converts are received into communing fellowship, the sign and seal of their incorporation into Christ. The New Testament texts connect the presence of the Spirit with baptism. The Gospel text claims that the very divine presence that came upon Jesus that day in the Jordan comes upon Jesus' followers. The Spirit is a powerful reality that cannot be domesticated or bought and sold like a commodity on the market. Baptism is also an acknowledgment of one's belonging to God. The voice from heaven at Jesus' baptism declares him to be God's own Son. He is the servant, the agent of God's reign, a sovereignty so eloquently praised in Psalm 29. His followers in baptism are also commissioned to be subjects of God's rule and empowered agents of reconciliation.

Questions and Thoughts for Reflection

- Read Isaiah 43:1-7. Do you allow failure to be an experience or has it become your identity? How can you use failure in life to recognize that you are a beloved child of God?
- Read Psalm 29. Who can you bless today by praying for them by name?
- Read Acts 8:14-17. What is the single most important step you can take to deepen your prayer life now?
- Read Luke 3:15-17, 21-22. In what ways do you evidence yourself as one of God's people "filled with expectation"?

Senior pastor, The Boston Avenue United Methodist Church, Tulsa, Oklahoma

Mark Twain's Huckleberry Finn says that he tried prayer and it did not work. He put a shoebox under his bed and prayed that it be filled with gold. He awoke in the morning, and the box remained empty. Definitive proof that prayer is of no use, he concluded.

Often people make resolutions for the new year, but studies show that most do not see them through. Just like Huck Finn we give up too quickly. Too many people approach prayer in just such a way. But prayer is not magic, is it? Prayer involves developing a relationship with God. For a relationship to develop we must invest in it and watch for changes over time. What change might unfold in your life if you resolved in this new year to deepen your prayer life?

Notice how the apostles start with the new believers. They pray with them. Recall that earlier in Acts Peter and John also head the list of those leading the Christ-followers as they were "constantly devoting themselves to prayer" (1:13-14). Prayer figures prominently throughout The Acts of the Apostles.

When I allow my priorities to shift and allow matters other than prayer to fill the top slot, then I am not devoting myself to prayer. Is prayer the first thing on your "to-do" list? What steps can you can take to deepen your prayer life now? A new year of God's grace beckons; a fresh start awaits.

O God, draw us by your Holy Spirit to turn to you with new resolve. Amen.

Our scripture offers clues as to how prayer can help us draw closer to God. The opening verse says, "The people were filled with expectation." Life with God, a life of prayer, works best when we *expect* God to be at work for our good—when we believe that God *can* and *will* work for our good.

Many Christians have lost the expectation edge; we have not made it a practice or a habit to expect God to do wonderful, fabulous, amazing things in our midst. But we can sharpen that edge this year. We can employ our eyes of faith and discover that when we look, we are more likely to see God at work.

The Holy Spirit receives mention in both of our passages and each bears witness to the Holy Spirit's work in the world. The one coming does not bring what most of us would consider to be good news: a winnowing. Then verse 21 tells us that Jesus is praying. As he prays, the Holy Spirit manifests in their midst. A voice speaks and affirms Jesus as Son and Beloved. Here we glimpse the triune God: Father, Son, and Holy Spirit. Prayer brings relationship with God, moving us ever closer to intimacy with the Three-in-One. Had you been on the riverbank, would you have seen? Would you have heard?

We in the church celebrate Epiphany tomorrow and continue that seasonal focus in the Sundays that follow. During this time we center on the many ways that Jesus Christ reveals God to us, affirming Jesus as the vehicle through which God has come to humankind, Jews and Gentiles alike. May we pray and remain expectant in order to see God's at work in our lives.

O God, renew our prayer life with expectations that you are at work for good. Amen.

Epiphany

The meeting had begun by the time I slipped into the room. As I entered, persons were introducing themselves. One after another stated that he or she felt a special call or commissioning by God to be in service to persons living with AIDS.

I seldom hear people speak that way. I seldom hear people say with assurance that God has prepared them or called them or led them to a certain kind of work. And here an entire group of people affirmed God's communication with them and a calling to particular service! They felt led to meaningful and purposeful work for which they were equipped. Their ministries would implement part of God's plan for reaching and loving all God's family. Each was commissioned as a child of God and knew it.

Paul expresses to the Ephesians a powerful sense of God's presence; God has commissioned him, blessed him. And like those persons mentioned above, his commission and call involves a particular group of people: the Gentiles. Paul writes from a Roman prison, identifying himself not as a Roman prisoner but rather a prisoner for Christ. Therefore, he shifts from victim to victor. And his inclusion of the Gentiles as fellow heirs with the Jews promotes a unity, a oneness.

Knowing who you are and understanding the work to which God has called you can instill purpose and confidence in you despite the circumstances. Who are you? How do you, like those noted above, sense your commissioning as a child of God? What is your call? What has God's grace commissioned you to do? Whom will you serve?

O God, shape me into a servant for the gospel by the gift of your grace. Amen.

Where do people turn when they encounter struggles in their lives? I know that some people withdraw. Some people turn to friends or coworkers. Some look for books that might help. Others turn to drugs. Yet others turn to pornography or gambling or other addictive behaviors. Some people look to initiate newer, less complicated relationships. Some turn toward God. Think about to whom or where you would turn in a time of difficulty and struggle.

In today's reading, the psalmist celebrates God's sovereignty and the power and strength that accompanies God's rule. I find it remarkable that he notes, "The voice of the LORD causes the oaks to whirl, and strips the forest bare; and in his temple all say, 'Glory!'" The psalmist encourages his people to see God's power, majesty, and glory exemplified in this amazing storm, in God's raw power simply by speaking.

Can we sense God's presence in the midst of struggle? Will we take the psalmist's counsel and look for the power and majesty and glory of God, even in the midst of turbulent life circumstances? The psalmist prays for strength and peace: "May the LORD give strength to his people! May the LORD bless his people with peace!"

If you find yourself in the midst of struggles, draw from the psalmist's wisdom and look for God at work in the midst of those experiences. If not, pray for people you know who are struggling. Personalize your prayer for them using the psalm: May the Lord give strength to _____ (*insert the name*). May the Lord bless _____ with peace! Whom can you bless today by praying for them by name?

O mighty and majestic Lord, bless us with renewed strength and abiding peace. Amen.

At the end of my second year of college I found myself in a depressed state. I had fallen in love for the first time, and I had also fallen out of love that year. I was burned out from attending classes and from the sense of overwhelming study. Feeling like I couldn't go on, I dropped out of college. I felt like a failure: I had let my family down. I didn't measure up.

The question that struck me during my time out of school was this: Is this feeling of failure now my identity, or is this emotion an experience along the journey of life? When have you allowed failure to define you?

The prophet Isaiah writes to a people who have gone through the terrible ordeal of being taken over and taken away by a foreign power. In the wilds of Babylon the people have to decide if this shift will define them and be their new identity or if this is simply an experience along the way. In this chapter, Isaiah tells them that exile is only an experience; their identity as God's chosen people remains. They are about to move from a time of exile to homecoming. The saving God who "created" them and "formed" them also redeems. Like Jesus, who in baptism learns to whom he belongs, this people in a foreign land hear of God's love for them: "Do not fear, for I have redeemed you; I have called you by name, you are mine."

I finally returned to school and fell in love again. I continued to follow God's leading in my life. I realized my identity as a beloved child of God and acknowledged my failure as one of those universal experiences we all have along the way. Just as Isaiah assured his people, I experienced God's assurance: "I have called you by name, you are mine."

O loving God, assure us once again that you are ever present with us. Amen.

During a season of restlessness, I came across a prayer by Thomas Merton in which he expressed his inability to discern God's leading. He hoped only that his desire to please God and to follow God's will would be sufficient.

I prayed that prayer for months. Then one night I got a call from my supervisor. It was time for me to move to a new position. Suddenly I began sweating. I had not expected a move; I didn't see it coming. After my initial shock, I realized that the opportunity to move came as an answer to prayer.

Prayer is a peculiar mix of confidence and mystery. It may not be as simple as we wish it to be. It may not be as quick a fix as we desire, but prayer does open up peculiar possibilities that I am convinced only come through prayer.

Earlier in chapter 3 of Luke we read of John's message to the people and of the baptism he offers (3:3, 16). Then in today's passage, Jesus prays after his baptism and hears God's affirmation of him as Son and Beloved. The coming of the Spirit commissions and empowers Jesus for ministry; he takes up where John has left off.

How have you prayed in a season of restlessness? What words of affirmation and assurance is God offering you? Thomas Merton in his book *Thoughts in Solitude* wrote, "I believe that the desire to please you does in fact please you." As we pray and seek to follow God's call, we too will receive God's affirmation and assurance. We then find ourselves empowered to take up our unique task in the world.

O God, pour out upon us your words of love and delight as we seek to follow you. Amen.

One of Oklahoma's United Methodist district offices added the well-known *Interview with God* video clip (www.theinterviewwithgod.com) to their website, and visitor usage crashed the site. Usually twenty-five or so people visited the district site—suddenly over five hundred thousand came to the site. The district communications team moved the presentation to a separate site, and it received over two million visits in the first month. I think such popularity signals the number of people who are looking for help.

Just like the millions of people who visit such Internet sites, these people in Acts come with needs. They are searching and ready for something different to happen in their lives.

The verses prior to today's reading tell us that the people have believed and been baptized. Yet, as noted in verse 16, the Spirit has not yet come upon them. Now these apostles take the next step. Verse 15 tells us that they go to Samaria. What is the first thing they do? They pray for the baptized. And what do they pray for? They pray that these new believers "might receive the Holy Spirit." And why would they pray for that? What role does the Holy Spirit play in a believer's life?

After prayer and the laying on of hands, the believers in Samaria receive the Holy Spirit. They have an experience similar to the believers in Jerusalem; they all become one body.

What obstacles block you from receiving the presence, guidance, and power of the Holy Spirit? Throughout the book of Acts, the Holy Spirit serves as the presence of the risen Christ that brings the guidance and the power believers need to live a life of love as revealed in Jesus Christ. What a great place to start the year!

Lord, help us receive your Holy Spirit anew this year. Amen.

What Concern Is That to Me?

JANUARY 11–17, 2016 • JANE MARIE THIBAULT

Scripture Overview: The Old Testament texts contain refer to "dawn," "burning torch" (Isa. 62:1), and "light" (Ps. 36:9), which are familiar symbols for the Epiphany season; and the miracle of changing the water to wine at Cana is a traditional text for this part of the Christian calendar. The common theme is the amazing generosity of God. The psalmist sings of it in terms of God's "steadfast love," which comes in times of opposition and threat. The voice of Isaiah 62 can hardly contain itself. Jerusalem's vindication is at hand. In the story at Cana in John 2, Jesus answers the emergency of a depleted wine supply with provisions that both quantitatively and qualitatively go beyond what the original host could supply. First Corinthians 12 reminds us of the abundant gifts of the Spirit, leading first to a confession of Jesus as Lord and then to a variety of services for the common good of the church.

Questions and Thoughts for Reflection

- Read Isaiah 62:1-5. How can you work in union with God for the redemption of the world?
- Read Psalm 36:5-10. Where in your life can you recognize God's steadfast love?
- Read 1 Corinthians 12:1-11. What gifts has God given you? How can you use those gifts for God's service?
- Read John 2:1-11. How can you remain open to the needs of others and respond to those needs without being judgmental?

Clinical gerontologist and professor emerita in the Department of Family and Geriatric Medicine, University of Louisville; spiritual companion and retreat leader; member of the Kentucky Institute for Aging

This is Jesus' first "sign" in the Gospel of John: water to wine. Jesus' response to Mary's communication that the groom has run out of wine seems somewhat harsh—yet it sounds so true to normal family life! Mary has recognized a safe situation in which Jesus can meet a human need by exercising the gifts that he alone has. She doesn't tell him what to do; she communicates the need, but he knows very well (as do most children) what his mother expects of him. It seems that Jesus isn't eager to be pushed into action. Perhaps Mary believes that Jesus needs a gentle but firm nudge. Perhaps she senses his procrastination about demonstrating his gifts. Maybe she knows his fear, while remaining acutely aware of her own.

At Cana, Jesus seems to be backing down from his display of confidence when inviting disciples to follow him. Now it sounds as though he's having second thoughts and needs encouragement through the confidence his mother has in him.

How often have we taken an action that seemed like a good idea at the time but found ourselves trying to back out after further reflection? How often have we excused ourselves with the thought, *What does that have to do with me?* When has the encouragement and support of others made all the difference?

God, help me recognize your call when it comes through other people. Guide me when I ask, "What does that have to do with me?" Amen.

Jesus—as obedient son—responds to Mary's suggestion that he help with the wine situation, and the Gospel writer tells us that by doing so he "revealed his glory." What glory did he reveal? That he had supernatural powers? That his humility brought obedience despite its not being the right time? What does he teach us about God's realm through his actions? That God's generosity extends well beyond need?

Followers of Jesus can learn much from his response to this situation. The lessons include the following:

- We remain open to being made aware of others' needs, especially when we are asked to help in some way.
- When our own needs seem to conflict with those of another, we need to discern and then decide who or what takes precedence. Sometimes that depends on the wisdom and trustworthiness of the one who asks us to help. In Jesus' case, he trusted his mother, put his own plans aside, and responded to her discernment of immediate need.
- We try to avoid judgmentalism about the worthiness of the person or situation we are being asked to help. (Cana was not a life-or-death situation as were some of Jesus' later miracles—family honor was important, but some might judge that need as trivial.)
- Once we decide to help, we help to the utmost of our ability without worrying too much about the results. (Jesus' gift of 120 gallons of wine might tempt us to ask, "Was that much wine really healthy for the guests?" But Jesus didn't ask, teaching us that God's superabundant gifts require our responsible use!)

Dear God, make me more aware of the needs of your children, as well as the superabundance of the gifts you give so that I may attend to those needs. Amen.

K nowing our spiritual gifts allows us to answer the question, "Of what concern is that to me?" As a spiritual director I frequently encounter people trying to discern God's call—from young people testing their first vocation to retirees finally feeling free to devote themselves unreservedly to God's work.

One guideline I offer is the saying, "Your spiritual gift occurs where your human passion and God's desires for the world meet." This counsel presents three criteria for discerning a spiritual gift: 1) it is a gift, not a skill or an innate talent; 2) it is a form of service for the good of God's children; 3) it demonstrates that it is God who desires and accomplishes the work.

Paul notes, particularly as he writes to the church in Corinth, that in the Spirit a plethora of gifts exists. Unlike the dispute over the gift of speaking in tongues as the "primary" gift of confessing Christians, Paul lists many that the Spirit gives. And the diversity of gifts is rooted in the nature of God. The qualifying use of all the gifts is for the common good.

A scientifically gifted woman earned her M.D. when few women physicians practiced. Specializing in ophthalmology, she went on to enjoy both a thriving, lucrative practice and a prestigious university appointment. A deeply faithful person, in midlife she experienced an irresistible desire to serve God as a full-time pray-er in a cloistered religious community. The call to leave her successful career to pray confounded those who knew her. But the spiritual gift of faith enabled her to believe that God needed her as a pray-er for the well-being of all God's children. Now, at eighty-six, she believes that her decision to leave her work of physical healing to devote her life to spiritual healing made sense only in the context of the belief that it was God at work in her.

Dear God, help me discern my spiritual gift(s). May I use them to the fullest. Amen.

When we are trying to decide how to respond to a given life situation, do we base our decision on our understanding of God's will for our lives or on some need of our own ego? Today's passage guides our thoughts. Verses 1-3 note that we first acknowledge the one whom we confess: "Jesus is Lord!" That confession comes "by the Holy Spirit." Only after affirming our basic commitment does Paul look at the gifts themselves.

We then ask if our response to a situation matches up with our particular spiritual gift(s)—the one(s) necessary for the job. The Corinthians strongly valued the gift of tongues, which even today some congregations tag as the test of true spiritual maturity. We may not be attracted to that particular gift, but do we ever neglect the ones we have, wishing we had other gifts?

I personally would love to have the gift of healing; I have a friend who helps others in profound ways with that gift. She visited me after I was diagnosed with cancer and spent two days laying on hands and praying for me. I truly believe that I have been in remission from stage 4 lymphoma in part because of her gift of healing.

So—what are our gifts? Since I've been a teacher throughout my life, in a variety of settings and in many different ways, I believe my gift is the "utterance of knowledge." This gift doesn't sound very exciting when compared with healing or prophecy, but it serves the people of God for the "common good." What gifts do you possess, given by God? How are you using them to respond to concerns that arise in your life?

Dear God, I am often tempted to envy the spiritual gifts of others. When I do that, I downplay and neglect the gifts that you have given me. Help me realize that you don't give your gifts for our benefit but for the building up of the body of Christ. May I acknowledge that you are the one doing the work when I participate with you in using my gifts. Amen.

How can we apply Isaiah's message to our lives when looking for an answer to the question, "What concern is that to you and to me?" This passage clearly states the task: "For Zion's sake I will not keep silent, . . . I will not rest." The messenger bears news of jubilation, news of vindication and salvation.

The word *Zion* has many meanings: the actual city of Jerusalem; a symbol of the world to come; the church as the bride of Christ; and, ultimately, the place of connection between God and humanity. The builder will marry Jerusalem, a city once named Forsaken and Desolate. So too our relationship with God develops. We come from various walks of life and disparate life circumstances. We begin with servanthood, proceed to discipleship, then to friendship, and emerge—through faithfulness—into an intimate spousal relationship.

Our mandate is to spend our lives as coworkers with God for the redemption of the world. In gospel terms we are called to work each day for God's reign to come, God's will to be done—on earth as in heaven. Our destiny finds fulfillment in the marriage of the Creator and the created. God delights in this union and proposes to us as individuals. When we accept this proposal, we—in union with God and others—work to make our planet a place of peace, harmony, love. It becomes the "kin-dom" where God and God's people live, love, work, and play side by side and rest together at the close of the day.

Dear God, grant me your vision so that I live for the unity in you of all persons, places, and things. Help me say with great desire and energy, "I will not rest." Amen.

"For Zion's sake I will not keep silent. . . . I will not rest." Isaiah's vision of God's kingdom ("kin-dom") continues to inspire. In Luke 4:16-21 Jesus announces his own purpose as fulfilling Isaiah's expectations of vindication, and he expresses the promise that salvation will prevail in communities of loving-kindness, health, and freedom from oppression and poverty.

What does this have to do with us? How do we help to establish the kin-dom? Can we also say, "For God's sake I will not keep silent. I will not rest"? Or have we succumbed to what Pope Francis has called "spiritual Alzheimer's disease"—the loss of memory of our first encounters with God? Often, individual and collective passion for the vision dies from neglect and/or suffocation, rather than through major crises of faith. Over time, the little things deplete us of energy for God's plan: sleep deprivation, failure to find daily time with God, overeating, becoming too physically and mentally comfortable, resistance to necessary change.

Sometimes a cluttered lifestyle suffocates spiritual vitality: too much to do at work and at home; too much entertainment —sports, music, media, games, hobbies, exercise; too much collecting of unnecessary information; too much interest in what others are doing.

All of these things in moderation are fun, relaxing, even stress-relieving. Some promote health and well-being. But they can also become addictive distractions that turn our thoughts and actions from our relationship with God. Our activities may keep us silent and give us so much rest that our spiritual muscles turn to flab. Then we lose the energy we once had "for Zion's sake."

Dear God, startle me into renewed energy for your work. Wake me from my spiritual drowsiness. May I not neglect my relationship with you. Amen.

As the number of people gifted with many years increases, those suffering from Alzheimer's disease and other forms of dementia also increase. Such suffering often precipitates a crisis of faith in God's steadfast love. As a clinical gerontologist specializing in work with dementia patients and their caregivers, I'm often asked, "Where is God in all of this?" and "Why has God abandoned me (or my loved one?)" Many affected by dementia find it difficult to believe in the psalmist's phrase "you give them drink from the river of your delights" or similar assertions of faith. After a few years of total immersion in dementia care, I also had begun to question God's faithfulness—until I discovered MaryElla.

The resident of a dementia care facility, MaryElla could no longer remember her own name. One morning, while Jeannie, her aide, was dressing her, MaryElla wailed repeatedly in distress, "What's my name? I don't know my name! I can't remember who I am!" Jeannie, angry with God because her own mother had recently been diagnosed with dementia, saw MaryElla's anguish as her own mother's future, and her anger at God intensified. Disguising her own feelings, Jeannie replied, "Your lovely name is MaryElla!" Upon hearing her name, MaryElla immediately calmed down, smiled broadly, and laughed, saying "Half the time I don't know who I am"—and then she pointed to the crucifix on her bedroom wall and exclaimed loudly and with great joy, "But he does, and that's all that matters!"

Jeannie saw the light of God radiating from the light and truth of MaryElla's testimony. MaryElla's witness to God's steadfast love restored Jeannie's belief in God's faithfulness.

Dear God, open my eyes to the many ways you exhibit your steadfast love, not only in the good times but also in the difficult circumstances of my life and the lives of others. Amen.

Held by the Power of God's Word

JANUARY 18–24, 2016 • LARRY R. HYGH JR.

Scripture Overview: It is appropriate that the people of God be reminded time and again that they live by the divine word, ancient but ever new. Nehemiah 8 records the beautiful story of the people of the reconstituted community of Israel gathered as one listening to Ezra read the Torah. It is that same delight in the Torah that makes it the object of praise in Psalm 19. It renews the soul, instructs the ignorant, brings joy to the heart and enlightenment to the eye. But it functions also to expose secret and proud sins so that God's servants can live in total dependence on divine mercy. The Gospel text reminds us that the word of God can also bring rejection and rage as well as delight (Luke 4). The epistle lesson from First Corinthians does not focus immediately on the word of God, but it depicts for us a community constituted by the word, a community grappling with the very diversity Jesus explained from the Isaiah text.

Questions and Thoughts for Reflection

- Read Nehemiah 8:1-3, 5-6, 8-10. What are obstacles that prevent you from gathering with other Christians for Sunday worship or other opportunities throughout the week?
- Read Psalm 19. What can you learn about God from creation?
- Read 1 Corinthians 12:12-31*a*. What special gifts and graces do you bring to the body for the work of ministry in God's world?
- Read Luke 14:14-21. What hinders you from sharing the gospel in your daily life and routine?

Religious communicator, United Methodist Churches in Northern California and Northern Nevada

With the blessing of Artaxerxes, the king of Persia, Nehemiah returns to help rebuild and repopulate Jerusalem. Those left in Jerusalem (a majority of the population having been in exile for decades) restore its wall in just fifty-two days. After such a feat, the people gather in the square before the Water Gate to praise the Lord for their blessings. The Water Gate on the east side of the city afforded a space in which both laypeople and clergy could gather to hear the word of God. Note that those included were "all who could hear with understanding." The people gather in the presence of the book of the law of Moses; they stand and listen for six hours. All remain "attentive" to the reading. This exiled and disparate people hear words that speak of God's work among them. These words empower.

We as God's people still respond to the call to assemble and to praise God in times of celebration and tribulation—to be imbued with the power of God through the word. On Sunday mornings our culture offers many alternatives to assembling in Christian community. Folks throw the golf clubs in the trunk and head out for a round of golf. Boats launch into lakes for a day of fishing. Children's organized sports give no heed to the sabbath. Some folks simply enjoy sleeping late on the weekend.

Christian assembly as a means of receiving the power of word and community still remains effective. And God still desires our attentiveness to God's law and gathering in community.

God of hope, help me to rise daily to give you the glory for all my many blessings. Amen.

With the renewal of the city, the people delight in hearing God's law read aloud. They realize that God's hand has been instrumental in the events that have led to their restoration. They listen attentively. They raise their hands in expectation and bow their heads in obedience and submission. Upon Ezra's blessing of the Lord, they respond with a hearty "Amen, Amen." They agree with Ezra's blessing of the Lord, and they accept the law as read to them.

Worshiping God and living by God's commandments lay at the center of Israel's existence. God's people rejoice as the words of the law affirm their covenant relationship with God and their keeping the commandments as an example to all the earth. They rejoice in God as their deliverer.

When the people gather, they come with a reverent attitude. Even as Ezra *opens* the book of the law, they stand. They acknowledge by their actions that they worship a God worthy of praise, honor, and glory. The gesture of their hands, the bowed heads and prostrate bodies indicate the attitude of their hearts.

Growing up in east Texas, I was taught to enter into worship reverently. My family took worship seriously. On Sunday, we gathered to give thanks and celebrate the holy of holies. We gathered as the body of Christ to grow and learn and then to disperse into the world to be the hands and feet of Christ. We wore our Sunday best to worship. I witnessed elders who prayed fervently on their knees. The choir sang praises to God, and the pastor preached for the transformation of people's lives.

How can we come to worship with an expectancy and obedience that leads to an Amen experience?

Almighty God, I offer you my worship and praise. May I experience the power of your word. Amen.

As a result of their time together in the reading and hearing of God's word, the people develop a clearer perception of God's will for their lives. They come with reverence, attentiveness, and active participation. Ezra and those assisting him read from the law and offer interpretation to enhance the people's understanding. Perhaps in hearing and understanding the law, the people realize their lives are far from measuring up to its standards; Ezra encourages them not to mourn or weep.

We affirm that God acts in our best interest. As we assemble in community for worship and Bible study, we gain an increased knowledge of God's will and leave with a determination to follow that will to the best of our ability

Ezra reminds the people of the holiness of their gathering. It will be a feast day. This passage ends with the phrase "for the joy of the Lord is your strength." And even as Ezra sends them away from their community in the square to feast, he encourages their remembrance of community and the need to assure provision for those who have nothing. Together or apart, the community exercises the responsibility of care for one another.

Still today, the joy of the Lord will be our strength. A rejoicing heart does not arise from a life that exists without difficulty but from a life that is rooted in faith as its foundation.

Despite our circumstances—whether exiled or lost—the joy of the Lord is our strength. We look beyond our struggles and doubts to the purpose for which God has called us. We see God's acts of restoration in our lives and experience joy and renewal.

All-knowing God, I come to you with reverence and attentiveness. Empower and invigorate my life to serve your will. Amen.

The psalmist calls us to join with all creation in praise of God: "The heavens are telling the glory of God; and the firmament proclaims his handiwork." The opening verses of this psalm present day and night as a continuous process of praise. The very heavens and firmament instruct us in the nature of praise and in bearing witness to the work of God among us.

I have traveled the world and often wonder how folks cannot believe in God. To me, if you've ever seen a sunrise or a sunset anywhere in the world, then you bask in the glow of God's radiance.

In the hustle and bustle that makes up our daily routines, we can forget to pause and notice God's handiwork all around us. Our constant electronic connections distract us from the world at hand. Work and hurry consume our days. How do we slow down enough to listen to creation's testimony and witness?

Most days I begin the morning with a short run. I time the run to coincide with my arrival at one of the small ponds near my residence, an area filled with ducks and geese. Each day, I pause near the pond and watch the sun rise while the geese take off in flight. Only God can make the sun rise each day and give new mercies every morning. When I lived in Southern California, I would often find myself at the beach in the evening watching the sun set into the Pacific Ocean. It's majestic and glorious.

In each of these instances, I took the time to see God's clockwork in the form of night turning into day and day turning into night. Take time, for "the heavens are telling the glory of God." Take time to listen to the silent speech of the universe.

Help me, God, to pause for a moment today and watch a sunrise or a sunset. Amen.

Psalm 19 has three sections. "The heavens declare the glory of God" begins the first section and concludes with verse 6 concerning the revelation of Creator God in the midst of creation. The second part begins in verse 7 and runs through verse 11, which commends God's law. The final few verses reflect the response of the person of faith to God's commands.

In verse 7, the poetry and focus of the psalm begin to change. The focus shifts to the "law of the LORD." The psalmist expresses great joy at being part of a people whom God has blessed with the law and its promises. While the transition seems abrupt, the psalmist understands that just as the sun encompasses all the earth with its radiance and heat, so nothing and no one can hide from God's word through the law, which enlightens all.

As noted by the psalmist, God's commands revive the soul, bring wisdom, rejoice the heart, and enlighten the eyes. These decrees, precepts, commandments, ordinances not only bring us joy, but our keeping them protects us from our transgressions and ourselves. We glimpse the good life that God has in store if we follow God's commands. The psalmist also issues a warning about the danger of turning our backs to those commands. The laws of the Lord are perfect and have stood the test of time.

This passage invites us to look at our lives and recognize the possibilities of joy more than judgment, healing more than condemnation, creativity more than legalism. The commands of God intend to help us lead good lives, orderly lives, and joy-filled lives. The psalm closes with a prayer that many preachers use to open their sermons, "Let the words of my mouth and the meditation of my heart be acceptable to you, O LORD, my rock and my redeemer." May it be so.

God of life, help me to follow your commands and turn from my transgressions. Amen.

We are all members of Christ's body, the church. The members of the Corinthian church seemingly disagree about the value of spiritual gifts; they have established a hierarchy of gifts and are perhaps choosing to stress one gift to the exclusion of the others. Paul reminds them that God creates the variety of gifts; therefore, differences enhance the unity of the body. God bestows gifts upon each of us; each gift brings certain aspects and values to the whole; each is useful and necessary for the other. Just as our physical body parts depend upon one another to function, all Christians depend upon others in order to function appropriately. The objective becomes the good of the entire body of Christ.

Paul's "still more excellent way" does not describe a gift to attain at the exclusion of the other gifts but a more excellent way of striving for those gifts. Christians are to "strive for the greater gifts," which Paul develops in chapter 13. Love becomes the binding force.

Have you ever been part of a team? In my growing-up years, I played little league sports and participated in a number of other team activities. I learned a lot about teamwork from these experiences. Whether executing a precision marching drill, drafting school policy, or trying to outpace an athletic opponent, each member of the team played a vital role. The end product depended on everyone working together to accomplish that stated goal. All then receive honor.

As members of the body of Christ, Christ's team, we care for one another with mutual affection. We affirm others' gifts, acknowledging our dependency upon one another.

Creator God, help me to use your gifts for the building up of the entire body of Christ. Amen.

Jesus emerges from forty days in the wilderness and goes to the region of Galilee, teaching in synagogues and getting favorable reviews. In his hometown of Nazareth he gathers with the men of the village at the synagogue and reads from the scroll of the prophet Isaiah, "The Spirit of the Lord is upon me, because he has anointed me to bring good news to the poor. He has sent me to proclaim release to the captives and recovery of sight to the blind, to let the oppressed go free, to proclaim the year of the Lord's favor." He then adds, "Today this scripture has been fulfilled in your hearing." With these words, Jesus challenges the status quo.

This story continues the emphasis on the power of God's word with which we began the week. Jesus proclaims that his coming fulfills the words of Isaiah 61. He is the long-awaited messiah who has come to usher in an era of good news—the kingdom is at hand. I find it interesting that Luke opens this bit of scripture with widespread approval of Jesus' teaching. Luke 4:22 notes that "All spoke well of him and were amazed at the gracious words that came from his mouth." Only in later verses when those in the synagogue realize that Jesus intends to bring release to *all* people do things turn ugly.

Having lived most of my adult life in urban areas, I have witnessed street preachers standing on street corners and in subway cars proclaiming the good news of release and healing. They enthusiastically and energetically offer the world the good news. Jesus claims Isaiah's proclamation as his mission; it remains our calling and mission today. What hinders you from sharing the gospel in your daily life and routine?

Eternal God, may I proclaim and live out your good news. Amen.

Leaning upon God from Birth

JANUARY 25–31, 2016 • KARA LASSEN OLIVER

Scripture Overview: This week's lessons affirm the reality and illustrate the remarkable results of being known, claimed, and called by God. God "knew" Jeremiah even before he was "formed . . . in the womb" (Jer. 1:5). Paul's teaching to the Corinthians about love is grounded in the affirmation that "I have been fully known" (1 Cor. 13:12). In language reminiscent of Jeremiah, the psalmist professes that it was God "who took me from my mother's womb" (71:6). The fulfillment of the scripture that Jesus announces in Luke 4:21 involves the claim of God on his life: "The Spirit of the Lord is upon me" (4:18). To be known, claimed, and called by God means to be equipped "to accomplish abundantly far more than all we can ask or imagine" (Eph. 3:20). The lessons offer an opportunity for us to consider God's claim on us. The good news is that a share of God's Spirit is ours as well, to equip and empower us in every circumstance to live and love in accordance with God's righteous purposes for us and the world.

Questions and Thoughts for Reflection

- Read Jeremiah 1:4-10. Consider in all humility what God has appointed you to be in your family, your church, your community, the world. Name aloud any protests and fears.
- Read Psalm 71:1-6. What attribute of God do you need to see in your life? Be bold in prayer, and ask God to reveal God's presence through wisdom, healing, power, and compassion.
- Read 1 Corinthians 13. How can you point to God in the life of a young person you know?
- Read Luke 4:21-30. God seeks to broaden our perspective, to help us see the needs of those beyond our immediate family, congregation, and communities. Where is God calling you?

Upper Room Books author; Director of Publishing for Discipleship Resources International, training writers in Africa

My fourteen-year-old daughter, Claire, leaves in a few days to attend boarding school. My husband and I have agonized that we have not finished teaching and preparing her—that she will leave our home speaking and reasoning like a child as she goes quickly to live independently like an adult.

The scripture lessons this week remind me that God's love surrounds us even in our mother's womb. God's love provides strength and refuge for us, and God's love can sustain us even when we face persecution—just as it sustained and gave Jesus courage. I want my daughter to know, have experienced, and trust in the breadth and depth of this love. How have we as family members pointed to God's love, demonstrated God's love, and allowed opportunities to stretch and test that love so that Claire believes that it will always hold and support her?

I had assumed that I would be present to help Claire navigate new academic and social situations that might appear to her as if looking "in a mirror dimly." I imagined wiping away the grime of peer pressure to see the truth underneath. I had hoped to stand behind her at the mirror and compliment her beauty and strength when she couldn't see them for herself. And to point daily to the love of God until she could discover it for herself.

Now I must learn again to trust that faith, hope, and love abide—even in a distant boarding school. I must also trust that the greatest of these, love, surrounded Claire before her birth and will be with her daily and forever.

Parent God, be with all parents who are separated from their children—whether by geography, misunderstanding, or unresolved conflict. May each trust in your love for the other. Amen.

Today we step into scripture and overhear Jeremiah's call to serve the Lord through an intimate conversation between God and Jeremiah. God calls to Jeremiah whom God formed in the womb, "I choose you. Consecrate you. Appoint you." And Jeremiah protests, "Uhhh, I don't know, God." Then follows God's assurance, "No, really. I choose you. Do not be afraid." And finally a sign (a touch to the mouth) and a vision (of plucking up and planting).

These verses record a unique and powerful moment in Jeremiah's life. But this particular story speaks to our universal reaction to God's calling throughout our faith story and in our contemporary lives. Consider Jeremiah, called to serve but afraid to speak on God's behalf. Yet God provides assurance, assistance, and a sign. The gift of this story comes in the reminder that when God calls we will likely be uncertain and afraid.

We stand in good company. Jeremiah and Moses protested; Sarah laughed at the promise of children; Esther struggled to believe the power of her place in history. But God knows us, loves us, and believes in our potential. God, who formed us in the womb, longs for our participation with God for good and invites us to use our unique gifts to bring the reign of God here on earth. God can transform our weakness and woundedness into strength and healing for the world.

I pray that you hear God's call upon Jeremiah as *your* call this day, a specific call, true for every believer. Read your name in verse 5, "(<u>Name</u>), before I formed you in the womb I knew you, and before you were born I consecrated you." Raise your concerns and then hear God's words of assurance, "Do not be afraid . . . , for I am with you."

Gracious God, grant us confidence that you know us intimately and love us unconditionally. Give us the humility to trust your call and the boldness to live it out. Amen.

My family and I had the privilege of serving with The United Methodist Church in Malawi. The most powerful time in worship for me came during the prayers of the people. Then the entire congregation would begin praying aloud, each in his or her native language—English, Chichewa, Shona, or French. Some people whispered, others shouted. Some clapped, some swayed. What struck me more than the cacophony of prayer was that in the snippets of prayer that I understood, congregational members were calling on God to remain faithful to God's own character.

A woman with a sick child would call on God the great Healer and demand healing for her child. A father would call on God as Teacher and plead for school fees for his children. And yet another requested that the Sovereign God resolve conflict in her life. Through the prayers of the people, I experienced a mutuality in prayer that I had not known before. The congregation knew God's attributes, knew the names of God; they held God accountable to God's nature.

It's the same in Psalm 71:3. The psalmist asks, pleads, tells God to be a refuge and strong fortress. "Be those things for me," I can hear a Malawian church member shouting during worship. Why? Because as the same verse states, "You are my rock and my fortress." I learned a profound lesson: The names for God—Almighty, Prince of Peace, Shepherd—are not randomly assigned or flippantly chosen. The names for God express God's demonstrated attributes, abilities, and presence in the lives of God's children. And we can count on God to display Almighty power, to bring peace, to provide. We can pray to God with great confidence.

Dear God, Rock and Redeemer, Light and Shepherd, demonstrate your faithfulness, forgiveness, and protection. We call on you, trust in you, lean on your character. Amen.

I long for a prayer life like the psalmist's. I long for an abiding trust in God that allows me to be so frank. I want a boldness that permits me to be so direct. I desire an intimacy that leads to prayer that is more conversation than words in the wind.

Read aloud verses 4-6. I imagine an elderly person, one who has prayed and lived faithfully and volunteered and sacrificed. Suddenly this person faces persecution, severe trial, and aggressive enemies. And in old age, confident of God's love, experienced in God's ways, unafraid of frank conversation with God, she stands with hand on hip and finger wagging, "Hey! I've leaned on you from birth. You created me and know my limitations. Rescue me now. I praise you continually."

The psalmist's prayer is not a last-ditch effort, a phone-a-friend moment. The prayer evidences continued conversation based on a lifetime of joys and trials, successes and failures that she and God have lived together. Nor is the prayer a threat. The relationship, trust, and confidence in each other will not fail based on God's response. The psalmist feels comfortable in her honesty with God.

And that's what I long for in my prayer life: that each interaction with God, plea and prayer, step forward and misstep, will increase our mutual trust and confidence. I know that God will continually be my hope and that God will rejoice as I mature from the womb, through my youth to adulthood, and into an elderly age when we talk as friends.

Dear God, let all my words to you be honest and true. Open my ears to hear your responses, equally honest and true. Rescue me. And my praise will be continually of you. Amen.

Ipreached the word of God but did not know God's love for myself. I protested injustice as a demonstration of love but not in response to my own belovedness. I have taught and witnessed God's love revealed to others while covering my eyes to the revelation myself. I have given away my possessions and followed God out of love for neighbor but always to prove that God loved me too.

And I gained nothing.

Not until I had no pulpit to stand in. No passion for the injustice around me. No one to teach. And I did not know the name of my neighbors. Then, when I could not do and demonstrate and point to evidence of God's love; then, without job or ministry; then when sadness and inertia enveloped me, I heard God say, "You are beloved."

In my life I wanted to live and enact and witness to the love of God. I dedicated my life to ministry—writing, preaching, ministry with youth. And I misunderstood that loving others is not the same as knowing I am loved. Speaking in the tongues of theology and Christian education without understanding my belovedness, I ran out of words. Clanging the symbols of injustice without the refilling love of God's power left my ears ringing, unable to appreciate the music all around me. When I gave away the physical trappings of my life, I found an empty soul.

And there, speechless, exhausted, and empty I was shocked to discover that God loved me. It wasn't the activity and bylines and sermons that God loved. God loved me.

Faith, hope, and love abide, these three; and the greatest of these is love.

God of love, come to us in the quiet moments, in the stillness, the nonactivity. Help us feel your deep, abiding love as pure as a parent for a child at the moment of birth—hope and joy and miraculous. Beloved. Amen.

Jesus grew up in a devout Jewish home. He read and studied scripture, observed the rituals and holidays. He became a teacher and healer, respected and admired. Word of his deeds and miracles has made it back to his hometown before he stands to read scripture in his home synagogue. And as he declares the scripture fulfilled in their hearing, they all "spoke well of him and were amazed at the gracious words that came from his mouth." But within the span of eight verses, the loving crowd turns against him, threatening to throw him off a cliff.

In his words after his reading of scripture, Jesus reminds the congregation that prophets of the past were called beyond their hometowns, that God used prophets to deliver people outside their social and tribal groups, that prophets healed those whom God chose. And the people "were filled with rage" that the young man they had helped to raise and train and whom they claimed as their own would not give them preference, would imply that God worked among people of all nations. And so they drag him to the cliff.

Listening to God in prayer, following the example of Jesus, obeying the prompting of the Holy Spirit can nudge us outside of our comfort zones to work for God's reign to come on earth. And that can make people uncomfortable, especially those who have invested the most in our spiritual formation and journey of discipleship.

We must continue to trust that the more freely we offer grace, the broader we spread love, the more deeply we work for reconciliation, the more all people sense God's presence.

God of grace, we trust that every scripture verse we read, every prayer we offer, every act in the name of Jesus Christ will form us more completely into your likeness so we may serve you faithfully and courageously in and for the healing of the world. Amen.

Discipleship Resources, International is a ministry of The United Methodist Church dedicated to providing church resources beyond the United States of America that are written by indigenous authors, addressing their particular ministry challenges, and providing the resources at prices that pastors and laypeople can afford.

Imagine the places in the world where a woman receives God's word without a journal or computer to record them; a place where only the few who have memorized the church hymns can sing them because the hymns do not exist in print. Consider the places where entire congregations and swaths of countries sing hymns in a second or third language because the hymns have not been translated into their native languages.

God tells Jeremiah that God will put words in his mouth, words powerful enough to destroy and overthrow, powerful enough to build and to plant. And those very words have been recorded, printed, mass-produced, and sold so that we can read them, learn from them, be inspired by them. Read them today, set them aside, and pick them up again tomorrow to read and gain inspiration.

God placed words in Jeremiah's mouth to call Israel back to the commandments and covenant made through Moses. And God continues to place words in the mouths of people around the globe. I have had the privilege of leading writing workshops where people record the words that live inside them in pen and ink for the first time, read them aloud, pass them around. And some, eventually, find their way into print. What a miracle of God's grace that the word can enter the world one person at a time and reach thousands.

Writer of the world, thank you for your Word made flesh in Jesus Christ, for the preservation of your word in holy scripture. Amen.

With Unveiled Faces

FEBRUARY 1–7, 2016 • DAVID L. EASTMAN

Scripture Overview: The texts for Transfiguration Sunday insist that glory is the right word for God as well as those touched by God's presence. The psalmist praises the exaltation of God above all people. The Exodus text depicts God's glory and its consequences for human beings. Moses, by virtue of speaking with God, under- goes a change so dramatic that the people of Israel cannot even look on his face. In the passage from Second Corinthians, Paul draws on this story of Moses to make the radical point that, in the Christ-event, God enables all to participate in the glory of God. All can see the glory of God (3:18) and, indeed, as Paul states in a verse that follows our passage, all believers have "knowledge of the glory of God" in Jesus' face (4:6). As Peter learns, God's glory can be neither reduced nor controlled.

Questions and Thoughts for Reflection

- Read Exodus 34:29-35. Where do you see or experience God's grace in your daily life?
- Read Psalm 99. What does it mean to you to know that the same God who defends and protects also desires intimacy with you?
- Read 2 Corinthians 3:12–4:2. How can you be more open to God's spirit working in the world? How can you reflect God's grace in the world?
- Read Luke 9:28-43. In what areas of life can you listen more to Jesus?

Assistant Professor of Religion, Ohio Wesleyan University, Delaware, Ohio

We can certainly imagine the scene. Moses, the leader of God's people, comes down from the holy mountain with two stone tablets. On them are written the Ten Commandments, the basic teachings of God about holy living. But the scene here is tainted, because this is not the first time Moses has come down from Mount Sinai nor is this the first time he has brought tablets.

Earlier Moses had received the Ten Commandments for the first time, but misbehavior in the camp below interrupted his meeting with the Almighty. The people back in camp had constructed a golden calf and begun to worship it as a god, thereby violating God's first commandment that they serve no other gods. Yet while Moses stands in God's presence, even as the glory of God covers the foot of the mountain, the people disobey. How can they break the first commandment with God so near?

And what about us? How many times do we break God's commandments at such moments? How many times on the way home from church do we speak ill of the pastor or worship leader or lose patience with our children? How often are we so near to God and yet so far away?

As we learn from this story, these moments grieve God— but note the divine response. God does not withdraw from the mountain or write off the Israelites. Instead, God sends Moses back with new tablets, as if to say, "Why don't we try this again?" Just as with the Israelites at the foot of the mountain, God offers us mercy again and again.

Dear Lord, thank you for not giving up on us. Amen.

When I was in seminary, one of my roommates fell in love with the woman he would eventually marry. I never had to ask if he had seen her on a particular day because I could see on his face the glow of having spent time with his beloved. He looked different.

Today's passage tells us that Moses actually looks different when he returns from God's presence. God's glory radiates from his skin. His face shines so brightly that everyone fears him. He finally decides to wear a veil in order to relieve their anxiety; yet in God's presence he removes the veil to bask fully in the divine brilliancy.

God may not call us away onto a holy mountain to meet, but as Christians we can commune with the Almighty anywhere. We can pray and talk with God in the privacy of our bedroom, in the car while driving our kids to school, at work, at our child's soccer practice, wherever.

When we meet with God in these places, how does that affect us? Do we look different? I'm not talking about physical appearance, as if following God means we have to smile all the time. (We don't. Just read the Psalms.) I'm talking about our entire being. Do our meetings with the Almighty through reflection, Bible study, prayer—even reading this devotional—change us in some visible way? When friends or colleagues need and search for hope, can they look at us and see the reflection of God's glory in our lives?

Dear Lord, may my meetings with you change me so that I will draw other people to you. Amen.

With Unveiled Faces

Often at the beginning of worship, the worship leader invites God's presence into the gathered assembly. When have you reflected on the significance of this invitation? Frequently we equate God's presence with a moving testimony or perhaps music that lifts our spirits toward heaven. We desire God's presence among us because we believe it will enrich our spiritual experience.

But in the Bible, God's presence does not always evoke warm, fuzzy feelings. As the psalmist here describes, this exalted Lord inspires overwhelming awe. People tremble, and the earth quakes because of the Lord's power. Our response is praise that comes from a recognition of how mighty and how holy God is. But God does not bully or remain distant and aloof. God answers those who cry out for help. God loves justice and fairness and has shown this on many occasions to the people.

The psalmist then reminds us that Moses had experienced God's presence in a tangible way. Recall the dark cloud that covered Mount Sinai while God met with Moses. God spoke out of this cloud, and yet the people could not come near the mountain lest God's glory overwhelm them.

Here, however, the psalmist issues a striking invitation: Come to this very mountain to worship. The psalmist encourages us to approach and share in intimacy with God—this glorious and holy God is accessible to us. The same God who defended the Israelites and forgave their sins waits to meet with us, to defend us, to fight for justice, and to forgive our sins.

O Lord, we are grateful for your awesome power—a power far beyond our imagining—that is able to forgive our sins and to equip us for every good work. Amen.

In this section of Second Corinthians, Paul emphasizes the powerful work of the Holy Spirit. Prior to this passage he has drawn a contrast between the law of God being written on the stone tablets given to Moses (old covenant) and the dynamic nature of the new covenant in Christ signified by the activity of the Spirit. The latter is greater and displays the glory of God more brilliantly. After spending time with God, Moses' skin glowed brightly. How much more will believers shine with Spirit power!

Because we have this Spirit, we may boldly proclaim God's truth and reflect God's glory. But Paul also offers a warning here. Even though the Israelites witnessed God's glory at Mount Sinai, they turned away from following God's laws. Their memories were short; soon they acted as if their time at Mount Sinai had never happened. Some of his Jewish brothers and sisters, Paul says, are hard-hearted. They may hear the words given to Moses, but they have forgotten the glory of the one who gave them.

For followers of Christ, God's glory has come in a greater form—the Spirit. Since we have this greater revelation, we should receive it without hindrance (without the "veil").

But do we? Do we accept God's teaching and the work of the Spirit openly, or do we create a barrier to obscure it? In what ways do we become hard-hearted? How do we prepare to receive God's instruction and follow the Spirit's prompting?

Lord, by your grace remove any barrier or obstacle that may stand between you and me. And allow me to receive from you with the veil removed. Amen.

The apostle is noted for using vivid imagery in his letters. He attempts to persuade his audience by employing metaphors to explain spiritual truths. In this passage he strongly emphasizes "seeing." Because the veil is removed when we turn to the Lord, we can all see the glory of God in a way that was not possible before Christ. But how do we see this glory?

Paul says that sight comes "as though reflected in a mirror," and when we look in a mirror, what do we see? We see ourselves. Not only do we behold God's glory, but we can reflect it. As we grow in our faith, our image grows "from one degree of glory to another." We more accurately reflect the divine image to those around us. This occurs not by our strength but by God's grace, which gives us strength to carry on in difficult times.

The other image Paul uses is that of transformation. As we approach the commemoration of the Transfiguration of Jesus, we keep in mind that transformation and transfiguration bear close relationship. The apostles observe an amazing occurrence involving Jesus, and Paul says that each believer undergoes his or her own transformation as well. Just as three disciples bore witness to the Transfiguration of Jesus, those around us bear witness to our transformation as we grow. Can others see this? What about our neighbors? our children? the server in our favorite coffee shop? May we never "lose heart," knowing that our lives direct others toward Christ as Christ continues to transform us.

Lord, by your grace help me vividly reflect your glory to all those around me and make me a mirror that shines more and more brightly. Amen.

The disciples seem to have a sleeping disorder. Every time Jesus asks them to wait with him while he goes off alone, they doze off. Do you remember that this will happen later in the garden of Gethsemane? Here Peter, John, and James have trouble staying awake and almost miss an amazing event. If we imagine the story, we might assume that the groggy disciples wake up when Jesus begins glowing and two men suddenly appear with him. At first they may have wondered if they are dreaming. *How can this be real?*

Overall the disciples do not come off well in this story, but they do understand the significance of what they witness. We as believers have received a rich inheritance. Moses represents for them, as for us, one who obeyed God's call despite overwhelming odds, led the people to freedom, and received the commandments that told God's people how to live. Elijah, a great prophet, spoke out against oppression and dared to challenge corrupt rulers. God worked powerfully through both these men. We, inheritors of their faith, follow the same God who empowered them. We stand in their shadows and on their shoulders.

In our modern world we can easily lose sight of our past and the legacy handed down to us, but the disciples hold this fact firmly in mind. The writer of Hebrews speaks of the "great cloud of witnesses" that surrounds us (12:1). Here the disciples catch a fleeting glimpse of those witnesses. What life experiences afford us glimpses of that great cloud?

Lord, I thank you for the many faithful women and men who have passed on the faith generation after generation so that eventually the gospel might come to me. Empower me to run my part of the race and to become part of the cloud of witnesses for others. Amen.

TRANSFIGURATION SUNDAY

The disciples, "weighed down with sleep," look up to see Jesus in dazzling clothes talking with two of the great heroes of the faith. Peter, as is often the case, speaks first. He states enthusiastically that he wants to erect shrines for Jesus and the two visitors. The Gospel writer indicates that Peter has missed the point. So what does God (once again in the form of a cloud as in Exodus) tell the disciples to do as a result of their experience? Listen to Jesus. The heavenly voice identifies Jesus as the Son, just as at his baptism. Now the voice also specifies that they need to listen. But what do they need to hear?

Immediately prior to this passage, Luke's Gospel recounts Jesus' prediction of his death and resurrection. Luke does not record the disciples' response, but Matthew and Mark indicate that the disciples do not understand Jesus' words or they try to silence him when he speaks of his death.

Is the prediction of Jesus' death the very thing the disciples have refused to hear? Even as Jesus stands transfigured before them and speaks with the two visitors about his impending departure, do the disciples still not understand? Looking back, we ask how they could have missed this bit of information.

In what areas of our lives do we need to listen to Jesus? What obvious things are we missing? How often have we responded to the Lord with enthusiasm and good intention, as Peter does, without taking time to listen? What might God want to say to us right now, if we would only listen?

Our Father in heaven, just as Jesus was made radiant with your glory, you desire to renew and transform each one of us. May I learn to wait on you and listen so that I may move in step with your Spirit rather than trying to run ahead on my own. Amen.

Gratitude for All We Have Received

FEBRUARY 8–14, 2016 • ELAINE J. W. STANOVSKY

Scripture Overview: What does it mean to call on God? Israel exists because it cries to God out of its bondage, and God delivers. The psalmist is convinced of the personal and profound manner in which he has offended God and shattered their relationship. In casting himself on God's grace, the psalmist acknowledges God's role as the unique savior of faithful people, and the result of God's intervention is a changed and redirected life. The story of Jesus' temptation offers a strong rejoinder to those who would claim that loving God and calling on God result in rescue in any and all circumstances. God's care is not a commodity to be gained by human beings through wheedling; it is, instead, a promise that no one ventures outside the realm of God's care. To call on God is not to ask for power to be dispensed but to acknowledge human finitude and divine providence.

Questions and Thoughts for Reflection

- Read Deuteronomy 26:1-11. How do you employ the three-fold method of (1) giving, (2) remembering and reciting, (3) celebrating and sharing?
- Read Psalm 51:1-17. Where in your life is God granting you courage to make a needed change?
- Read 2 Corinthians 5:20-6:10. In what ways can you receive God's grace in times of trial?
- Luke 4:1-13. Trials often accompany blessings. How can you use the blessings and trials in your life to show God at work in a life-giving way?

Bishop, Mountain Sky Area, The United Methodist Church, Denver, Colorado

MONDAY, FEBRUARY 8 ~ *Luke 4:1-13*

Blessing comes with temptation. Every time we receive some encouraging sign of God's work in our lives, we run the risk of becoming spiritually cocky. Of all those who came for baptism, only Jesus gets the Holy Spirit's stamp of approval. Doesn't it mean he has arrived? That he no longer needs to be vigilant in self-examination? No. Blessing comes with temptation.

John is out in the wilderness preaching repentance and inviting people to mend their ways—to change the way they live. As a sign of people's commitment to change their lives, John baptizes them in the river.

When John baptizes Jesus, the heavens open and the Holy Spirit says in effect, "You get what I'm talking about. You are OK!" And then Jesus gets put to the test. Instead of setting him loose on the world, the Holy Spirit leads him into the wilderness where the not-so-holy-spirit tempts Jesus to trust himself. If he has the Holy Spirit's endorsement, why shouldn't he use his power to turn stones to bread, to exercise authority over all of creation, to demonstrate his power by throwing himself from the pinnacle of the Temple. The temptation to self-reliance is strong.

If Jesus had said yes to the devil, he would have become an agent of the old order of greed and self-interest that God was leading people out of. By saying no the devil, Jesus powerfully demonstrates that he serves as an agent of a new way of life.

God, lead us from death to life. Help us know ourselves as you know us. Lead us not into temptation, but deliver us from evil. Amen.

When a person breaks an arm or a leg, if it isn't set straight the bone may grow back crooked. It may even be necessary for the doctor to rebreak the bone in order to set it straight. It isn't any easier when it's our spirit that needs correction.

We have trouble thinking about our faith journey as bone-crushing. But that's what the psalmist describes. Along the path of life, we have some serious breaking-and-mending work to do. At times we need to break bad habits, break out of narrow attitudes, make a clean break from unhealthy relationships.

We may need to mend our ways, our relationships, and even the threadbare social fabric that binds us one to another. Poet Robert Frost describes spring mending-time when neighbors walk the stone wall that marks the boundary between their properties to replace stones that may have fallen during the year.

When we join the psalmist crying, "Create in me a clean heart, O God, and put a new and right spirit within me," we admit that the choices we have made, the life we have drifted into, the spirit that we have invited into our hearts may be unacceptable to God. We may have wandered off from the way of life and truth. We may need God to help us break out of the confining and unhealthy way we have chosen and to mend what is torn or worn out.

It takes courage to change.

God, I have sinned and done what is evil in your sight. And yet I don't want to change. Break me of my willful spirit so that I may grow true in your way. Melt me, mold me, fill me, use me. Amen.

Ash Wednesday

Today Christians begin the forty-day journey of Lent that ends at Easter. For centuries Christian seekers and believers have observed this as a time of self-reflection, sacrifice, and repentance. Some Christians make this a season of fasting, prayer, or another spiritual discipline.

Every Christian needs to pause now and then to listen again and anew to God and to assess their life path and decisions. Prayer is the practice of placing ourselves in the presence of God. At its best, the practice of fasting reminds us that we do not need all that we want and invites us to rely again on the spiritual sustenance of God.

But even prayer and fasting can become corrupted. The prophet warns about pious practices with an ulterior motive. It is *unacceptable* to fast and pray in order to win favor with God, to "make your voice heard on high." Christians don't take on spiritual disciplines to win favor with God but to draw near to God. Can you hear God crying out in the psalm—if you want to draw near to me, draw near to your neighbor through acts of mercy and justice.

As Christmas break approached at a nearby college, a pastor-friend of mine invited church members to drive students to the airport for their trips home. They picked the students up, drove them to the airport, and sent them off with a bag of goodies for the flight. The pastor invited them to simply "practice being Christian" with no expectation of benefit to the church.

Dorotheos of Gaza describes how when you draw near to others you draw near to God and when you draw near to God you cannot help but draw near to the people around you.

Let my love of you, dear God, draw me nearer to the people around me. Amen.

When I was growing up, my pastor introduced the collection of the offering each Sunday with these words, "With gratitude for all we have received, let us offer our gifts to God."

We receive life as gift. Isn't that what Deuteronomy says? We may have sweated and toiled to produce this crop, but growth comes only with God's providence—and don't you forget it!

To be sure we don't forget, God instituted a ritual of giving away the first and best of everything we receive and reciting our history of how we came to be where we are: "A wandering Aramean was my ancestor; . . . alien, . . . treated . . . harshly, . . . afflicted." The story reminds us of our checkered past and all that we have received so that we never take it for granted. All is a gift of a generous God: every breath we take, every moment of pure delight, every sweet and juicy fruit, or tender caress we receive. We cannot generate any of it. It comes as gift—even if it requires labor to create and generosity to share.

Many people don't live by the rhythms of planting and harvesting, so what does God expect of us? How are we to show our gratitude? What sacrifice is required of us?

First, God wants us to give away a portion of what we have as an act of self-sacrifice and gratitude and for the benefit of others.

Second, God wants us to remember and recite the story of our dependency upon God's grace and the generosity of others.

Third, insofar as we receive and enjoy God's providence, God wants us to celebrate and share God's bounty with people in our communities who are wandering, alien, afflicted, and dependent upon the generosity of others.

Now, O God, with gratitude for all I receive this day, lead me to share with others. Amen.

Gratitude for All We Have Received   61

Every time a server sets a meal before me in a restaurant I wonder about this passage. Jesus instructs us not to make a public show of our piety. And yet I live in an age and a nation where many people take their food for granted, where moments to pause and reflect are rare, and where many people are not part of any faith community and never pray in public or private.

Isn't there a place for a public witness to faith and faithfulness? I wonder how Christians in a secular society make their faith visible to others, offering even a glimpse of the joy of a life lived in relationship to God. How can Christians be a "contrast" community if we never appear to differ from the people around us? I feel caught between not wanting to put my faith on display and wanting to put my lamp on a lampstand.

In my own practice, I try to pause and pray before my meals taken in public as a reminder and a witness that life is sacred, that every meal is a blessing, and that we participate in the richness of creation when we practice gratitude and wonder. Maybe others who see me pray will remember that their meal is a gift too. Maybe they will remember those who have no meal to be thankful for. But that's not why I do it. I do it simply as a practice of living gratefully and attentively.

And yet I hear Jesus' caution: *Beware* of practicing your piety before others in order to be seen by them. Make sure it comes from the heart and not from a need for the approval of others.

God, as our prayers travel from our hearts and lips to your ears, may our lives invite others into abundant life with you. Amen.

As a young pastor I remember reading that people in the Bible not only *act out* their feelings; they also act their way *into* feelings. When a tragedy occurs, they rend a garment and put on sackcloth and ashes as a way of acting their way into appropriate feeling. And when a blessing is bestowed, they tell it abroad and offer a sacrifice in order to experience the feelings of joy and blessing.

When Christians fast—when we take on a discipline of self-denial—it shouldn't lead us to whine and whimper. We do not act like it is a big sacrifice, that we suffer from it. Instead, if we act as if we are experiencing abundance, we can experience God's abundance, even though we practice self-denial.

Have you ever noticed that people's happiness seldom has any relationship to how much stuff they have? People in Africa or other parts of the world may live in conditions of rampant poverty, disease, and violence; still they do not appear to let suffering define them. Churches in communities with few resources often serve as gathering places for singing and dancing in a spirit of exuberant joy. Physical circumstance does not determine spiritual health. Joy can overcome adversity.

In Haiti, following the 2010 earthquake, I saw people who lived in refugee tents with no water or sewer systems, walking to work or to school. Dressed in clean and pressed clothes, they stood straight and walked with purpose. People who had every reason for despair lived out of a spirit of abundant life. They strode into the work day with confidence and hope.

How we behave can affect how we feel. If we pray and work and prepare for a hopeful future, we will find hope all around.

Savior Christ, teach us to live in hope so that we experience hope in you. Amen.

First Sunday in Lent

We urge you also not to accept the grace of God in vain." God does not promise that our lives will be easy, only that they will be blessed. Afflictions, hardships, calamities, beatings, riots should not surprise us or discourage us. They become the occasions for putting our faith to work. Just as the Holy Spirit drove Jesus into the wilderness to put his faith into practice under difficult circumstances, so too God raises us up in faith in order to walk into the lions' den.

Don't receive God's grace in vain. Don't give up on grace in times of trial. God's grace exists for the trials. Put God's grace to work in those times. This understanding is the great paradox of Jesus Christ.

Appearances may deceive. What we feel may not reflect reality. Trouble may be blessing. Despair may bear seeds of hope. An empty vessel may contain all we need for abundant life. The desert may blossom. Death may give way to life unexpectedly, impossibly.

As a young mother and pastor, one Holy Week I was telling my young son the story of the passion of Jesus. When I got through Jesus' death on Good Friday, I moved on to tell how on Sunday he rose from the grave and lived again. My son almost jumped out of my lap. His eyes sparkled as he shouted with glee, "He tricked them, didn't he? He really tricked them!"

Jesus "tricks" people every day, not just Easter Sunday. He connects us to a deep river of living water that makes sorrow flee away. Taste and see that God is good. God's steadfast love endures forever. If we keep silent, the stones will shout out this great good news.

Resurrecting God, give us eyes to see your blessing all around us and courage to live abundant life even in the midst of great distress. Amen.

Do Not Be Afraid

FEBRUARY 15–21, 2016 • JACK EWING

Scripture Overview: The contradiction between appearance and reality runs through several of the readings. Hearing God's assurance of protection, Abraham reminds God that he and Sarah are childless. Hearing God's promise once again, Abraham believes; but he believes in the face of all the evidence. In Philippians, Paul employs the powerful language of citizenship to explain that Christians live as citizens of another realm; believers live out of an allegiance that cannot be witnessed with ordinary vision. "Herod wants to kill you," Jesus is warned. Yet Jesus' death will not prove an end to the threat he poses to either Roman or religious authority. If Psalm 27 does not so clearly distinguish between appearance and reality, it is because the psalmist knows on whose side reality lies. He anticipates a time when things will appear the way they actually are; that is, when he will live in God's very presence.

Questions and Thoughts for Reflection

- Read Genesis 15:1-18. When have you doubted God's promise to you?
- Read Psalm 27. When have you felt surrounded on all sides by "enemies"? How has entering a holy space brought calm to your soul?
- Read Philippians 3:17–4:1. Who models the Christian lifestyle for you? What would need to change for you to be more like them?
- Read Luke 13:31-35. What aspects of your life do you fear but know that you have to endure? How can you approach those with the confidence of God's presence and strength?

Executive Director of Lake Junaluska Conference Center, North Carolina

For a third time God reveals to Abram that God has chosen him, selected him to receive a vast amount of land and to have countless descendants. Neither promise makes any sense. The land promised is not where he lives, and his wife, Sarai, cannot have children. In chapter 12 God told Abram to leave his home and go to "a land I will show you." With God's first intiative of "go" and "I will show" and the promise of a great nation and blessings in chapter 12, things seem to look up for Abram. Abram does as God commands and goes. He and Sarai have many adventures before God reaffirms the promise of heirs and land in chapter 13. Now in chapter 15, Abram and Sarai remain childless—clearly a disconnect between God's promise and their reality. The "chosen" ones must wonder about the benefits of their specialness to God.

When have you felt chosen by God for a task? How did that chosenness manifest in your life?

In my early forties I served as an assistant dean at a university. I felt a clear sense of being chosen by God to be the president of a nearby university. I knew I was too young, too inexperienced, and not ready to take on the responsibilities of leading a university. But one Sunday morning, before the selection process had commenced, I experienced a deep assurance that God had chosen me for this task. The committee selected me for the position, and I have served in executive positions ever since. Being chosen by God does not mean our work will be easy or the benefits evident. Understanding that God has chosen us boosts our confidence in the possibility of promises fulfilled.

God, thank you for our unique gifts that we employ to make the world a better place. Help us to know and use our gifts for your purposes. Amen.

How could Abram possibly question God? God has twice promised Abram the blessings of land and descendants. Here God, once again, clearly communicates with Abram and tells him that "his reward will be very great." Despite all this interaction and communication, Abram responds to God's latest promise with a bit of an attitude. While verse 6 makes it clear that Abram believes the promise, he seems ready to have some assurance that the promise will come to fruition. God patiently tells Abram to look up at the sky and the thousands of stars and assures him that he will have many descendants. These promises will materialize. God and Abram engage in a covenant ritual to confirm the fulfillment of vows, particularly to instill confidence in Abram that God will make good on the promises.

Many of us have experienced God's presence. It may have been during a worship service or during a time of personal prayer and devotion or while on a walk around a beautiful lake. God's presence was real; God's words may even have been clear. We may have told a family member or friend about the experience or written about it in our journal. But like Abram, perhaps we have forgotten that sense of clarity of God's presence. The memory may have faded, and we may have questioned the validity of the experience. Take time to remember these moments of presence and recognition of God's promises while acknowledging that trust and hope in the Lord forms the bedrock of our relationship. God is faithful.

God, you reveal yourself to us in a myriad of ways. Forgive our failure to remember your constancy and faithfulness. Amen.

The Bible attributes many of the psalms to David, a shepherd boy who became king. As a great warrior, he led his armies against foe after foe. Understandably, he had enemies who plotted against him. The reality of his enemies trying to defeat him often engaged his mind.

I can imagine David as one who spent the early hours of each day meditating on God, on the challenges that he faced, and on his reliance on God as deliverer. One morning as the sun rises, these words come to his mind: "The LORD is my light and my salvation; whom shall I fear?"

Whether written by David or another psalmist, this poetry resonates with many of us. It begins with a profession of faith, an affirmation of God as light and stronghold. Only in verse 7 does the psalmist mention his request for help; we read the imperative words of command: *Hear, come, do not hide, teach, do not give me up, wait.* The psalmist seeks God's face and in that seeking, God—the light, the stronghold—sustains and strengthens.

All of us in leadership roles have felt a little like David when persons have questioned our leadership, intentionally worked against us, or falsely accused us. Then the words of this psalm become our words.

The psalmist praises God and reflects utmost confidence in God's ability to save. These affirmations are followed by a sense of God's distance: "Do not hide your face from me, . . . do not forsake me." Even at our best, we often express total confidence in God but then let doubt creep back in. However, we "wait for the LORD"; our strength and courage depend on God's goodness.

God of light and salvation, forgive us for failing to have total confidence in your presence and love. We need you. Thank you for being our hope and our strength. Amen.

The psalmist alternates between fear and faith. In the midst of his praise, he makes one request of God: that he may live in the "house of the LORD" forever. We can relate to this desire to experience God's presence and peace. Only in God's presence will we know joy and abundant life.

Soon after graduating from high school, I entered one of our country's service academies. Throughout my growing-up years my parents assured me of their love daily. That was not the case at the academy. In fact, I experienced the opposite. I heard few words of affirmation and certainly no words of love. I felt miserable; I lived with a constant knot in my stomach. That is, except for one hour each week when I attended worship in the chapel on campus. Oh, the euphoria of being in that space! I don't remember the order of worship or the music or any sermons, but I vividly remember the joy of being in the "house of the LORD," a time and place that relieved my anxiety, reassured my confidence in God's continued presence with me.

I, like the psalmist, experienced the stark contrast between my world outside of God's house and the peace of being in God's presence. Is it possible that we can praise God even more when armies surround us, when the troubles of our lives weigh us down? We certainly don't seek those troubles, but they do come. In those times in our lives, we need more than ever to enter into the house of the Lord, to experience the joy of being in the presence of God, our light and our salvation.

God of peace and joy, may we feel your presence when we enter your house. Amen.

Paul writes to the Philippians while in prison, not knowing whether he will face release or death. He has every reason in the world to feel sorry for himself. Instead, he writes a letter full of thanksgiving and encouragement. He clearly has developed a relationship with the people in the church at Philippi, and it sounds as if he is hearing of some disunity among them. So he writes to assure them of his well-being and also to thank them. Paul could easily have berated the Christians at Philippi for their selfishness and their forgetfulness; instead he gently but firmly motivates them with words of encouragement and example.

In chapter 2 Paul encourages the believers at Philippi to imitate Christ and in today's passage, he encourages them to imitate himself. Paul, a highly disciplined and confident person, does not hesitate to hold himself and Timothy up as examples that others may emulate. On the one hand it appears that Paul is violating the words he wrote earlier: "in humility regard others as better than yourselves" (2:3), but we recall that he is trying in every way to encourage and motivate. In the previous verses of 7-16, Paul has described the ways that he has allowed the knowledge of Christ to take hold in his life. He desires to be an example of Christian living, an example others may follow.

In some ways the letter to the Philippians is like a letter that a parent writes to a child after hearing that the child is not living the way he or she had been reared to live. In effect, Paul says, "That's not the way we do things in our family. Let me remind you of the way you were raised." And Paul does so in a gentle and affirming way.

> *Gentle and loving God, may the example of your son, Jesus Christ, and the mature Christians who have gone before us inspire our living. Amen.*

After Paul has held up examples worthy of imitation, Christ first and then himself, he identifies those whose example the Philippians should *not* follow. He refers to this group as "enemies of the cross." He goes on to state that "their god is the belly." Is Paul suggesting that people who consume more food than they need are enemies of God? I hope not, for then many of us who strive to be followers of Jesus are in trouble.

I believe Paul employs the term *enemies of the cross* to refer to people who lack self-discipline. We read about these persons who live a life of self-indulgence and gluttony when we read First Corinthians. They interpret Paul's stating that they are not under the law as a gateway to immorality. They set their minds on earthly things.

But Paul reminds the Philippians that "our citizenship is in heaven." The Philippians, while Roman citizens, owe an allegiance to an even greater commonwealth: heaven. Christ shared in "the body of our humiliation" that we may share in "the body of his glory."

Followers of Christ are encouraged to live a disciplined life, not a life of selfish indulgence. We accept the challenge of practicing "spiritual" disciplines—daily Bible study, prayer, and reflection. Few of us are as disciplined in our lives as Jesus or Paul. But most of us strive to be more disciplined in our times of devotion, worship, and physical self-care, which of course includes habits of eating.

How often do you allow earthly things to consume your thoughts and actions? What disciplines will help you redirect your focus to heavenly citizenship?

God of our whole lives, help us imitate Jesus and Paul in our living. May we ever be mindful of our citizenship in heaven. Amen.

SECOND SUNDAY IN LENT

The New Testament refers to the Pharisees almost one hundred times; a vast majority of them are negative. And yet, here in the passage from Luke we find the Pharisees warning Jesus about Herod's intentions to kill him. Clearly, not all Pharisees have ill intentions toward Jesus. In fact, this passage indicates that a group of them feel concern for Jesus' well-being. Even so, they miss the point.

Jesus' response to the Pharisees is both enigmatic and instructive. Jesus understands his work as a part of a broader and more significant mission than any plan of Herod or the Pharisees: "Today, tomorrow, and the next day I must be on my way." Jesus still has work to do, and he will not allow a threat from Herod to detract from this mission. Jesus ignores the advice of the Pharisees but reveals that his mission will lead him to death. Even in this instance, Jesus holds the power by choosing the location of his death: "It is impossible for a prophet to be killed outside of Jerusalem." Jesus will not usurp Herod's power; he will be empowered by the cross.

How easily we, like the Pharisees, forget Jesus' true intentions. We get wrapped up in divisions within churches, whether based on style of worship or theological understanding. Jesus continues his work of healing as he moves toward his death. As we make our way through the season of Lent, may we keep in mind Jesus' mission. His mission led him to suffering and death on the cross while culminating in his saving work on earth.

God of the universe, may we ponder your healing work among us as we walk with Jesus toward the cross. Amen.

Lessons from the Desert

FEBRUARY 22–28, 2016 • JOAN CAMPBELL

Scripture Overview: The need for introspection and repentance looms large during this season of the church year, yet there is also room for joy. The joy that issues from the Isaiah text is generated by the prophet's realization that God's mercy is close at hand and available to any who will draw on it. Psalm 63 expresses a strong confidence in God, praising God for past outpourings of mercy. The longing for sustenance is transformed into a "rich feast," which satisfies the innermost being of the psalmist. Paul views the lives of his fellow Christians in Corinth against the background of ancient Israel's experiences of exodus and wilderness wanderings. The Corinthian believers are exhorted to learn from the example of these Israelites, lest they too be judged by God. Paul balances the warning with a promise: God's grace is active, even in times of greatest pressure to forsake God's calling. The Luke reading stresses the urgent need for repentance.

Questions and Thoughts for Reflection

- Read Isaiah 55:1-9. When have you been the most aware of your own smallness in contrast to God's greatness? How did you react?

- Read Psalm 63:1-8. Consider how earnestly you take your relationship with God. Do you seek God halfheartedly or with deliberate intent?

- Read 1 Corinthians 10:1-13. In what ways is our culture similar to that of Corinth? How have we let the world's culture creep into our churches and lives?

- Read Luke 13:1-9. When have you experienced Christ's pruning? What fruit did you bear?

Trainer and mentor for Media Associates International; member, Discovery Methodist Church, Johannesburg, South Africa

Deserts are harsh places. Survival is a daily struggle for plants, animals, and people alike. Deserts figure prominently in the Bible. Cast out of lush Eden, Adam and his descendants lived under God's curse of "thorns and thistles" (Gen. 3:18). The Israelites wandered for forty years in the desert. David hid from Saul, John the Baptist preached, and Jesus faced temptation—all in the desert.

The desert of Judah inspires the words we read in Psalm 63. The words of the opening verse resound with a profound sense of isolation and a deep longing for God. In that vast desert, the psalmist expresses his need for God's closeness and provision. His physical thirst emphasizes his far greater spiritual thirst.

The season of Lent invites us to become desert sojourners— to slow down and survey the harsh world around us, sensing our own and others' thirst. It invites us to recall Jesus' desert wanderings—his first steps on the journey to the cross—and the oasis that his death opened for us all. We are urged to drink deeply at this oasis, finding rest and sustenance in God alone.

We can learn from the psalmist who seeks God earnestly. We are to seek God with deliberate seriousness and intent, not halfheartedly and distractedly as we sometimes do. Times in the desert may feel dry and bleak. But as the psalmist discovers, in the desert we realize our desperate need for God, which leads us to search for and encounter God in meaningful ways. Thorns and thistles can give way to an oasis of refreshment.

Lord, impress on me the need to seek you earnestly, and refresh me during these times. Amen.

Our journey in the desert continues as we hear God's voice calling people to come and drink at the waters. Written almost six hundred years before Christ's birth, Isaiah's words point to the everlasting covenant and reign of the Messiah. The words issue an invitation of salvation and blessing, echoed by Jesus when he offers the Samaritan woman his "living water" (John 4:10-14).

Unlike the psalmist who acknowledged his deep thirst for God (Ps. 63:1), Isaiah urges his readers to act. The repetitive use of verbs such as *come, listen, spend,* and *eat* call them from apathy to action. These verses express a warning worth heeding. What keeps us away from God's life-giving water is ignorance of our own deep need for God. Verse 2 deals with one factor that can lead us to this dangerous position—trying to quench our thirst and satisfy our hunger with "that which does not satisfy."

As a parent, I've often had to warn my children against eating sugary candy before dinner time; if they do, they will lose their appetite for my nourishing meal. Similarly, Isaiah's words warn us away from things that are "not bread."

We find ourselves surrounded by empty treats that, like brightly colored candies, look inviting and entice us to temporary fulfillment. These temptations differ for each of us. As a writer I struggle with the allure of people's recognition and praise, which may offer a temporary "sugar high" but ultimately does not satisfy. The Holy One has to remind me to use my writing to honor God alone rather than fulfill my need for approval.

Let us use this Lenten period to identify prayerfully the "candy" in our lives, those things that are "not bread" and do "not satisfy" and keep us from thirsting and hungering for God.

Lord, show me what I use to try to quench my thirst and assuage my hunger, instead of turning to you. Amen.

Each of us will face seasons in the desert—times of intense hardship and sorrow. You may be in such a place in your life right now. My friend is navigating the harsh landscape of loneliness and confusion after her husband of twenty-four years left her. Another friend received a diagnosis of cancer and is wading through the unknown, fearful quagmire of operations, chemotherapy, and radiation.

Know that no matter where you find yourself today, God has promised never to forsake us. However, grief and pain may well blind us to God's presence. The psalmist shows us how to cling to God in the desert, employing three practices:

First, in verse 1, the psalmist reflects on his personal relationship with God and his deep need of the Lord. If you find yourself in a barren place right now, remind yourself that you are God's son or daughter. If earthly parents care for and protect their children, how much more will God care for and protect you?

Second, in verses 3-5, the psalmist praises God. Praise is a powerful spiritual force. William Thrasher* says, "Satan so hates the genuine praise of Christ that his fiery darts of discouragement are not effective against us when we respond in praise." Offer praise in the desert today, no matter how dry and cracked your voice, and you may well sense a cool, soothing breeze blowing through your heart.

Finally, in verses 2 and 6, the psalmist meditates on God. When our path becomes uncertain, it helps to look back and recall how faithfully God has journeyed with us in the past.

So today, begin meditating on your Father. Cling to God and know that wilderness seasons do not last forever.

---

*www.christianquotes.info/quotes-by-author/william-thrasher-quotes/

Lord, open my eyes to see and trust you in the desert seasons of my life. Amen.

How easily we take something for granted. Water, for instance. Water is a precious commodity on my continent of Africa. More than 300 million of the 800 million people in sub-Saharan Africa live in a water-scarce environment. Because I only have to turn on the faucet to access clean water, I have come to take it for granted, unlike other Africans who realize the value of every drop. My privileged access to water has led to complacency.

Privilege led the Israelites to complacency too. In his first letter to the Corinthian church, Paul looks back on Israel's desert wanderings. Before his warning that God will not tolerate sin, Paul establishes some of the privileges God has bestowed on the Israelites. Paul invites reflection on all God has done for them. The Israelites, God's chosen people, have been redeemed from Egyptian captivity. They stood on the shore when the sea miraculously parted before them. They drank fresh water pouring from the rock and ate sweet manna that faithfully rained down from heaven. They followed the cloud and pillar of fire—God's constant presence with them. Our lavish God provides not just the necessities but "wine and milk" and "rich food." Yet, the Israelites took these gifts—and God—for granted.

Believers are also a people of privilege. We too have been redeemed from captivity, fed by the word of God, and guided by the Holy Spirit. Let us pay careful attention to the warning in Paul's letter and never take for granted the position and blessings we have in Christ; if we do we, like the Israelites, could fall into the sin of complacency.

Today allow the simple act of turning on a faucet remind you of God's abundant privileges.

Lord, thank you for my many blessings. Forgive me whenever I take them for granted. Amen.

If the psalmist's life and words in Psalm 63 illustrate how to approach time in the desert, the Israelites' wilderness wanderings illustrate how not to. In writing to the Corinthians, Paul urged the immature church to pay careful attention to the lessons of Israel's past.

Many problems plague the Corinthian church, partially due to its location in an idolatrous and hedonistic city. Little wonder immorality has crept into the church. Among the issues Paul addresses in his two letters to the church are the factions and in-fighting and the fact that the Lord's Supper has turned into a selfish, raucous feast.

The people, times, and places may differ, but we see in verses 6-10 that the sins of the Corinthians strongly resemble those of the Israelites. It appears that sin and human nature vary little through the ages. Complacency and a sense of entitlement in the Corinthian community has blossomed into full-blown sin: revelry, sexual immorality, testing, and grumbling against God.

We may stand and peer through the dusty veil of time, shaking our heads and tut-tutting in disbelief at the wickedness of the Israelites and the waywardness of the Corinthians. We may think, *I don't do any of those things; I'm much better than everyone else.* If these are our thoughts, Paul speaks his closing words to us: "So if you think you are standing, watch out that you do not fall."

Friends, let us use this Lenten season to come humbly before God, asking for the revelation of our own complacency and sinful attitudes and actions. Then, we can take comfort in the sanctifying work of the Holy Spirit—our wonderful privilege as believers—as well as rest in God's faithfulness.

Lord, reveal to me any sins that I have been blind to and accept my confession. Amen.

In South Africa, news reports recite a litany of stories related to crime, corruption, trade union strikes, political unrest, and other human tragedies. At times the bad news feels so over-whelming that I have to "unplug" from the media.

How surprisingly familiar it feels to read of people bringing Jesus a "breaking" news story, one of murder and persecution. In their conversation, another news item is raised—the tower collapse that killed eighteen. The people are trying to make sense of unexpected death and tragedy, as each of us does when we watch the news. Interestingly, Jesus doesn't give them clear-cut answers, except to say that the suffering and death did not result from the victims' sins. Jesus does, however, use the stories as a call to self-examination and repentance.

The parable that follows reminds us that fruitfulness indicates genuine transformation. Repentance and productivity are expected. Like the gardener in the parable, Jesus patiently tends us—watering, fertilizing and pruning our lives, nurturing us to bear fruit for him. Yet, just as the fig tree, we may remain unfruitful and be cut down.

Yes, we live in a world inundated with tragedy and hardship. From Jesus we learn that our appropriate response does not involve discouragement or denial. Rather, we bring our sorrow and confusion to him; we examine our lives closely, ensuring that we are allowing the Holy Spirit to develop fruit in us.

The antidote to the bad news in the world is for Christ's followers to live fruitful, righteous, and engaging lives and to bring light into a dark world. As we do this, we will make some joy-filled breaking news stories of our own!

Lord, help me not to be discouraged or indifferent to the happenings around me. May my life reflect your love and light to a hurting world. Amen.

THIRD SUNDAY IN LENT

Icy desert nights bring clarity to the view of the sky. I slept outside one winter's night at a youth camp in a remote location. Near midnight I awoke, cold and uncomfortable—but I released both feelings as I opened my eyes. I had never seen a sky like that before: deep layers of stars, clusters and constellations that crowded out the dark with their brightness. What an astounding thought that those same stars shone every night, but I had never seen them.

Today we end our week in the desert by looking to the heavens, seeking God anew. God's ways and thoughts are far higher than our own partial and limited ones. Just as we perceive only a portion of the night sky, we perceive only a hint of God's majesty. Yet, even this incomplete glimpse will convict us of our desperate need for God and fill us with reverent awe.

"Seek the Lord; . . . call upon him; . . . return to the LORD." The prophet gives voice to an urgency: seize hold of repentance and restoration *now*, for our God "will abundantly pardon."

Through Isaiah, God calls each of us out of our slumbering states. We are to awake from the superficiality that has infiltrated our lives and rise above the ingratitude and complacency that have taken root, even in the midst of abundant blessing. We then examine our lives for spiritual fruit. If we lack that fruit, we must return to the vine to allow Christ's life-giving sustenance to flow through us again (John 15:5).

Let us not tarry to bring ourselves and others to God, for now is the time that God is near!

Lord, turn my eyes toward you and draw me out of sleep into a fruitful relationship with you. Amen.

Finding Your Rhythm

FEBRUARY 29–MARCH 6, 2016 • DJ DEL ROSARIO

Scripture Overview: A common theme of these passages is that of joy over the restorative love of God. Joshua 5:9-12 describes the first celebration of Passover in the land of promise. God's promise has been realized; the goal of their lengthy journey is beneath their feet. The psalmist, aware of the devastating nature of human sin, celebrates the reality that confessed sin offers a means of reconnecting with God. Paul acknowledges certain consequences of Jesus' death: (1) the cross opens up a new way of knowing, (2) to see with the eyes of the cross is to see a new world, (3) God's reconciling love is clearly revealed, and (4) Christ's followers are commissioned to engage in the ministry of reconciliation. The familiar parable of the prodigal son is concerned with matters of recognition and nonrecognition. The younger son comes to his senses about his own situation, and his repentance is recognized by the father.

Questions and Thoughts for Reflection

- Joshua 5:9-12. How am I being rooted and grounded in this very moment to acknowledge the presence of God?
- Psalm 32. When did you last experience the joy of forgiveness that only God offers?
- 2 Corinthians 5:16-21. When have you failed to treat others as persons of sacred worth?
- Luke 15:1-3, 11b-32. With which character do you most identify? Where do you see God in this story? How would you respond if you found yourself in the role of the elder son?

Senior pastor, Bothell United Methodist Church, Seattle, Washington

In the Hebrew Scriptures, we tend to focus on the daring escape of the Hebrew people from Egypt, fast-forwarding through the many adventures of the people during their forty-year wilderness trek. Here in Joshua 5, we discover a generation of Hebrew people who experience God's promise fulfilled. They celebrate the Passover in the land of promise and praise the saving work of Yahweh from generation to generation.

The Hebrew people during their wilderness wandering lived day to day by relying on the grace of God who provided for their needs. Here in chapter 5, they taste the first fruits of Canaan. "The manna ceased the day they ate the produce of the land." A new day dawns.

In this season of Lent, we make our journey to the Cross and the grave. We may be tempted to fast-forward to the end where we stand on Easter morning singing God's praises.

This week, we have an opportunity to appreciate the sacred moments of the in-between—times when the Hebrew people experience God's provision again and again, moments like this when we center ourselves in God who is present with us in this very moment. Maybe you have had a taste of God's promises fulfilled and are excited for the next steps. Maybe it's your lack of fulfillment that causes you to hunger for enough daily bread just to make it through the next few hours.

How are you being rooted and grounded in this moment to acknowledge God's presence?

God of yesterday, tomorrow, and this very moment, may I experience all that you are with all that I am. Amen.

Afriend once said that forgiveness doesn't simply mean for-getting. Forgiveness also conveys the quality of wishing the other person well. It often takes an extraordinary act of grace to forgive—much less to accept forgiveness of this sacred kind.

In reading the psalmist's words, we realize the true bless-edness of the recipient of God's forgiveness. We worship a God who loves us completely, who forgives transgression, and who covers our sin completely.

The psalmist, like some of us, experiences physical illness as a result of his unconfessed sin: his body wastes away, his strength dries up. But then he confesses his sin to God.

Words, spoken or unspoken, offer an opportunity to commu-nicate to God not only our sin but also the deep longings of our hearts. We worship a God who knows the choices of our past, a God who knows the choices others have made on our behalf. These choices linger today; some may still haunt us.

The psalmist confesses his sin and receives forgiveness after his time of crisis. God forgives the guilt of the psalmist. Far beyond a temporary feeling that can melt as fast as a pint of ice cream on a hot day, the joy of the Lord can sustain the weary.

Today you can experience the steadfast love of God. Set aside your unwillingness to call upon God for help; "happy are those whose transgression is forgiven."

How can you experience the joy of forgiveness that only God offers today? Are you ready in this moment to acknowledge to God how you are really doing?

God, this time is your time; it always has been. May I experi-ence your forgiveness and grace today. May it begin here and now. Amen.

In the city of Seattle when the sun comes out you can sense a shift in people's mood. It's not that folks expect it to rain every day; it's just that people don't often anticipate the sun during the rainy season. Folks seem genuinely happy when an unanticipated gift like sunshine breaks the monotony of gray days on end.

The psalmist has experienced a "grayness" of illness, "groaning all day long." But then he acknowledges his sin to God, and the sunshine of forgiveness lights his life.

This amazing ray of "sunshine" shifts the psalmist's mood; God preserves him from trouble, surrounding him with deliverance. This shift is life-altering, so much so that the psalmist goes on to bear witness to others of the difference God can make in a life. From his experience of steadfast love, he steps out to instruct, teach, and counsel others, encouraging them to entrust their lives to God's care.

Verse 1 alludes to those who are "happy." By the end of the psalm, there is joy—joy in God's steadfast love. I perceive a difference between joy and happiness. I often experience happiness as a fleeting moment: a hot-fudge sundae with peppermint ice cream makes me happy while I eat it. But no matter how much or how often I delight in this treat, that feeling will dissipate too.

Happiness is temporary. Joy lingers in our hearts and souls, a ray of sunshine on the gloomiest of days. When did you last experience joy?

Forgiving God, thank you for moments of happiness. May I experience the joy of forgiveness today through your son, Jesus the Christ. Amen.

My beloved, professional baseball team signed a big-name player from the New York Yankees. His contract was worth an enormous amount of money for about a decade worth of commitment. The first time his new team traveled back to play his former team in New York, a famous talk show set up a cardboard cutout of the player on a booth to give local New Yorkers a chance to boo their former Yankee. New Yorkers had no idea that the man himself stood behind the cutout.

I found it fascinating to watch local New York baseball fans change their demeanor when the baseball player came out from behind the cardboard cutout. Equally intriguing was the way the baseball player handled the situation with grace and poise, shaking the hands of people as he thanked them.

In our world and culture, we often value people for what they produce or achieve. We may perceive the gospel message as promoting accumulation of things and wealth. In this season of Lent, however, the cross looms ever closer as an expression of God's love for all and Jesus' death for all. "From now on, therefore, we regard no one from a human point of view."

It's easy to treat people poorly, to devalue their existence by considering them as nothing more than a cardboard image. It's a completely different matter to be face-to-face with someone, face-to-face with someone for whom Christ died. The cross changes everything.

God doesn't view us as cardboard cutouts. We worship the God who reconciles all things through Christ. Christ changes our worldview and offers us peace and reconciliation with one another as well.

In this Lenten season, reflect on how Jesus' death on the cross affects your perception of others as persons of sacred worth.

Lord, thank you for loving us as your created beings. Amen.

The main character in the French novel *Les Misérables* is Jean Valjean, an ex-convict haunted by his past. Like Valjean, we make choices that we wish we could take back. Choices of others may have harmed us, and we bear the scars today. We all bear physical and emotional wounds that require healing. We yearn for a new creation.

In Christ, "everything has become new!" Christ's death has reconciled God to all people. This reconciliation ushers in a new way of knowing one another, no longer regarding one another "from a human point of view." We receive a "new creation." We are reconciled to God and, perhaps more importantly, God asks us to participate in the ongoing ministry of reconciliation. We move into the world to relay the news that all are friends of God, having been reconciled through Christ.

In the film version of *Les Misérables*, Valjean's last words are these: "To love another person is to see the face of God." Despite his haunted past, his wounds and scars, the love he experienced gave him a glimpse of a world made right. We too have the opportunity to be reconciled to God—and not only reconciled but to become reconcilers, ambassadors of Christ.

May our lives reflect the story of the good news that we read in this passage. Jesus came into this world for one person and for all people. May the love of Christ fill us.

When did you last feel God's presence in such a way that you knew without a doubt that God knows you and loves you deeply? How did you share that love with others?

Holy One, may we see your face today. May we reflect your grace this day, and may our lives encourage others to fall more deeply in love with you. In the name of your Son, Jesus, we pray. Amen.

Today's parable is one of the more developed parables that Jesus tells. Let's review this story from the perspective of the three main characters. The elder son's perspective: This is the story of two sons. One son remains faithful to the father (him), and the other is a wastrel.

The younger son's perspective: This is the story of a son who squanders his inheritance (him), and the father's love that draws him back into the family. Note that the younger son and elder son *never* interact in Jesus' story.

The father's perspective: This is the story of a son who demands his inheritance before his father's death—an unacceptable demand to which the father gives in.

And so we begin reading the story. The younger son asks for his inheritance in advance of his father's death and then spends it all in riotous living. He becomes a servant for another in order to live. Finally he comes to his senses and decides to return home. He practices his apology; over and over again he confesses his sin and acknowledges the forfeiture of his position as son.

When the father runs to meet his younger son, the translation denotes a sense of rush and hurriedness. Some theologians wonder if the father runs to protect his son from the scorn of the village. The father does not wait for explanation or confession; he never judges the sincerity of the younger son's confession. Thus it is that the lost son and the "lost" [bereft of relationship with the younger son] father reunite.

With which character do you identify most? Where do you see God in this story?

Lord, thank you for your never-failing love. May I experience your grace today. Amen.

FOURTH SUNDAY IN LENT

Some people refer to this parable as the parable of the lost son, in keeping with the two preceding parables about the lost sheep and the lost coin. The younger son and father in their estrangement from each other are indeed lost. And perhaps it is not too far-fetched to consider that the elder son is also lost. He may feel lost *from* the father's love, lost *in* resentment of his brother.

But the father runs to meet his older son just as he ran to meet the younger. He does not offer an immediate "fix" for his son's feelings and perceptions. He listens to the older son, letting him vent his frustration and anger. "This son of *yours* [and we could add our own, 'this daughter, this friend . . . ']" indicating his unwillingness to accept his brother back into the family. The father listens and does not argue or disagree with the son's assessment.

Many of us would understand if the father lost his temper just this once. If he got even a little upset with one of his sons, I wouldn't blame him. Instead, he responds to the elder son's pain and hurt with compassion and persuasion. He refers to his elder son as *teknon,* a word we would translate from the Greek as "child." We may interpret it as a term of affection that affirms their familial relationship. In the Filipino language of Tagalog, I would use the word *mahal,* a term that expresses a deep love of the other.

The father pleads with the elder son, extending compassion and inviting him to the party. He attempts to confirm family ties by referring to "this brother of *yours.*" We don't know the elder son's decision. How would you respond?

Loving God, thank you for your incredible grace. May the life I lead reflect the grace you offer every day. Amen.

From Dawn to Dancing: A Pilgrimage

MARCH 7–13, 2016 • KATHY EVANS

Scripture Overview: The Isaiah text portrays God's redemptive activity that is about to be introduced into Israel's life. All paradigms lie shattered before the enormity of God's grace! The joy of Psalm 126 is occasioned by the memory of God's (unspecified) act of redemption in the past and also by the anticipation that a similar intervention is imminent. Paul's autobiographical sketch directed to the Philippians confesses the change that has come into his life as a result of "knowing Christ Jesus my Lord." The story of Mary's anointing of Jesus' feet must be read in the context of Jesus' looming passion. Jesus sets Mary's actions in their proper perspective by linking them to his own death, even as he deflects Judas's counterfeit compassion.

Questions and Thoughts for Reflection

- Read Isaiah 43:16-21. How do God's past actions help you to imagine the great gifts God will provide in the future?
- Read Psalm 126. When has God's grace restored the desolate circumstances in your life?
- Read Philippians 3:4b-14. When you look at past experiences, how do these motivate you in your continued journey with Christ?
- Read John 12:1-8. How can you listen and recognize others' needs? In what ways can you respond to those needs?

Director of Music Ministries, First United Methodist Church, Cookeville, Tennessee

Any early riser will agree that the darkest hour of the night is just before the sun peeks over the eastern horizon. The reality of that darkness and the pain and sorrow it surrounds touches all of us at some point. Lives full of joy and laughter are suddenly thrust into overwhelming darkness.

The night of weeping has lasted until dawn. The thought of ever knowing joy again seems far away. The strong and faithful have fallen under the weight and have pounded the tabletop as they cry out, "Why, God, why?"

Both the psalmist and Isaiah address the matter of God's redemptive activity. Drawing on the Exodus event, the prophet alludes to God's saving action in the past. God made a "way in the sea, a path in the mighty waters." The prophet asks the people to hold that image in mind even as he asks them not to "remember the former things." For all of God's mighty acts in the past, what's coming is even bigger and better!

Just as the sun slices through the darkness and offers the hope of the new day, the scripture announces God's new thing. Circumstances will change; situations will grow better. The road from the darkness of pain to the brightness of joy may be longer than we desire. The important matter at hand is that we see the road and take the journey. As hard as it may be, we must carry our faith as a cherished seedling. We water it with our tears, fertilize it with our pain, and let the love of God shine on us as we make the journey toward the dance of joy.

Be with us, God, on this journey from the darkest hours before dawn to the sunlight of joy that awaits us. Amen.

The psalmist asks God to change his circumstances, but he doesn't give God a deadline. Our instant-gratification culture tricks us into believing that everything changes at the same speed as our state-of-the-art cell phones. Our unrealistic expectations often pave the way for disappointment and heartache.

As we embark on the journey from darkness to joy, we acknowledge that pain and sorrow depart more slowly than they enter. The circumstances of life that leave us spent of energy and joy most often take us down much faster and harder than we can imagine. We fall far, and we fall hard. And then we begin that slow recovery process of regaining our strength, assessing our options, formulating our pathway, putting one foot in front of the other, and maneuvering the journey one hill at a time.

The people in the psalm cry out to God for a restoration of fortune. They recall the dry watercourses of the desert, which fill rapidly with water when the rains come. So the people express their confidence in God's ability to affect their future, bringing them refreshment in the dryness of their lives. Their anticipated joy becomes a current reality.

The refreshing rains of God's grace saturate our parched lives. The cherished seedlings of faith sprout, and we affirm, "The LORD has done great things for us." Our inner being strengthens, and we grow like those seedlings. Our dreams become visions of a hopeful future, and we rejoice.

Thank you, God, for your refreshing rains of mercy and grace. Amen.

Mary and Martha certainly have experienced sorrow and pain in the death of their brother, Lazarus. After his resurrection we find the family hosting a dinner, and Jesus is present. The joy of having Lazarus among them plays out differently for the two sisters. The hostess duties fall to Martha as she serves the guests. Mary turns all of her attention to Jesus, anointing his feet with expensive oil. Judas Iscariot chastises her for not having sold the oil to give money to the poor.

At some point in our journey from darkness to dancing there comes a time to reawaken our awareness of the world around us. Mary moves from the darkness of death to the light of resurrection. Her awareness awakens in her a realization of the path Jesus will take. Only she, of all those gathered, perceives what awaits him, and she expends her oil in a mission of honoring the one she loves. Mary and Martha take different routes, but they have one thing in common: They both honor Jesus and care for those around them. How would our lives change if we were to do the same?

Widowed much younger than I had ever expected, I asked my children: Why me? Why did I have to be the first in almost every circle of friends and family? Their wise response: Maybe so you can help others. A large part of my own healing has come from my intentional awareness of others and their needs. Sometimes it takes being a Martha, cooking or cleaning. Often, it requires the listening Mary, whose intuition will be borne out in Jesus' crucifixion and death—an awareness of others' needs and responding in some way. We give thought and take action because, like Mary and Martha, opportunities may not present themselves more than once.

Loving God, give us an awareness of those around us and the grace to respond to their needs. Amen.

The first time the nearsighted young woman put on glasses, her response was, "Look, those trees over there have leaves too!" Her world greatly changed when everything came into focus. So it is on our pilgrimage toward healing and joy.

The Gospel writer contrasts the constant presence of the poor with Jesus' soon-to-be absence. Jesus will be with the disciples and his friends for just a little longer. Only Mary seems aware of his impending departure. And the poor remain. Jesus' statement defends Mary's action and speaks to Judas's feigned concern for the poor.

Like the little girl with the new glasses, things have come clear for Mary. She views matters from a different perspective, sees things in a new light. Judas remains myopic.

And like Mary, we can come clear about our focus. Situations and people offer opportunities for our intuition and service. We become anointers. We become aware of the struggles and needs of friends and family, and we anticipate ways of helping and healing. Each party gains strength from the other, and the burden carried by two people lightens the load.

We begin to let go of our ancient history, and new things begin to spring forth—a new way in the desert. God charts the course through the desert, providing rivers of refreshment not only for the journey but also for the journey of those we serve.

O God, may we become anointers, aware of needs and taking action. Help us perceive the new thing you're doing. Amen.

When we walk through the darkest days of our lives and we feel there is no hope, we know in our hearts that God has not forsaken us and that Christ walks with us. But we experience moments of overthinking and underknowing that cause us to question and to doubt. As we transition out of the depths of grief and pain and back into the arms of Christ, we realize that nothing compares to our life in Christ.

One day we awaken and realize that our thoughts and actions once again center in knowing Jesus Christ and that our faithfulness in Christ guides our journey. The challenges, the fears, the questions, and the concerns pale and fade from sight. We focus on the challenges Christ puts before us.

Paul lays out his religious credentials in these verses. His relationship with Christ has generated a total reversal of values: The matters of gain and loss have changed dramatically. Paul asserts that gaining Christ involves us in his suffering and his resurrection. Our greatest knowing of God in Christ comes through our suffering. And because Christ Jesus has made us "his own," we press on in active anticipation and hope.

Have we finished the race? No way! But we remain in pursuit of the goal. As we pursue the goal that lies before us, we can look back over our shoulder and see the road we have traveled, the potholes we have missed, the speed bumps we have crossed, and how far we have come. But we set all that aside because we still have a long way to go. We do not lose sight of the heavenly call of God in Christ Jesus. That call keeps us moving forward with eagerness.

Heavenly Father, we pray for the fortitude to pursue the goal of your high calling and for the strength to grasp the prize. Amen.

Throughout many years of teaching young musicians and working with church choirs, I have always reinforced a theme: Recovery is everything! There is no perfect performance; there is no perfect race. We as human beings will have setbacks and stumbles. How we handle those setbacks is the most important thing—think on your feet and think quickly!

We are going to stumble on this journey, but how we recover makes all the difference! We can collapse, or we can choose to do some fancy footwork, regain our balance, and dance on! Everyone knows if we collapse, but few realize we have stumbled if we come up with fancy footwork and move on toward the goal.

Paul himself notes that he has not won the race or reached the goal: "I do not consider that I have made it my own." But he still strives and presses forward. Yet he, like us, can acknowledge that we need not run anxiously, for the end is assured. We know the outcome. In this race, everyone wins because Christ has made us his own. Circumstances may offer the opportunity to take a step back. Obstacles will appear along the pathway, but we simply press on.

When challenges arise and seemingly impede our progress toward being the hands and feet of Christ and responding to his calling on our lives, we tie up our laces and continue to press on "toward the goal for the prize of the heavenly call of God in Christ Jesus."

Mighty God, I pray for wisdom and stamina to turn my stumbles into dances as I strive toward the prize of your call in Christ Jesus. Amen.

FIFTH SUNDAY IN LENT

The psalmist records a pilgrimage song in Psalm 126: a pilgrimage from desert and wilderness wandering to being a people restored by God's grace who relish life-giving water. The journey from the darkest hours of the morning to the celebration of the harvest is a long one, requiring faith and strength.

The joy of the harvest comes when we step out of the night of darkness, move beyond ourselves, and begin to focus on others. We see and experience circumstances differently: a clearer path, a direction, a need, a response. We acknowledge that our seeds of faith are growing and taking root.

We grow stronger and then one day we realize it has been a pilgrimage, and it will continue to be a journey. The seedling has grown into a tall plant and bears fruit. There is a harvest that calls for celebration!

In this season of Lent, we sow the tears of crucifixion and death, yet we reap the joy of God's work through the resurrection of Jesus. We recall God's efforts on our behalf in the past and in the present and look forward to the future with joy. We are bearers of memory and hope.

And joy of joys, the plant of the harvest is a perennial that will grow and produce for many years. There will be many harvests, many celebrations. Our sorrow has turned into joy and celebration. Party on!

Rejoice and be glad, for eternal life in God's kingdom belongs to those who run the race and dance when they stumble.

Bone-Deep Despair

MARCH 14–20, 2016 • MARY DONOVAN TURNER

Scripture Overview: Palm/Passion Sunday is a time of celebration over the coming of the King, but it is also a time of foreboding because the celebrants know that the King will soon die. This King is a king like no other, yet he goes almost unrecognized by those over whom he rules. Isaiah 50:4-9 portrays a servant of God who is aware of deep trouble yet faces it with bold confidence. The confidence emerges from a sense that the servant is doing the will of God, but this does not diminish the hostility or render the servant less vulnerable to it. The servant's single purpose is to affirm the rule of God. Psalm 118 celebrates the reality that the rejected building stone "has become the chief cornerstone" (v. 22). The epistle passage sings of Christ's humiliation and exaltation. Luke narrates Jesus' entry into Jerusalem: Jesus enters as king and his greeters extend to him a royal welcome.

Questions and Thoughts for Reflection

- Read Isaiah 50:4-9a. When have you received a word of wisdom from an unexpected place—a child, a rival, an enemy?
- Read Psalm 118:1-2, 19-29. How do you understand the word *salvation*, and when have you known moments of deliverance in your own life?
- Read Philippians 2:5-11. When have you or those you know felt forsaken by God?
- Read Luke 19:28-40. How do you imagine the Palm Sunday story? When have you known the joy of those who stand beside the road waiting for Jesus to enter Jerusalem? Where is God trying to enter the life of your congregation or community of faith?

Ordained minister in the Christian Church (Disciples of Christ); Carl Patton Professor of Preaching at Pacific School of Religion, Berkeley, California

The psalmist calls us to thanksgiving for God's enduring love and faithfulness. Over and over again the psalmist affirms the love of God, God's *hesed*, which never lets us go. Praise and gratitude saturate the psalmist's words as he affirms that this God is his God. They belong to each other in an unconditional bond of respect and support.

When we read the omitted verses of Psalm 118, we realize that the life of the worshiper has not been an easy one. He has experienced distress, hatred, enemies on every side. He had thought he might die. In the midst of the psalmist's despair, God answered him and became his helper, his strength and might, his salvation.

The worshiper gives thanks to God not because life has been easy, untouched by human dilemmas and seemingly insurmountable challenges, but because God actively helped him resist the naysayers and his physical oppression. His vibrant songs of praise issue from his experience of God's faithfulness. God is the source of his immortal gladness, which transcends circumstance, time, and space. God answers, grants success, causes light to shine, and calls forth another day.

When we hit our limits, when fear and anxiety break into our awareness, then comes our realization that dependence on anything other than God can fail us. Not surprisingly, the church reads this psalm every year on the Sunday that ushers in the difficult and challenging stories of Holy Week.

Limitless God, be with us as we make our Lenten journeys. Speak to us in our despair, and remind us of your undying compassion and care. Amen.

Today's passage comes from Isaiah's third servant song. In the servant songs, Israel or the prophet testifies to the calling God has given—the calling to live out and bear witness to God's presence in the world. In this song, the servant says, "The Lord GOD has given me the tongue of a teacher, that I may know how to sustain the weary with a word." Certainly we consider this task part of the calling of a servant of God. A servant notices the weary, then speaks to sustain those most vulnerable to despair.

The servant of God speaks to sustain; yet in these verses, the servant primarily listens. "Morning by morning he awakens my ear." What happens when we make our Lent a "listening Lent"? Where do we hear wisdom? Might it come from the weary ones we have sustained? from those who have gone before us, the ancestors on whose shoulders we stand? Our grandmother who used to sing "My hope is built on nothing less than Jesus' blood and righteousness"?

If we listen to the world around us we may be confronted with questions that pierce the armor of our denials, rationalizations, and self-deceptions. We may find ourselves listening to someone who challenges our closed circle of certainty, the ways that culturally incarcerate and bind us.

When we are servant listeners, something fresh can break through. We may find new alternatives, new solutions to dilemmas, or new answers to questions. Then the way opens so that we can hear, feel, and respond with communal wisdom and courage. There is the possibility of genuine hope. We listen. We learn. We are revived, and we find new ways to be God's servant.

Loving God, open our ears to hear the wisdom of those around us, those who are different from ourselves, perhaps even our enemies. Amen.

The psalmist says that his life is "spent with sorrow." In all likelihood this does not reflect his entire existence; but at this particular moment, his experience is real and seemingly pervasive. These words depict the painful parts of our living. Much like a country song that is sung with a twang of despondency, the psalmist gives voice to a bleak existence. He is in distress: his eyes grow weak, his soul and body grieve; he is in anguish and is groaning. His strength fails; his bones grow weak. Each description becomes a different verse of the same song of despair—graphic lyrics that paint the portrait of his humiliation.

Humiliation and despair, however, are not the final word. This song has a chorus that provides an antidote to the current plight of the worshiper: "But I trust in you, O LORD; . . . You are my God. . . . My times are in your hand."

As in many of the laments in the Psalms, the one who seems lost, overwhelmed, and disoriented finds foundation, a solid place to stand. The psalmist knows that God is with him.

In the end, it is not only important that we believe in God. It is important what kind of God we believe in! In the first eight verses of the psalm, the psalmist stacks metaphor upon metaphor and image upon image to communicate the kind of God he trusts in and in whom his hope lies. This God is refuge, deliverer, rock, fortress, guide, redeemer, and steadfast love. This God listens and sees the psalmist's despair.

We cannot say for certain that bad things will not befall us. However, the guarantee is that God's gracious hand has already been extended. Distress and depression, betrayal and ridicule, acute contradictions—even crucifixion—do not have the final say.

Faithful God, we look back on the tumultuous and chaotic times in our lives and realize that you have always been with us. We are grateful. Amen.

Let the same mind be in you that was in Christ Jesus." These daunting words begin the song found in Philippians 2, a song that does not glorify Jesus' divinity or his superiority but rather the humility and humanity of the one Paul calls Lord.

We customarily think about Jesus' divinity during the Easter season; we use words like *triumphant* and *victorious, resurrected one.* But these verses from the letter written to the church in Philippi invite us to pause for a moment and think about the Jesus who was mortal, who became like us, who walked upon the earth, and who ultimately knew the suffering and despair of death on the cross. He did not exploit his exalted relationship with God but emptied himself, becoming servant to those around him.

"Let the same mind be in you that was in Christ Jesus." What does that mean? It means we are called to resist contemporary expectations and to embody a different kind of community than we see and experience around us. In a world where greed, the accumulation of wealth, and staying on top are the primary goals; a world where trickery and scam, appearances, deception and illusion are the dynamics of everyday life, we are called to be different. This is not a call to become celebrity or to hold a "me first" mentality. This is a call to release our arrogance and become servant . . . of all. This is a call to lose our lives.

How then do we allow God's powerful weakness to work its way into ourselves and our communities? What does a faith community look like when survival and celebrity are not its primary goals, when the congregation willingly loses itself for the sake of those in the community, those most vulnerable among it?

God of expectation, we get drawn into and conform ourselves to the world around us. Give us the courage and wisdom to live our lives as followers of Jesus. Amen.

The Lord is my strength and my might; he has become my salvation." Wisdom about God comes from the mouth of one who has known distress and despair.

The word *salvation* is an important one in the Hebrew Bible, but its Hebraic meaning has been largely lost to us. Like other Hebrew words for redemption, righteousness, and justice, popular and contemporary definitions have lost the substantive grounding we find in the Old Testament texts.

Salvation in the Hebrew Scriptures is largely a poetic word, most often found in the Psalms and in the poetry of the prophets. Nearly half of the psalms contain one or more occurrences of this word. Salvation was considered primarily communal and had an "of this world" character. The psalmist in 118 sings a song of praise because God came to him in his despair and saved him. Salvation, the Hebrews believed, could come time and time again when the community needed deliverance.

Some relate the word *salvation* to other Hebrew words meaning "spacious" and "wide"—connoting a hopefulness that God can deliver us from what restricts or oppresses us, those times when it is hard to breathe because the world seems to be caving in around us. We are given room, a liberating space within which to live. This implies a God who actively participates in the life of the community and in the lives of individuals. Our God listens and hears the cries of distress that arise from our human living. It implies God's willingness and desire that we be given a full and wide berth to live abundantly. The word bears witness to God's willingness to come to us and to continue coming to us as the world brings us tragedy and despair.

God, we thank you for the times you have pulled us forth from the restrictive stretches and places in our lives so that we could breathe in the fullness of life you desire for us. Amen.

Jesus experienced all our human emotions. As he moves toward Jerusalem for the last time, he teaches through parables; he heals; he calls to Zacchaeus. Then he sends two disciples to find a young colt. They bring it to him. Jesus gets on the colt and begins what we call his "triumphal entry" into Jerusalem.

Hearing this story as a child, I had imagined that people standing along the roadway had been alerted and notified that Jesus was headed their way. I could imagine fliers being distributed, calls made, everyone on board as to what was about to take place. If they stood by the side of the road, if they got there early and found a good place to stand, they would get a glimpse of the parade that was passing by.

But, of course, it is not that way at all. People standing by the side of the road are probably in conversation with family and friends, shopping at the markets, going about their daily chores. And then, perhaps, one person notices Jesus passing by. *Is that Jesus?* Yes, though they have only heard stories about him and have never really seen him. One person takes notice and tells another. And then another. People begin to look, and energy rises. His followers begin to shout and sing, praising God for what they have seen and heard, giving thanks for God's work among them.

Lent calls us to a greater sensitivity, a greater vulnerability, a greater awareness. The "triumphal entry" occurs in the middle of life marked by good memories and not so good ones; in the midst of unlikely conversion experiences; wise investments; neglect, betrayal, and pain. Now is the time to open our eyes, ears, and hearts to the ways that God is trying desperately to enter our lives, our communities, our world—ways we do not expect and that we may not at first recognize. God can surprise us.

Open our eyes, God, so that we can see what in the world you are doing among us. Amen.

PALM/PASSION SUNDAY

We stand on the threshold of the complexities of Holy Week. Our readings this week have invited us to think about the intimate relationship between despair and hopefulness, sadness and joy. The worshipers in Psalms 31 and 118 know the depth of tragedy and challenge; their unwavering trust and hope in God inspire. Isaiah knows the calling and the satisfaction of living faithfully, though he has experienced resistance and violence. And Paul in Philippians 2 speaks of a Jesus who comes to know death but who lives resolutely and steadfastly.

These texts prepare us for the gritty, complicated, textured stories that await us, stories like the Passover meal Jesus shares with his disciples. This meal is grounded in the narrative about a delivering God but a "last meal" tinged with forewarnings of death, betrayal, and denial. There joy and sadness comingle. Every event taking place around the disciples suggests God's abandonment and absence! Have they misplaced their trust? Has Jesus really been "forsaken" as he shouts out this shocking word from the cross?

Our texts for Palm/Passion Sunday cry out a resounding NO. There is no abandonment here—only the testimony of many who can speak of God's presence in the midst of the overwhelming realities that face us. The prophets and psalmist whisper words of assurance as we travel over the rocky terrain of the week to come.

God is here. God is compassionate. God hears our despair. God is our helper. God will have the final word.

God, we despair about local and world events. They bring us to despair. Reassure us that we do not travel alone. Amen.

Loving as Jesus Loved

MARCH 21–27, 2016 • JEREMY T. BAKKER

Scripture Overview: [*This Scripture Overview accompanies the lections listed for Easter Sunday.*] The common themes of death's reality, the powerful intrusion of the delivering God, and the manifold responses to resurrection run prominently through the texts. The psalmist rejoices at an occasion of divine deliverance, remembering death as a threat from which God has provided rescue. In the Gospel passage, Mary acknowledges the devastation of death and begins to come to grips with her grief and consternation. All four texts announce God's deliverance from death, the divine "power play" that brings life not only for "the one ordained by God as judge of the living and the dead" (Acts 10:42) but also for God's people (1 Cor. 15). Jesus' resurrection makes possible a radical style of new life.

Questions and Thoughts for Reflection

- Read John 12:1-11, 20-36. How can you be more aware of those who experience quiet suffering? In what ways will this awareness require sacrifice?
- Read John 13:1-17, 31*b*-35. Where in your life can you be more open to and forgiving of the shortcomings and flaws of family and friends?
- Read John 18:1-19:42. We are called to live in a world of ambiguity. How can you resist self-certainty that leads to manipulation?
- Read John 20:1-18. The Resurrection allows us to live as Jesus lived. In what ways can you accept this truth and live full of knowledge and truth?

Scholar in Residence, Upper Room Ministries, Nashville, Tennessee

Jesus arrives in Bethany six days before the Passover. We have just learned that the authorities plan to put him to death. (See John 11:53-57.) And we can scarcely envision any alternative to his ultimate fate. We read of it as early as the first chapter (John 1:29, 36), and Mary's anointing in chapter 12 seals it. But we are all the poorer if we fail to consider the intricacies of the story that leads up to the cross.

Many interpreters draw a singular connection between Mary's anointing of Jesus and his burial. Jesus defends Mary's act by proclaiming that she bought the ointment "so that she might keep it for the day of my burial." But to focus only on the connection between anointing and burial in John's Gospel is to miss Mary's anticipating Jesus' foot washing. Mary, a woman, epitomizes discipleship in the Fourth Gospel by fulfilling Jesus' love command before he speaks it. (See John 13:1-35.)

As we begin this journey through Holy Week, many of our minds will turn to consider once more whether we can bear the true cost of discipleship. If we strive to live as Jesus lived, we must prepare to die as he died—and many of us have much to lose. But I wonder whether the journey of Lent remains incomplete unless we also recognize the quiet suffering of those who fall victim to oppression and social derision. They, like Mary, bear the marks of discipleship even before the season demands it. And they often have no one who calls attention to their plight.

As fear about our own fate calls for our attention, let us be mindful first for those who suffer in silence this day.

The Jesus in this Gospel troubles me. In the other three Gospels, Jesus wavers before the cross—but not in John. Pondering the cross he asks, "What should I say, 'Father save me from this hour'?" Then he answers his own question, "No, it is for this reason that I have come to this hour."

Reading these verses, I miss the Jesus described in the Synoptic Gospels who prays for the cup to pass from him. That Jesus has doubts like I do. His hesitance to march headlong toward death makes him more human, more like me.

Much of my discomfort with John's version stems from Jesus' charge to the crowd—and to the rest of us—that "those who love their life lose it." In the other Gospels, I also hear that call to discipleship, but the life-or-death consequences aren't quite so loud or clear. Take up my "cross"? It's just a metaphor, right? Well, at least that's what I can tell myself.

John's Gospel leaves no room to rationalize. There is no denying the connection between discipleship and painful sacrifice. A kernel of wheat must die to give life. Those who love their life will lose it. Those who hate it will keep it. Disciples follow Jesus as he marches headlong toward a place of unfathomable pain and suffering.

In this scripture, Jesus invites us to probe our discomfort. He also bids us to look closely at our commitment to our faith. Discipleship comes at a price. But we can pay it with the assurance that God's gift of selfless love has prepared us for times of trial.

God, when we pray for deliverance in times of trial, assure us that your love abides. Amen.

Jesus has just finished washing the disciples' feet when he jolts them with the news: "One of you will betray me." The disciples look at one another. Who could Jesus be talking about? The scripture wastes no time convicting its readers. Even those closest to Jesus could be an accomplice in his death.

Imagining myself as one of the disciples, I'd like to think I could feel assured Jesus wasn't talking about me; I suppose we all would like to feel the same way. But then my doubts creep in. And I wonder if some of you are unsure.

As we read, we can join the beloved disciple who asks, "Lord, who is it?" confident that we too warrant a special place next to Jesus. But in our living we have to wonder whether we might run off into the dark night with Judas.

Jesus responds, "It is the one to whom I give this piece of bread when I have dipped it in the dish." The disciples still do not understand. Evil enters a man who has just participated in a symbolic act that identifies him as the betrayer. And the disciples miss it. Their guilt-laden introspection blinds them to the evil swirling around them. While wondering whether they could be the culprits, they overlook evil incarnate. So it is with us.

We are on the march toward the cross. Jesus has told us that we must go with him if we are to be his disciples. The invitation certainly warrants introspection. We must consider the cost and our willingness to pay it. But our quest for internal assurance must not blind us to the external powers that assail the world. The disciples look inward and miss the external tragedy. May we learn from their mistake. Systemic evil abounds, and God calls us to confront it at the risk of losing our very lives.

When life forces us to look inward, O God, draw us out. When the world demands our immediate action, O God, draw us in. May we find balance in you. Amen.

MAUNDY THURSDAY

The one command Jesus issues to his disciples alone stands at the conclusion of today's reading. "By this everyone will know that you are my disciples," he tells them, "if you have love for one another." Following on the heels of Jesus' washing his disciples' feet, his command to love exhorts them toward sacrificial devotion to the well-being of others.

However, unlike other Bible passages, the injunction in John to love is limited to insiders. There is no command to love neighbor, and, at first glance, it may seem as though John has softened the commitment required to be a disciple. But it is not so.

Today's reading is hollow. It contains the introduction and conclusion to yesterday's episode (John 13:21-32). Unless we consider that story at the same time as today's text, Jesus' ethical imperative can appear to be little more than an exhortation toward service: Jesus washes his disciples feet, and we should do likewise. Humble service becomes the mark of love.

In its entirety, John 13 places the love command in the context of Jesus' death and betrayal. It teaches us that discipleship is predicated upon our learning to love those among us who openly betray the ones we love or who remain woefully ignorant of their own contribution to evil, suffering, and death in this world.

It is relatively easy to love neighbors. It's easy to say we "love our neighbors" when we don't have to interact with them. But to love our friends and family with all their flaws and shortcomings requires us to recognize that we too are culpable. For we act in ways that require our friends to give of themselves selflessly. None is above reproach. Lord, have mercy on us.

Kyrie eleison, Christe eleison, Kyrie eleison.

GOOD FRIDAY

At the conclusion of the Farewell Discourse (John 14–17), Jesus goes with his disciples to a garden in the Kidron Valley. There, on the east side of Jerusalem, Judas betrays him to the authorities, and John's narrative pace quickens. It takes Jesus three chapters to bid his disciples farewell. Within the eighteenth chapter alone, Jesus is arrested, tried three times, and condemned to death.

At the beginning of chapter 19, Pilate declares that he has found no case against Jesus. The Jewish authorities beg for a crucifixion, and Pilate responds in so many words, "Do it yourself." Resolute, the Jewish authorities press their case, accusing Jesus of blasphemy. His fate rests in a game of political intrigue.

The Jewish authorities have just abdicated their legal right to the death penalty while standing before Pilate. (See Leviticus 24:13-16.) And they have done so in order to manipulate the Roman leader into doing what they have been unable to do. They use knowledge of their religious traditions to exploit Pilate, who is not as well informed.

I wonder how we often we do likewise. From the perspective of the twenty-first century, the biblical texts often seem flexible enough to allow us to shoehorn our own agenda into them. The breadth and depth of the Christian tradition often allows for justification of many ideas and actions that others find unorthodox.

Holy Week compels us to examine our own role in Jesus' Passion. May we find ourselves faithful in love when expedience calls us to manipulate another with our own self-certainty.

God of great mystery, empower us to live faithfully in the ambiguity of your world as we await the day when we will know fully. Amen.

We first meet Nicodemus in chapter 3 of John's Gospel. He seeks Jesus under the cover of night in order to learn from him, which—on the surface—seems an admirable deed. A leader of the Jews, Nicodemus goes to Jesus at great personal risk. But his initial foray into discipleship is superficial, and John makes no room for halfhearted discipleship. Nicodemus, it seems, is among those John condemns at the end of chapter 3 when he writes, "This is the judgment, that the light has come into the world, and people loved darkness rather than light because their deeds were evil" (John 3:19). Nicodemus seeks the light. But he cannot bring himself to abandon the dark.

As the Gospel account proceeds, Nicodemus gains confidence. In chapter 7, he makes his second appearance, tepidly defending Jesus in the open. As the Temple authorities debate the best way to deal with Jesus, Nicodemus asks, "Our law does not judge people without first giving them a hearing to find out what they are doing, does it?" (v. 51). It's hardly an open proclamation of fidelity to Jesus. But it's a step in the right direction.

Nicodemus secures his attachment to Jesus following the crucifixion. Today's reading shows Nicodemus bringing what amounts to one hundred pounds of ointment to prepare Jesus' body for burial. Recalling Mary's anointing of Jesus, Nicodemus's excessive attention to Jesus' body bears witness to his irrepressible love for the man. By the end, Nicodemus has come full circle. His story attests to the later Johannine proclamation that "perfect love casts out fear" (1 John 4:18).

That, for me, points to the invitation of Holy Saturday. The world is dark, and there is much to fear. God incarnate lies dead in the tomb. Have we the courage to love as Jesus loved?

O God, when the dark world beckons, call to us so that we might walk forth toward the light. Amen.

EASTER SUNDAY

"Christ is risen, he is risen indeed!" This shout of exultation often marks the arrival of Easter, but I have never resonated with it. When I studied today's passage, I understood why.

For many, the story of Christianity is the story of Easter, and the story of Easter is the story of the resurrection. I, on the other hand, have centered my faith in the story of the Incarnation. To paraphrase Athanasius, God became flesh so that we might become divine. (See John 17:19-26.) For me, the path to Christian perfection becomes possible not through the Resurrection but through the Ascension.

The key proclamation of John's Easter story comes in Jesus' command to Mary. He tells her, "Go to my brothers and say to them, 'I am ascending to my Father and your Father, to my God and your God.'" Unlike Matthew and Mark, who recount Jesus commanding Mary to tell the disciples of his resurrection, here John focuses on Jesus' ascension. His return to the Father opens for us the possibility of knowing God in a new way, for his God is now our God.

John's Gospel begins with the proclamation that "No one has ever seen God. It is God the only Son, who is close to the Father's heart, who has made him known" (John 1:18). The Gospel winds down with Jesus telling his disciples that he is ascending to "my Father and your Father, to my God and your God" (John 20:17). The joy of Easter is not simply that we will rise as Jesus rose. By means of his death, resurrection, and ascension, we can live as Jesus lived, beloved of God, full of knowledge and truth.

God of new life, draw our eyes heavenward that we may live beyond the shadow of the cross and into the divine community marked by love. Amen.

Our Great God

MARCH 28–APRIL 3, 2016 • PHILIP HUBER

Scripture Overview: The texts help us grasp what it means to be "witnesses" of the resurrection. Acts 5 depicts the apostles in Jerusalem announcing both the resurrection of Jesus to those who shared in his death and his exaltation as Savior. The apostles witness by means of a verbal proclamation, through which the Holy Spirit functions as divine authorization. Revelation 1:4-8 continues the theme by declaring Jesus as "the faithful witness, the firstborn of the dead, and the ruler of the kings of the earth" (1:5). Identification with Jesus produces a body of people that intercedes before God on behalf of the world and stands before the world on behalf of God. John 20 records the transformation of Thomas, for whom analysis and debate give way to confession: "My Lord and my God!" (20:28). The psalm's call to praise becomes a summons to live one's life in the context of God's powerful rule.

Questions and Thoughts for Reflection

- Read Psalm 150. How do you prefer to express praise to the Lord?
- Read Revelation 1:4-9. How do you offer others access to God?
- Read John 20:19-31. What does Jesus' offer of peace mean to you?
- Read Acts 5:27-32. How do you bear witness to Christ's presence in your life?

Shepherd, Inlet Community Church; retail manager, living in the Adirondacks in upstate New York

In six short verses the psalmist offers a succession of a dozen entreaties to praise the Lord. These staccato phrases express the where, why, how, and who of praise—with emphasis on the *how*. *How* can we offer adequate praise for God's superlative greatness? In this case the answer comes through a cataloging of means. We are to match God's overwhelming greatness with our exuberant praise, the instrumentation adding variety and intensity. Every type of instrument is employed—wind, string, percussion. In this symphony of praise, each instrument adds its unique sound. Layer upon layer, they form the song, one instrument complementing another. The psalmist weaves the visual aspect of dance into the auditory fullness of the score. Nothing is held back.

The psalm rises to the crescendo of clanging cymbals, twice mentioned in verse 5, as if to double the volume of an already blaring chorus. The psalm begins and ends with the shout of "Praise the Lord!," a verbal concentration of overflowing praise.

Psalm 150 invites us to hold nothing back in our worship. We express our adoration with our voice, our expression, our imagination, our instrumentation, and our joyful exuberance. Variety and creativity are essential elements of our praise. While our ability to express God's supreme worthiness has limits, in worship we strive to push those limits as far as we can.

Almighty God, may I reflect your greatness in my praise. Amen.

Some movies end with a door left open to a sequel. The writers wrap up most of the plotlines but leave one conspicuously open. This will become the launch point for the follow-up. In a way, the book of Psalms ends in this manner. The final psalm comes to a close, but it leaves a loose end dangling.

Psalm 150 is a psalm of closure. It is the last in a group of five songs (Psalm 146–150) that begin and end with the Hebrew phrase *Hallelu Yah* (Hallelujah!), which means "Praise the Lord." It completes the book of Psalms, a fitting doxology with an extended call to praise. But it also concludes the fifth book in Psalms, stretching from Psalm 107–150. This book does not close in quite the same way as the other four books in Psalms.

The first four books of the Psalms end with "Amen," a word of tight closure that means "so be it." (See Psalms 41; 72; 89; 106.) It is a fitting capstone to what has gone before, a latch to close the door tightly on all that has been expressed in the preceding collection of psalms. There is agreement to what has been expressed. But Psalm 150 has no "Amen." Instead it ends with *Hallelu Yah*, an invitation to praise the Lord.

This leaves the psalm surprisingly open-ended. The psalmist issues a summons to praise with no response given. God awaits our RSVP. This catalog of 150 songs has not exhausted our praise. Everything that has breath receives an invitation to join in the chorus of praise and add its voice. The praise that unfolds throughout the Psalms will continue beyond the confines of the book. Our own praise becomes the sequel, an opportunity to add our own psalm to the collection. This ongoing worship expressed by those who accept the invitation will be the "Amen" that has been left unsaid.

"Let everything that breathes praise the LORD."

My family recently moved to a community situated on a lake in the Adirondacks of New York. Rustic cabins that overlook the water and the surrounding mountains dot the lake. Recently as my family and I rode our bicycles along the road encircling the lake, I noticed that most of these properties had signs posted. PRIVATE PROPERTY. NO TRESPASSING. The signs emphasized the boundaries. Outsiders were told to pay attention to the fences.

We noted one exception: A group of rental cottages had a sign at their entrance with the words VISITORS WELCOME in large lettering. Lured in by the invitation, we cycled down the driveway. When we reached the parking area, a man greeted us and encouraged us to ride down to the shoreline and take in the view, bragging that it was the best around.

What a stark contrast. Instead of focusing on boundary markers, this man's interest lay more in inviting people to experience what his rental property had to offer within its boundaries. All were welcome to come and take in the view.

It is easy to portray the gospel as a message of restriction, where fences and boundary markers become the focus. But John introduces Jesus as the one "who loves us and freed us from our sins by his blood" (Rev. 1:5). The very first mention of Jesus in a book known for its heavy-handed judgment emphasizes grace and freedom. God's love is preeminent, making us to be priests, a privileged position of those who have access to God.

Instead of pointing out the fence lines, we are being invited to come and enjoy the view. In his love, Jesus has freed us from our sins, poured his grace upon us, and given us direct access to God. We rejoice in this blessed relationship.

Lord, help me to erect the sign that invites people to discover the freedom that is found in you. Amen.

Zechariah had predicted a day when the inhabitants of Jerusalem would look on the one they had pierced and mourn for him (12:10). Their sensibilities would stir them from their spiritual stupor. They would come to their senses, realizing what they had done in crucifying the promised Messiah. The grief of guilt would replace the bliss of ignorance.

In the book of Revelation, the reach of this realization extends to all people. "Look! He is coming with the clouds; every eye will see him, even those who pierced him." The most resistant heart and the most rebellious spirit will break.

Yet amidst the feelings of grief and mourning shared by the people of John's world and ours, this greeting from John to the seven churches (and to us) comes: "Grace to you and peace from him who is and who was and who is to come." Though we suffer from the guilt of our sin, God brings peace. The greeting comes also from "him who loves us and freed us from our sins by his blood." This same Jesus Christ has made us, even in our sin, "to be a kingdom, priests serving his God and Father."

Paul wrote to the Philippian church, "At the name of Jesus every knee should bend . . . and every tongue should confess that Jesus Christ is Lord, to the glory of God the Father" (Phil. 2:10-11). Surely the choice to repent of our waywardness and disobedience is ours. Will we continue to search aimlessly for some kind of life that holds purpose for us? Will we still be searching when the One "who is to come" returns?

Our search will be over when we bow before God and allow God, the Alpha and Omega, to be the beginning and the end of each of our days.

Lord, I bow to you today in submission, anticipating a day when every knee will bow. Amen.

Fear hangs heavy in the air. The authorities have brutally executed the disciples' leader. Clearly the authorities intend to squelch this burgeoning threat. How far will they go with this crusade? With the leader removed, will they search for the key followers in order to nail the coffin shut? In fear, the disciples hide behind locked doors.

The disciples have put their confidence in locks; their security hinges on latches and bolts. But even locked doors do little to calm their anxiety. *What if their hiding place is discovered; what if there is another way in; what if the lock doesn't hold?*

They feel anxious and fearful. Then Jesus appears, undeterred by any hindrance. The lock not only indicates the disciples' fear but sets up Jesus' miraculous arrival. The lock makes Jesus' sudden appearance that much more amazing; locks are no match for him! Jesus turns a locked door into an opening for the joy of his presence.

Jesus conveys a message—a message twice uttered, "Peace be with you." The locks, which bring a measure of security, prove inadequate to subdue the disciples' fears. But where locks fail, Jesus succeeds. He offers his peace to overcome their fears. The disciples can find their security in him. As fear dissipates, joy replaces sorrow.

Jesus makes this same offer of peace to us. We may employ all manner of earthbound solutions to quell our fears, but all will prove inadequate. With doors tightly locked, fear can still overwhelm us. Locks cannot ease the barrage of "what ifs." But Jesus can bring peace and ease our anxieties. The resurrected Lord has defeated death; surely he can defeat the sources of our fears!

Lord, I invite you to bring peace to calm my fears. Amen.

Istarted a new job recently, working in a retail environment where I was basically starting over. I had much to learn: same field, new company. The new work overlapped some with my former job, but I had to learn which aspects were the same and which differed. The broad training process didn't prepare me for many specifics. When I felt unsure, I asked someone.

I learned quickly that I got contradictory answers from various people. I had to choose to whom I would listen. The weight of the answers I got lay in direct proportion to the person's authority on the job. When I got conflicting answers to taking action, I would listen to the person who had the most authority.

The apostles deal with this very issue when the Sanhedrin issues a warning not to teach in Jesus' name. They realize that they have already received a command from a higher authority. Jesus has charged them to be his witnesses starting in Jerusalem (Acts 1:9). They cannot obey both; they must decide. Peter and the apostles reply, "We must obey God rather than any human authority."

Each of us faces pressure regularly to compromise on what God has revealed. We can justify shortcuts and easily manufacture excuses as to why following God's instruction is outdated or irrelevant. But we must make the choice: follow God or obey any other voice. God honors the decision of the apostles by expanding the reach of their ministry (Acts 6:1). He will honor our decision to follow also, even if that means disobeying lesser authorities.

Lord, give me courage to obey you, even if that means disobeying or disappointing others. Amen.

When we hear the word *witness* used in a religious context, we think in terms of a verb—something we *do*, a spiritual obligation that overwhelms us with feelings of inadequacy. But in this passage *witness* functions as a noun and refers to something we *are*. Witnesses testify to their personal knowledge, relating firsthand experience. In a courtroom, witnesses establish the facts based on what they saw. In defense of their unwavering proclamation of the death of Christ, Peter and the apostles declare, "We are witnesses to these things." They testify to their personal experience.

Each person's living generates unique experiences. While the disciples serve as witnesses to the death and resurrection of Jesus, Paul as a witness has his own encounter with Christ on the road to Damascus (see Acts 22:15). His experience differs but with no less transformative effect. These individuals have personally experienced the power of God to transform. Each person bears witness to his or her own encounter—the disciples do it; Paul does it; we do it. If we have come to know Christ as our Savior, we have our own experience to draw from, our own story to tell, our own encounter to testify about. Out of that personal experience we share our story.

How has Christ changed your life? How has he helped you deal with disappointment, fear, or anxiety? How has he healed hurt in your heart? How has he comforted you in grief? How has he broken the chains of addiction? How has he guided you through difficult decisions?

Start there with your personal encounter with the Savior. Then bear witness and be a witness to Christ.

Lord, I pray for an opportunity to share with someone a story of my personal encounter with you. Open the door, and give me boldness to walk through. Amen.

New Roads, New Beginnings

APRIL 4–10, 2016 • DARIAN DUCKWORTH

Scripture Overview: Moments of disclosure can free us to go on with life. Such a disclosure happened to the disciples after a long night of unsuccessful fishing. They hear a voice directing them to let down the nets on the right side. As they do so and find an enormous catch of fish, they wonder who has such insight about the waters. The beloved disciple voices the revelation, "It is the Lord!" Just so, the light that flashed on the Damascus road and the voice of identification constituted such a moment of disclosure for Paul. In reflection, the psalmist sings about such a moment for himself. These texts relate revelations of the divine mystery. The scene in Revelation puts it most clearly. The scroll that not only explains the final events of human history but sets them in motion is to be opened, but who is worthy to do it? "The Lion of the tribe of Judah, the Root of David."

Questions and Thoughts for Reflection

- Read Acts 9:1-6. Where do you see God's light overtaking your life? How can you, like Paul, allow time and space for God to work in your life?
- Read Psalm 30. When have you failed to respond to God's "pull"?
- Read Revelation 5:11-14. Whose song will you join as you surround the throne?
- Read John 21:1-19. What in your life reminds you to run toward Jesus' friendship rather than away from it?

Pastor, St. Luke United Methodist Church, Cleveland, Mississippi; Yahweh yoga instructor

When the alarm wakens us in the early morning hours, we reach for a lamp switch. The sudden entrance of light causes us to blink—and maybe yawn. When the closing credits of a movie roll in a darkened theater, we push the bar of the EXIT door to the parking lot. From darkness to sunshine, we have to cover our eyes and reach for sunglasses. But when the holy light finds Saul on the road to Damascus, more than his eyes react. God's light doesn't stop at the eyes. "A light from heaven flashed around him," overpowering his body.

Behind the light is a force that knocks an adult man off his feet. Years of anger, homicidal thoughts, hatred, jealousy, and pride begin to drop off his shoulders. This light desires all five senses. He sees it. It touches him. Then it speaks. He hears. His desire for the taste and smell of food weakens to the point of fasting. While everyone thinks that Saul has gone blind, God is actually opening his eyes from the inside out.

We often speak of Saul's Damascus road experience as a spontaneous conversion. In the course of one chapter, Christ transforms him from a murderer of Christians to a worshiper of Christ. We fail to note how long his conversion took. "For three days he was without sight, and neither ate nor drank" (Acts 9:9). The light is powerful, but sometimes we take days to surrender to its loving power. Saul's journey was not one of instant change. His change took time, patience, and fear of the unknown. Where are you on your Damascus road? How has God's light overtaken your life?

Jesus of Damascus road, transform me today. Amen.

Lord, I'll do anything for you—but. . . . " How easy disciple-ship seems without a Saul.

Ananias, a disciple who has divine visions and hears the Lord's voice, seems to know God well. He even questions God's request of him, a sign of authentic friendship. Perhaps this close-ness encourages God to trust Ananias with a difficult task: "Go . . . look for a man of Tarsus named Saul." Immediately Ananias recognizes the name, and he trembles in fear. God directs him to go to a man who has killed Ananias's friends—and might kill him too.

When have you felt pushed out of your comfort zone? How has the Spirit nudged you toward a person from whom you want to run? We often limit what we will and won't do for God. We say that we'll do anything, but eventually we state a "but"—fol-lowed by a fear. Ananias offers a solid argument, citing the word on Damascus's streets about Saul.

Yet Ananias does not say no. He honestly expresses his misgivings, and God honestly tells him what he has in store for Saul. For a second time, God tells Ananias to "go," and he obeys.

How long the journey to Judas's house on Straight Street must have seemed! As stunned Saul stumbles into Damascus, led by the hands of his companions, Ananias now travels on familiar roads to unfamiliar territory. Each of his footsteps traces a path of faith, a belief that God knows what God is doing even when we only fearfully obey. Faith spurs us out of our comfort zones to a place where miracles happen: "Immediately something like scales fell from [Saul's] eyes, and his sight was restored. Then he got up and was baptized."

Lord of Straight Street, draw me out of comfortable discipleship and into your miracle-working kingdom. May I too receive my sight. Amen.

Long before Jesus of Nazareth healed people with a touch, the God of David healed with a pull: "I will exalt you, LORD, because you pulled me up" (CEB). Pushing and pulling are a part of everyday life. We push grocery carts down the aisle. We pull a towel off a high shelf. Pushing and pulling can also indicate a struggle. We discipline children who push one another on the playground. We chastise the little boy who pulls the pigtails of a little girl sitting in front of him. In the wrong hands at the wrong time with the wrong motive, pushing and pulling can become dangerous. In the right hands at the right time with the right motive, pulling can save a life.

The hands of the Lord have pulled David out of his enemies' reach and drawn him out of the grave. David cried out to God to save him. Now he celebrates the answer to his prayer in an assembly. God has saved him with a pull.

What would have happened if David had resisted the healing God offered? If someone is in a literal pit, and a hand reaches down, the person at the bottom of the pit has to reach back if he or she wants out. Rescue is much easier for the rescuer if the "rescuee" responds to the offer to be pulled out.

Pits and potholes litter our lives. We fall into some, and we create others. Sometimes it's easier to set up residence in the ditches or to live "among those going down to the pit" (CEB). We'd rather live in misery than risk a struggle. We'd rather push than give in to God's pull. Healing of our souls requires effort and endurance. But when God is the one pulling and bringing us up, a morning of joy awaits!

Today I will not resist the hands that are lifting me to new life.

By the end of Psalm 30, David has made a difficult vow. God has pulled him to safety and turned his tear fest into a dancing festival. Rescued, David composes a song to express his gratitude. With his gratitude comes a promise: "My whole being might sing praises to you and never stop. LORD, my God, I will give thanks to you forever" (CEB).

Does David really use the words *never* and *forever*? What absolute words with lofty goals! David is not saying that he will literally sing "hallelujah" in his sleep until the day he dies. Perhaps he is trying to find words that give voice to his gratitude. It is hard to express in words, and "forever" is the best we can do in the limitations of language and song.

Forever is a long time. Forever encompasses everything—both the good and the bad. We use the word so often that we forget its weightiness. A newly married couple vows fidelity to each other forever. Someone does us a favor, and we say that we're indebted to her forever. A company meeting drags on for hours, and we whisper to a colleague that we've been in that room forever. God heals a loved one or answers our prayer, and we promise to serve God forever.

Forever does not constitute a flippant promise. It is a commitment to praise God even when we don't know what to say. Forever calls us to look back on the times that God "took off [our] funeral clothes and dressed [us] up in joy" (CEB). When we vow our forever to God, we see that in Christ Jesus God gives us forever too.

Today I will give thanks for God's presence in my life. Tomorrow, I will give thanks again. The day after tomorrow, I will give thanks yet again. . . .

The end of the New Testament begins a new song. Amid the letters, visions, beasts, and riddles of Revelation are these spoken verses set to music over the centuries. They are choruses that praise a slaughtered Lamb, the center of John's "dream," who rises victorious over all kingdoms and powers in heaven and on earth.

Think about the largest choir you've ever seen. How many people stood on those risers or lined those pews? How many voices did you hear? Sometimes even a small group of people can create a sound much bigger than what the eye can see. Now imagine that choir growing exponentially as more voices join in. The "choir" of Revelation is grander than anything we can imagine: "They numbered in the millions—thousands upon thousands" (CEB). That's only the census of those around the throne of God. Add to their count every being from the story of creation in Genesis—the swoosh of every fish, the whistle of every leaf, the howl of every wolf, the voice of every person—all created by God. The cosmos can't contain that splendor.

No matter how great the numbers, John describes hearing all these individuals as "a loud voice" (CEB)—one single, united sound. Every rustle and roar unite in words of worship. With so many denominations, traditions, theologies, and divisions in the church, we long for unity. On what can we agree when we face so much disagreement? From this passage, we can discern two truths. To God belongs all power. To the Lamb who laid down his life as a sacrifice belongs all worship.

Unity does not mean that every voice is identical. John celebrates diversity around the throne and on the earth. Unity arises from hearts, eyes, and ears fixed on Jesus Christ—the center of all worship.

Lamb of God, tune my voice to be part of your song. Amen.

We take comfort in familiarity. For Simon Peter, fishing is familiar. We assume that he's already seen the risen Lord with the other disciples. But there's been no specific mention of Peter since he stood in the empty tomb, puzzled by Jesus' abandoned grave clothes. He cannot remove the guilt and blame of his denial of Jesus from his soul as easily as he can take the robe from his back. So he goes fishing. His friends come along. They try to return to life before Jesus, before the upper room, before the garden, before the crow of the cock.

When we feel let down, and life doesn't play out as we hoped, the easiest route is back the way we came. Like Peter, we cling to something that helps to pass the hours and occupy our minds. When we feel like we've failed God and strayed too far from God's grace, we feel drawn to old ways of life.

The funny thing is that Peter's not very good at fishing anymore. He's tasted heavenly power but tries to get by on his own power. The results? Empty nets and frustrated, sleepy friends—until a stranger yells advice from the shore. The nets fill, and Peter recognizes the mysterious fishing adviser. Instead of cowering in a corner of the boat, ashamed of his past, Peter leaps toward his Lord. He swims toward a second chance that awaits him on the land.

Jesus already has breakfast on the "stove." He wants what they have too, saying, "Bring some of the fish that you've just caught" (CEB). Jesus feeds them, and the disciples feed him in a fellowship of forgiven friends. It's easy to run from a new beginning. But when we choose to run toward the beginning, what awaits us is a familiar friend.

Today I will let go of shame and guilt. I will accept a new beginning.

Awkward conversations occur often. You round a corner in a bookstore and bump into an ex-boyfriend—who introduces you to his new girlfriend. You sit next to an acquaintance at a dinner party who asks about your political leanings. Your mom asks why you and your spouse haven't had a baby yet. We've all been there; we probably looked for the nearest exit.

On the shore of the Sea of Tiberius, Simon Peter has no exit. Breakfast is over, and Jesus looks at him. He calls him by his old name and asks if he loves him. What a perfect opportunity for redemption! Peter responds quickly and well, "Yes, Lord, you know I love you." Jesus gives him instructions. Peter must breathe a sigh of relief. His denial slips farther into the past.

Jesus asks him the same question again. Maybe Peter shifts uncomfortably. Perhaps the other disciples excuse themselves to wash dishes. Does Jesus need proof of his love? He answers the same, and Jesus gives him more instructions.

When Jesus asks the third time, it's enough to make the grown man visibly sad. Jesus still does not call him by his new name, and he asks the same question over and over. The conversation turns awkward in its repetition. Does Jesus not believe his sincerity?

The third time, Jesus goes into more detail. He describes the future. Jesus and Peter need this conversation so Jesus can tell him what lies ahead.

We go through "awkward stages" of physical and emotional development. They are not always pleasant, but they are necessary. These stages and conversations help to shape and form us into caregivers of one another in God's kingdom.

Lord, you know everything. You know that I love you. May all my experiences fashion me into your servant. Amen.

Faith and the Power of Community

APRIL 11–17, 2016 • ROY M. CARLISLE

Scripture Overview: All four passages voice the providential care of a loving God whose concern reaches out to needy folk. The widows in the Acts account are saintly but are also vulnerable in the broader society and subject to manipulation by ruthless scoundrels. Peter becomes an instrument of divine mercy for their leader, Dorcas. In the vision in Revelation, the great, diverse host of people "have come out of the great ordeal"; they now experience deliverance, shelter, and a way to the "springs of the water of life" (7:17). Both Psalm 23 and John 10 relate God's providential care. To be a part of the shepherd's flock means to be watched carefully so that no foe can snatch the sheep from the hands of the divine caretaker.

Questions and Thoughts for Reflection

• Read Acts 9:36-43. Where do you experience true friendship and community?

• Read Psalm 23. How could times of trouble provide opportunities to develop the discipline of faith?

• Read Revelation 7:9-17. Where do you experience the diversity of racial, cultural, and ethnic issues most often? How has that diversity broadened your perspective?

• Read John 10:22-30. How do your works testify to your desire to heed Jesus' words?

Acquisitions Director, The Independent Institute; cofounder, Academy of Christian Editors; Oakland, California

We all yearn for community: a place to belong, a place where our personal welfare is considered important by others and where we can depend on the charity and grace of others. Tabitha's friends evidence this longing. They have lost a dear friend. They care enough about her to ask Peter to come to her bedside. And Tabitha's care for her friends was reciprocal. She cared about all of them, as her gifts of clothing and her good works indicate.

This depth of commitment may seem simple enough, but it is actually quite elusive in modern life. We often substitute social niceties, even at church, for true community. But in Joppa friendships ran deep and were heartfelt.

Deep personal friendships always involve acts of trust, honesty, vulnerability, and faith, which in turn build communities that care, even in the midst of tragic loss. Faith that has the power to affect lives, even dramatically, takes root in these honest and trusting communities.

The friends bear witness to God's providential care for those in need, especially for those who have no other recourse. As a member of a faithful community while in seminary I learned that faith is never a private affair but meets our deep need for belonging when it is a part of an honest community. I hope you find or build yours.

Jesus, help me build friendships that will encourage and enliven my faith. Amen.

When we belong to a faithful community we find that serving others comes naturally. Clearly Tabitha had discovered this and offered herself to the community in good works. Joppa, a coastal town, probably had its share of widows and orphans due to the loss of seafaring husbands and fathers. So Tabitha made clothes to express her faith and her friendship.

Those who have benefited from Tabitha's generosity are in genuine mourning at the loss of their friend—no paid mourners for Tabitha. Peter comes to the room, dismisses the mourners, and prays. Rather than copious words and pleading, Peter speaks only the woman's name and "arise" (rendered "get up" in the New Revised Standard Version). The Greek word for arise is the same one used in affirmation of Jesus' resurrection. Tabitha sits up and is restored to her community of "the saints and widows."

My experience of deep community in seminary made it possible for me to serve writers and produce books of spiritual nourishment. But once I left that seminary community I knew I had to find another group of true friends in order to continue to serve. The vital relationship between the depth of my communal experience and the authenticity and power of my service or work was not lost on me in seminary. Over the years I have built small communities around every activity I was involved in: work, family, running, writing, and even reading. It has not always been easy to be vulnerable and open to the cycles of friendship, but the gospel stories always put community right in the center of spiritual works. The community of the faithful can serve as a channel of resurrection power that brings new life. And it is a lesson that we all must learn over and over again.

Jesus, give me the courage to be open and honest in the midst of life's vicissitudes. Amen.

Inevitably, all of us will walk through dark times. The nature of those dark times, whether it be overcoming cancer as my older brother did in six successive bouts or recovering from the devastating loss of a love relationship as my friend did after four years of joy or confronting the lack of a palpable sense of God's presence year after year while faithfully preaching and teaching is less the psalmist's concern than finding out he is not alone in the universe. For most of us the modern question is not, "Does God exist?" but "Does God exist for *me*!"

The psalmist chooses to believe that the Divine Presence is here and now. And he also knows that he will more readily experience that presence if he dwells "in the house of the LORD" or chooses to live in faithful community, to put the phrase into the vernacular.

In "rugged individualistic" Western culture, we often find that it goes against our grain to reach out for companionship and divine presence when life is dragging us down. But the psalmist says he is going to do that even when he is surrounded by enemies or misfortune or calamity or hopelessness. We too can hope for comfort, no matter what darkness swirls around us; the promise is here to lift our hearts and souls: Even when I walk through the darkest valley, I fear no danger because you are with me" (CEB).

Jesus, I need courage to face the darkness that rolls through all of life. Amen.

If dark times are inevitable, can we believe during good times? For those whose natural predisposition is optimistic, the struggle of faith seems rather easy. For those who hold a pessimistic attitude toward life, the struggle can seem insurmountable. But optimism and pessimism—even as common as those predispositions are for most of us—differ markedly from what I call the "work of faith." Some people have the "gift of faith," but that is not true for most of us. Most of us must "work" at faith. In other words, growing faith is more like exercising for an athletic or health benefit.

As a runner and diabetic I run almost every day. I help manage my diabetes with this discipline, and I find that if something precludes my daily run I pay a price. But my longtime discipline gets me back on the running paths. If I miss more than a day or two then I really suffer, and I have to remind myself that the pain of recovering my conditioning is worth the effort; and it is.

The psalmist opens with his profession of faith: "The LORD is my shepherd, I shall not want." He lacks for nothing; God furnishes provision for food, drink, shelter. God leads him, teaches him, just like a good personal trainer or coach. And the perks of getting into "faith" shape is that certain benefits accrue: comfort, goodness, mercy. For some a fearlessness emerges. I want all of these benefits in my life, and my desire is the beginning of faith for me. I am glad the psalmist continues to remind me of this spiritual reality.

Jesus, help me exercise my faith and grow in that discipline, so that I grow closer and closer to you. Amen.

Understanding the value of diversity is a great struggle and a great theme in modern life. But two millennia ago the story of civilization as recorded in Revelation offers preview. Eventually we will gather around Someone worth gathering around. In the fractious and conflict-ridden history of humanity this poses an outrageous idea. We can hardly imagine it. And we all have notions about who should not be allowed to be part of this gathering.

But the good news is that we will have some help getting prepared for this all-inclusive social network. Most rational people would admit that we need help in preparing. The bad news is that a lot of people think they know best who should be included in this standing-room-only crowd. I would suggest a rethinking of that position.

The biblical text testifies that we are not the ones who will be deciding the makeup of this group. Right off the bat we have one hundred forty-four thousand who are "sealed"—people from diverse tribes who stand before the throne robed in white. But verse 9 reminds us of the scope of God's people: "a great multitude that no one could count, from every nation, from all tribes and peoples and languages." All we can do is say yes and move toward God and become part of the divine congregation or say no and move away from the Someone into light years of loneliness.

Don't forget the words, "These are they who have come out of the great ordeal" because they serve as an honest appraisal of the difficulty of spiritual life. We will struggle, experience dark times, and suffer, but if we have exercised the muscle of faith we will join that throng before the throne to say, "Salvation belongs to our God who is seated on the throne, and to the Lamb!"

Jesus, help us run the race and fight the good fight and do it for as long as we live. Amen.

Jesus says, "The works . . . testify to me." Spiritual leaders, politicos, government authorities, and corporate moguls know how to spin a good cover story, but can we trust their words? We all know better, but the temptation is great. It takes effort to find out what certain people or governments or companies actually do, so we let it slide. Jesus emphasizes works not because they are miraculous and testify to his messiahship, but these are the works of the Father. Jesus' works testify to the fact that "the Father is in me and I am in the Father" (John 10:38).

Those who state the request "If you are the Messiah, tell us plainly" must have felt puzzled by Jesus' response: "You do not believe, because you do not belong to my sheep." What? Ask for a straightforward answer, and you get sheep. Jesus says that a rather important dimension of spiritual life encompasses paying attention to what is happening around us.

I take comfort when a leader says words that I like to hear. In this specific instance the Jews are hoping to hear certain words, but it doesn't really matter what is said. They don't want to "hear" what the actions say either because that requires change on their part. When I pay attention to what Jesus is saying in this passage, I get uncomfortable because I resist change, as we all do. Perhaps we will hear Jesus' words and follow. Listen to his words closely: "You do not believe, because you do not belong to my sheep. My sheep hear my voice. I know them, and they follow me." I wonder, *Do my works testify that I have changed—that I belong in Jesus' flock?*

Jesus, help me to listen and watch, to hear with more than my ears and to be willing to change. Amen.

The religious leaders have trouble believing that Jesus is the Messiah. But what is hard for me to believe or even imagine is the aspect of eternal life and never perishing. Not that I would have recognized Jesus for who he really was back then either, but it would have been this odd and new idea of life everlasting that would have boggled my mind. Many authors have written novels about life after death. Each portrays a different vision.

The New Testament also offers hints about this reality, but usually those hints are perplexing. And why should it matter? Well, one theme that runs through all the novels is that our life now prepares us in significant ways for the next. That theme is less overt in the biblical text, but it is implied often enough.

This passage highlights the benefits of being a sheep who hears the voice of Jesus. Those who do will not perish or be snatched from his hand. A comforting thought that Jesus' power and ability stems from his relationship with his all-powerful Father. Given by God, we remain God's.

Only those who hear Jesus' voice and follow receive this offer of eternal life. It comes to those who experience a reorientation from outside to inside, who move beyond the words. So what does this mean for those within the fold? Like those in Revelation, a great throng of people stand in the fold: "There are no ordinary people. You have never talked to a mere mortal. . . . But it is immortals whom we joke with, work with, marry, snub, and exploit" (*The Weight of Glory*, C. S. Lewis)—and none will be snatched from Jesus' hand.

Jesus, I want help in becoming a long-term goal person, especially when it comes to eternal life. Amen.

God's Dwelling among Us

APRIL 18–24, 2016 • CHERIE R. WHITE

Scripture Overview: The New Testament witnesses affirm the radically new era ushered in with the advent, death, and resurrection of Jesus Christ. It is a time of excitement and expectation. In the Gospel of John, perplexed disciples are instructed by Jesus before his departure; they are given "a new commandment." Peter learns about the new and inclusive strategy in a dream. The contention between the old and the new sometimes reaches a fever pitch. We receive the promise of a time when the conflicts between old and new will have completely faded (Rev. 21:1-6). In the light of Easter and the anticipation of a new heaven and a new earth, Psalm 148 becomes for us a marvelous expression of praise to God. Voices from heaven and from earth; voices of angels, animals, and humans; voices of women and men, young and old join in a splendid harmony to the One who makes all things new (Rev. 21:5).

Questions and Thoughts for Reflection

- Read Acts 11:1-18. What changes in your life can open you to God's surprising new paths?
- Read Psalm 148. What parts of God's creation move you to praise the Creator? How can you be more attentive to these aspects of creation?
- Read Revelation 21:1-6. Imagine the time when God will dwell among us. How does that vision of promise and hope affect your living in the present world?
- Read John 13:31-35. Where in your life do you see or express self-giving love?

Retired United Methodist missionary to Chile and Mexico; professor, the Methodist Seminary in Mexico City

This praise psalm enthusiastically declares God's sovereignty over the heavens and the earth. It uses an imperative "praise" form of the verb eleven times, thus urging us to action. Go and do! Saint Francis's "Canticle of the Sun" echoes this even earlier hymn, Psalm 148.

In this psalm we sense the scope of God's creative essence as each part of the known universe receives the call to acknowledge and praise God. It calls upon not only human beings but also inanimate elements of creation to praise God. I can just see the psalmist whirling around in a joyous dance of recognition of all that is good and praising the Creator for it.

In reaching out to human beings, the psalmist covers the whole spectrum from rulers to all people and becomes even more specific naming men, women, young and old. He leaves no one out. This gamut of people is called upon to "praise the name of the LORD," which leads us to ponder God's name.

What's in a name? To many of us, naming a child can represent our hopes for him or her, or it may serve as a way of recognizing a family member or a friend. In many cultures, a baby does not receive a definitive name until the child has evidenced his or her character. So what does this psalm tell us of God's character? God's name revealed to Moses was "I AM WHO I AM" (Exod. 3:14). God refuses to be pinned down. Here we can see God as creator and feel the joy of relationship and, in naming God, feel God's presence.

May we never cease to praise God's name and being.

This story must be important because it repeats what the previous chapter has already told us. Namely, that Peter has had three consecutive visions about food. We know that Peter seems to need to hear things several times before the message sinks in. In this passage he learns to loosen up, listen, go and see for himself, discern, respond, and accept. Many of us are also slow on the uptake, so we are in good company and grateful for God's patience.

Most cultures offer food out of hospitality or love, so the one to whom it is offered must not reject it. When we visit or live in other cultures, we have to learn new customs, to understand what is polite or not, and to eat new foods with unfamiliar tastes. Once when I lived in Chile as a missionary I was offered a boiled chicken neck with head attached for breakfast as the only piece of meat available. I was baffled as to how to eat it. But because I had already learned to accept anything, I now know how tender the meat is in a chicken neck!

Peter also faces a learning curve when he comes to realize that God's love reaches beyond the confines of Peter's "in" group. He learns that Gentiles also receive the Holy Spirit and benefit from God's grace. How often are we surprised by God in terms of who will accept God's word? How often do we preach or evangelize and then are astounded when an unexpected person accepts it? This is often when our "buts . . . " begin, and we end up reversing gears, reconsidering, and responding to God's priorities.

God, do not let us become complacent. Prod us into surprising new paths. Amen.

When our youngest son was about six or seven years old, my husband and I were commenting on the dire situation of the world. Our son piped up to say, "Well, God already created the earth and is now busy somewhere else." He also implied that the task of caring for creation now fell to us. I affirm the truth in his statement, but Revelation offers a reminder that God has not gone far.

This text calls us to imagine a time of promise and hope when God will dwell among us, and all will be God's people. Part of God's dwelling involves being with us: wiping tears and eradicating death, mourning, crying, and pain. As I write this, with the devastating epidemic of ebola in Western Africa a frightening reality, this promise of a new earth would be welcome right away. We can think of many other endemic health situations or hunger or violence that create great suffering throughout the world.

The good news is that God responds through people, churches, and agencies that rise up to face these challenges. In Mexico, where I live, many people are saying that violence is not the last word, and they are organizing to create awareness. Families who have lost loved ones due to the war on drugs have organized the Movement for Peace with Justice and Dignity. And because hundreds of women have died violently because of their gender, women have organized to combat this scourge. Farmers losing their land to large business interests have organized to defend their way of life and the ecology of their ancestral lands.

God's word is active and all-encompassing, a beginning and an end that frame reality, saying a loud NO! to pain and realities that are a living death to people everywhere. God's new heaven and new earth offer a clean slate.

God of life and new beginnings, use me in spite of my limitations. Amen.

We have a saying in Mexico that states, "Oh, Mexico, so far from God and so close to the United States." This is not a blessing. Sharing a three-thousand-mile-long border has meant tensions across time. Currently the flow of undocumented persons over that border from Mexico and Central America has created a major crisis, especially with the new reality of children crossing as they flee hunger, poverty, and drug gangs in their countries.

This text imagines a "new Jerusalem," a Jewish concept and longing from ancient times. The temple in Jerusalem was God's dwelling place and thus symbolized God's presence on earth, which completely upended all unjust realities.

The promise of water as life hearkens back to Jesus' encounter with the Samaritan woman at the well, and we rejoice that a new earth with springs of refreshing, life-giving water is possible. It will also not be temporary but permanent. When the text declares that "It is done!" it implies that it is not simply an end but a goal, and goals require conscientious work on our part to achieve them.

What does God's dwelling in our midst therefore demand of us, especially in the face of an unjust world? From the Old Testament prophets we learn that there can be no peace unless there is justice, which we can then surmise to be a basic element of creating a new earth.

This text reinforces that life begins and ends with God and that God's words are "trustworthy and true." God's new creation will entail God's presence among us; God is near, accompanying, creating—and that gives us hope!

God of justice and hope, help us to be aware of the foreigners in our midst. Amen.

Jesus calls his disciples to love one another as he has loved them. Sounds easy, right? But knowing that the disciples did not always get along and that Judas's walking out to betray Jesus immediately precedes this text, we need to rethink what is involved in this call to love.

In Greek the word used for love in this text is *agapeo*. As a verb it signifies action, specifically self-giving action—the kind where a person gives his or her life. We find it tough enough to love our enemies, which Jesus has already commanded; but giving our life is almost incomprehensible. Jesus did it, and we have had examples throughout history where people have followed his example, often becoming saints. In Latin America, Archbishop Oscar Romero from El Salvador is an often-cited example. A man who did not agree with Romero's support of the poor and oppressed assassinated him in 1980 as he performed mass. I have come to discover that this incredible type of love is not exclusive to Christians.

Agapeo as it refers to God's self-giving love means to be in relationship with God. Jesus' *new* commandment to love one another emphasizes the life-giving aspect of mutual love and support within the circle of the disciples. Earlier Jesus washed the feet of his disciples. Peter was slow on the uptake at that point, but he will catch on, realizing that here and elsewhere Jesus is making an ethical demand.

History is filled with examples of hatred, hurt, and betrayal. This text asks us to lay all that aside and practice *agapeo* love. Can we respond to this challenge? Eventually, Peter did. How about you?

God of love, strengthen us to live love as you have taught us. Amen.

Jesus uses the word *glorified* (or some form) five times and the word *love* four times in these five short verses. Jesus also says farewell, explains who he is in terms of his relationship to God, and presents an ethical demand to his disciples: "Love one another." Judas's imminent betrayal and Peter's upcoming denial of Jesus bracket these dual themes of glorification and love, creating a perplexing situation. How can Jesus proclaim his death and then calmly ask the disciples to love one another in such a setting?

Glorification, understood as Jesus' death on the cross and subsequent resurrection, is closely tied to his relationship with God. Jesus the human being is at the same time God's son and will share in that glory. God's glory is also understood in texts such as Exodus 16 where God's actual presence resides in the midst of God's people. Thus we can see that Jesus' physical presence on earth and his future presence with God make him a constant presence and a reference point to God.

Even though Jesus will soon physically depart from the disciples, he calls upon them to act as he has with them: "Love one another. . . . as I have loved you." This will not be easy in his absence as they may also face betrayal and death, but he enjoins them to practice unconditional love. This love will sustain them in the challenging days ahead, while exhorting them to be an example to others. And this love of one another will be the distinctive way the church will be recognized in the world.

God, may your love dwell in us, so that we demonstrate your love to the world. Amen.

God continues to surprise us. In this story Peter faces several surprises. One comes in the acceptance of unacceptable people in the "in" group. A Jewish sect that is in the process of becoming Christian because its members follow Christ comes to realize that God's love and grace go out to others, far beyond their familiar boundaries.

Then when those "others" believe in God, have a vision, and reach out to Peter, the Holy Spirit pays a visit and God grants "repentance that leads to life." As Peter notes, "Who was I to hinder God?" The Spirit works freely, unhindered by anyone. Not only must Peter accept this, but he then has to convince the rest of the disciples of this truth. He carefully crafts a full explanation of how the conversion took place. They receive his report in silence but then begin to praise God for the expansion of their ministry.

At this time I am concerned about "excluders"—people and groups that insist on exclusion, on limiting membership, on employing strict rules about right and wrong. The general stance of an excluder is this: "If you are not with me, you are against me," which attempts to give legitimacy to a personal stance.

When certain groups of people are excluded in any situation, I suspect that the excluders may be working against the Holy Spirit. But "who [are we] to hinder God?" Who are we to say that God forbids anyone from full participation or inclusion? The call to discipleship is a mandate for all who believe, and God's Spirit moves in awesome ways.

Be ready to embrace the life-changing surprises that God has in store for you.

Visions of Transformation

APRIL 25–MAY 1, 2016 • GEORGE R. GRAHAM

Scripture Overview: The heart of the gospel is that God so loved the world, and the Easter proclamation is that Jesus Christ died and rose for the sins of the world. The texts warn us against the persistent temptation to make our God too small. In Acts, Paul takes the gospel to Macedonia, which fulfills Jesus' commission to the disciples "that repentance and forgiveness of sins . . . be proclaimed in his name to all nations." Psalm 67 also reminds us of the wideness of God's mercy. Revelation states that the immediacy of God's presence will be recognized by "the kings of the earth." In John 5 the unsolicited and undeserved healing expresses the "unprovoked grace" that flows from God's limitless love for the world and all its people.

Questions and Thoughts for Reflection

- Read Psalm 67. When have you been aware of God's transforming you or your community of faith?
- Read Acts 16:9-15. When have you acted promptly on a "nudge" from God? How did your action affect your life or that of another?
- Read Revelation 21:10, 22–22:5. When have you been transformed by someone different than you?
- John 14:23-29. When do you struggle most to lead with love? To whom are you called to serve as mentor?

Development Officer with University Hospitals, Cleveland, Ohio; ordained minister in the United Church of Christ

Psalm 67 is clearly intended for use in worship. The psalm follows the contours of our prayer and our encounter with God in worship. We move from saying what we hope God will do (verse 1) to addressing God directly (verses 2-5) and finally to making our petitions to God (verses 6-7). Within the psalm there seems to be a movement or almost a dance between what we pray for, the answer God gives, and our human response to God's answer. Our encounters with God seem to follow these steps; as a result, we are ultimately transformed.

This psalm links us to congregations of worshipers who have prayed it for thousands of years, who recognize that transformation depends on God's grace and blessing. But the psalm also makes clear that transformation depends on human recognition that God has acted and is the source of the transformation.

The process of transformation may begin with our feeling the warm blessing of God's face shining upon us, but it then leads to more challenging journeys of knowing God's way (verse 4)and experiencing God's saving power through life's valleys. The psalm speaks not just of the transformation of an individual or community. Rather it envisions the possibility of all nations being glad and singing for joy about God's equity in judgment and guidance of all people. God brings about the harvest each year, a reminder of God's desire and ability to transform the whole world.

May your face shine upon us, O God of light. May we know your way and experience your saving power. Transform us. Make us new again. Amen.

Paul and Timothy are eager to spread the gospel but have been struggling with their next move. The Holy Spirit has forbidden them to go to Asia. The Spirit of Jesus has prevented them from going into Bithynia. Paul has a dream in the night and experiences a vision of a man pleading with him to come to Macedonia. This dream provides the needed direction, and they immediately get up and make their way to Macedonia.

What impresses me about this story is the immediacy of their action. Paul has a dream, and the next day they move. When I decided to relocate, the discernment process took a couple of years and filled most of a journal. The actual move—finding a new job, selling the house, packing and moving, and then settling into a new house—took the better part of a year. Rather than taking time to reflect, much less form a committee and do strategic planning, Paul makes his decision based on a dream of where God wants him to be. What opportunities might Paul have missed if he had not acted immediately? Some commentators note that Paul's trip to Macedonia, part of modern-day Greece, led to the first account of conversion on the continent of Europe, a critical step in the establishment of Christianity there.

A powerful vision can transform our journey—if we are open to it. In turn, living out God's vision can transform the world around us. If we lack openness, what opportunities might we miss? Of course, we also can make rash decisions, which differs from following a vision. Perhaps the key comes in remaining open to God's direction and measuring our plans against it. Paul receives a dream that sets his course for Macedonia, and he pursues it.

Be our vision, O God. Help us open ourselves to your direction. Transform our journeys. Amen.

Paul has a vision of the man of Macedonia, and he immediately follows that vision. He never finds the man who came to him in a dream. Instead, he finds a woman named Lydia, "a worshiper of God," which likely means that she is not Jewish but a God-fearer. She gathers with a group of women by the river for prayer since the Jewish population in Philippi is likely not big enough to support a synagogue.

We may suppose that Paul will be looking for a man, as he dreamed. So isn't it unusual for him and those with him (presumably male) to be talking to a group of women? The vision that Paul had while asleep gives way to a new vision when he awakes. He has dreamed of a man but finds a woman. Paul's words open Lydia's heart, and in turn she offers the traveling evangelists what they need. She opens her home to Paul and those with him. As a dealer in purple cloth—the fabric of royalty, rulers, and the rich—Lydia is a woman of means whose hospitality may have fanned a spark of faith into a flame that spread to Europe.

Paul opens himself to the vision that God gives him in a dream, and he remains open to God's unfolding vision. He does not get hung up on the literal image of the man from his dream but rather lets God speak to him through a woman who is new to the faith.

Just like Paul, God's vision for us might find fulfillment in a different way than we imagine. God may be trying to speak to us through others, especially those who seem to be unlikely messengers.

God of surprises, help us open ourselves to the way that you speak to us through unlikely people. Help us recognize your transforming vision. Amen.

Love comes first; keeping God's word flows out of that love. Loving God and loving others—those closest to us as well as strangers—is the first measure of faith. With this love as the source, we naturally follow God's word.

Putting love first is important for my family to remember after a tough day at work for the adults and a long day at school for the young people. We all feel pretty out of sorts when we first walk in the door, and there is a rush to get dinner ready quickly. Our attitudes usually get better after we eat, but tempers may flare later as fatigue sets in just before bedtime.

At times like these, I think about the fact that *how* I say something is as important as *what* I say. I try to lead with love, whether I am at home, work, or church. I know that when I speak lovingly my words will more likely be heard and taken to heart. But I often fail—I get hungry and tired like everyone else, and my tone becomes sharp.

I remember a pastor friend who used to introduce the Lord's Prayer in worship by saying, "When we don't have words of our own, we pray the words that Jesus gave us." When we don't seem to have love of our own, we lean on God's word to guide us back to love and invite God to be at home with us.

More than anything else as a parent, I want my children to love God and to know that they are loved by God. I want God to be at home with my family and for my family to be at home with God. By remembering to put love first—and leaning on God's word to find a way back to love when we don't feel loving—God comes to us, transforms us, and makes God's home with us.

Come, Lord Jesus, be our guest. Make our home your home. Amen.

Amonth ago, the man I regarded as my mentor died after a brief illness. He had given me an internship my last year of graduate school, which led to full-time work in ministry after I graduated and set me on my vocational path. For eight years we were colleagues with offices next to each other, and he provided guidance as I came into my own. After a new position took me to another city and state, we did not talk frequently; but I knew that I could always turn to him when I needed direction or advice. He would adeptly ask the right questions in order to pay attention to God's leading for me. Even after I moved, knowing he was just a phone call away gave me a sense of assurance. His death has left a huge hole for me and I am sure for others as well.

Jesus is preparing the disciples for the time when he is not physically present with them. He tells them that the Holy Spirit "will teach you everything, and remind you of all that I have said to you." If their spirits are troubled and they feel afraid, he reminds them of the legacy of peace that he has left with them.

These words echo from the years of the early church with disciples unsure how to navigate without Jesus' leadership through the generations, as each experiences the loss of the previous generation. These words comfort me as I still work through the loss of a mentor and listen for the Advocate, the Holy Spirit, to guide me. Even when those who mentor us in faith are gone, the Holy Spirit works to transform us into the people God calls us to be and helps us know how to guide the next generation.

Holy Spirit, when we feel troubled, alone, or afraid, give us your peace. Lead us in Christ's way. Amen.

I live in Cleveland, Ohio, which has a rich and diverse religious heritage. The immigrants who built the city also built houses of worship to honor God. Whenever I drive downtown, I marvel at all the steeples, domes, and towers I pass. They are especially beautiful at night when they are lit.

In Revelation 21, the author gives us a vision of a different kind of city—the new Jerusalem—descending from heaven to earth. In that city there are no steeples, domes, or church towers. In fact, there is no need for a temple. There is no need because the whole city serves to honor God. And the steeples do not need to be lit because the glory of God is the city's light, and there is no night. Like Psalm 67 that we read at the beginning of the week, in the new Jerusalem the light of God's saving power transforms all nations.

Another mark of the vision of the new Jerusalem is the fact that the city's gates always remain open. Modern cities do not have gates that close, but more and more individual buildings and housing developments are secured, which tends to separate us from people who are different from us.

Where city gates do not exist, perhaps a more fitting parallel in our day is the national border. Borders in our country and elsewhere are policed and defended like never before. The story of Paul entering Macedonia in Acts 16 reminds us that transformation can occur by entering a new land. But transformation can also occur when people from other nations come to us. Relating to people who are different from us can give us an experience of "the glory and the honor of the nations"—a foretaste of the new Jerusalem.

God of all nations, help us walk in your light. May we keep our gates open to those who are different from us. Transform us by the glory of the nations. Amen.

Revelation 22 is the final chapter and offers the final images in the Bible, so it seems especially important to pay close attention. Before I took the time to read this passage about the river of life and the tree of life carefully, I always thought of the tree of life as I had seen it rendered by artists: a single, proud, tall tree with strong branches and plentiful fruit.

But a careful reading of this passage in Revelation reveals another image of the tree of life. This tree of life cannot have a single trunk but rather multiple trunks because it grows on "either side of the river." How can this be? Perhaps its roots extend underneath the river that provides its nourishment and gives it life. Perhaps like giant redwoods, roots that interlock strengthen the tree against storms and wind. The tree of life seems more like a grove than a single trunk, spanning both sides of the river with branches bowing to each other.

Most artists' interpretations of the tree of life do not include the river of life. If I had had to picture it prior to studying this passage, I would have put the river of life in the foreground and the tree of life on the far shore. But according to this passage the river runs through the middle of the tree of life.

So much of life seems to be aimed at getting to the other side of the river, whether that is job, family, or simply getting to the next phase of life. But God's grace is not relegated only to a distant shore. This vision of the tree of life reminds us that God's grace flourishes on both sides of the river, always in our midst. We are fed in each season by its fruit, and God's life-giving power can transform us right where we are.

Holy God, remind us that we can find shelter in the tree of life wherever we are on our journey. Amen.

Moving from Ending to Beginning

MAY 2–8, 2016 • L. CECILE ADAMS

Scripture Overview: The continuation of the church when Jesus is no longer present is an acute issue. This fearful, waiting community, which is anxious and bewildered, has no power of its own. And yet, oddly, power is given that causes this fragile little community to have energy, courage, imagination, and resources completely disproportionate to its size. How can one speak about this changed situation that can only be attributed to the inscrutable generosity of God? The psalm breaks out beyond reasoned explanation into wonder, awe, amazement, and gratitude. God's new rule is beyond our logic. We only see its effect in a transformed community. That community is not certain what has happened but is sure enough to affirm its identity and embrace its proper work.

Questions and Thoughts for Reflection

- Read Acts 1:1-11. When have you actively awaited God's work in your life? How did your active waiting affect the outcome?
- Read Psalm 97. How does your worship of God find expression?
- Read Revelation 22:12-14, 16-17, 20-21. Jesus acknowledges and describes his imminent return. How do these words lead you to make changes in your life?
- Read John 17:20-26. Reflect on a time when someone prayed aloud for you in your presence. How did this experience help you acknowledge the unity of believers?

Life coach and retired local pastor, Iredell and Cranfills Gap First United Methodist Churches, Central Texas Annual Conference

Both of these psalms, placed in a category called "enthronement psalms," describe a pattern of worship that recognizes and honors God as the Lord, the Most High, the ruler of the whole world. The first psalm is full of kinesthetically glorifying God: clapping, shouting, singing, sounds of rams' horns and trumpets. The second psalm focuses more on visual acclamations of God: clouds, consuming fire, melting mountains, lightning, moving figures, a holy throne. "God reigns!" is the inescapable theme. God is over all and loves all! God will prevail!

Perhaps you have attended a religious concert, joined a group in a multilingual worship service, walked in quietness among ancient tall trees, looked into the depths of a clear lake, or volunteered for a service project and experienced yourself celebrating God's sovereignty. These experiences—and others—can create in you a deep well of love, joy, hope, and trust from which you may draw holy sustenance for yourself and others.

Turning the statements in these two psalms into wonderings can expand your experience of and walk with God. Possible wonderings might include the following:

- What is needed for me to become more righteous and just as God is righteous and just?
- How does God guard my life and rescue me from the wicked?
- What could it mean for me to claim more people as sister or brother?

Awesome God, I come to you, clapping and singing your praises. Raise me up and send me forth to witness to your amazing love. Amen.

A fter the resurrection, Jesus leads the disciples through Witness 101—a fast-track course in how they will become his earthly successors, inviting others to join God's realm. The twelve appear clueless. They plaintively ask Jesus, "Lord, is this the time when you will restore the kingdom to Israel?" Jesus replies in effect, "Wait. God has a promise yet to be kept in store for you. Power is coming—not just to you but upon you, not just upon you but visible through you. The Holy Spirit will empower you to tell people what I have taught you, what you have seen me do, what we have shared together. You won't have time to wonder about the coming. You'll be too busy with people who want to hear good news!" He reminds them to wait in Jerusalem to receive power. Then he ascends and disappears as the disciples watch.

The disciples in this passage hold up a mirror for us today. We often seek our own agenda while remaining unaware of or ignoring God's agenda. What we don't "get" about God's promises usually trips us up. Too often we forget that active waiting may be the best current strategy. We fail to expect God's active involvement in what is going on and to remember that our work entails prayerful discernment. Some possibilities for reflection are these:

- where active waiting has been missing or present in my life and the results of either,
- when looking inward is more important than looking up or outward,
- some results of paying attention that have come to me through spiritual disciplines.

Creative God, open me to anticipate and receive the power you send to support my witness in the world! Amen.

In this story, the term *slave* applies to various people. The girl is a slave to her owner and the demon possessing her. She calls Paul and Silas "slaves of the Most High God" (16:17), a phrase used by the worshipers of Zeus to describe themselves. The owners are slaves to the money generated by the girl. The magistrates and the crowd are slaves to keeping things the same. The jail keeper is a slave to the system.

"What must I do to be saved?" also has several meanings. Initially, the jailer may mean to ask what will save him from the wrath of and punishment by his superiors—perhaps even from his execution. Yet, he obviously recognizes in Paul and Silas a centeredness, a power for good that he wants in his life. Note that the jailer is the only one in the story who asks this question.

The words of Paul and Silas hit home with the jailer and his family: They are baptized immediately. The hospitality of the jailer toward Paul and Silas testifies to his newfound faith, even as this story testifies to the power of the Holy Spirit in and through Paul and Silas.

Some possibilities for reflection are these:

- What captivates or enslaves me?
- How would I answer a person's question about what he or she needs to do to be saved?
- When, where, or how has my witness had seismic results or "rocked the foundations"?
- How has my life become caught up in the greater story of God's redemption of the world?

Saving God, use me through your provision of opportunities to rock the foundations of this world by sharing the simple truth of your love for all creation, including us. Amen.

Some people refer to this passage written to the Christians in Ephesus as "Paul's Prayer." Paul writes to commend the congregational members' faith and love toward all the saints, a love widely known. Paul also reassures them that he thanks God for their witness and prays for their growth in the faith. Paul refers to God as the Father of glory, a reminder of God's glory as expressed in the two psalms from Sunday's reading.

Paul prays that the eyes of the saints' hearts be enlightened so that they may know "the hope to which [Christ] has called [them], . . . the riches of his glorious inheritance among the saints, . . . and the immeasurable greatness of his power for [those] who believe." This power came to fruition when God raised Jesus from the dead and then raised him in glory to sit at God's right hand. In fact, Paul reminds his readers that God's plan of salvation has existed from the beginning and is for all time. His words exponentially expand awareness of God's power and glory and generate hope.

Some possibilities for reflection are these:
- what "the eyes of your heart" see in this passage and in your own life,
- how you would describe the hope to which you are called,
- how the "spirit of wisdom and knowledge" is at work in you and in your congregation,
- your particular place or gifts (as you understand that/those today) in the body of Christ,
- those saints (individual and/or collective) for whom you give thanks.

Glorious God, enlighten the eyes of my heart so I see you everywhere. Infuse my heart with hope. Amen.

Tomorrow's passage from Luke 24 is the last of Luke's Gospel; the reading today is the last in the book of Revelation. Both passages focus on ending and beginning. The Common English Bible titles today's passage "Jesus is coming soon"; the New Revised Standard Version calls it "Epilogue and Benediction."

The speaker in verses 12-14 paints a lush, bright, eternal picture of what is coming—a repayment or blessing for the faithful. The faithful are those who have followed God's commandments, being devoted witnesses regardless of temptations. They will have access to the tree of life and enter the city through the gates.

Jesus identifies himself as the speaker in verse 16. He is the sender of an angel with these words for the churches. He is of David's lineage and the star that heralds the beginning of the day. Responding, the Spirit and the bride implore Jesus to come and invite others to add their voices as well. Those who are thirsty—who want what has been promised—are to come and drink of the water of life. A liturgical response and a benediction follow the words "Surely I am coming soon."

Read this passage again silently. Then read it aloud or ask someone to read it to you. Listen for (1) familiar words, (2) words that you hear in "bold print," (3) words that puzzle you, (4) words that comfort you and give you hope.

Possibilities for reflection are these:

- robes you have washed that bear witness to your faithfulness,
- the thirst that you would like the water of life to quench,
- how the words you identified above lead you to make a change or changes in your life.

Come, Lord Jesus, come and pour your grace on me! Amen.

Before beginning his ministry, Jesus spends forty days in the wilderness in preparation. After his resurrection, Jesus spends forty days preparing his disciples for their ministry. He takes them through a review, "opening their minds to understand the scriptures," especially how scriptures have been fulfilled through him.

Jesus commissions the disciples to witness to what they have seen and heard, know in their hearts, and understand with their minds. Jerusalem is the starting place for them, and the whole world is their mission field. Jesus promises them power for ministry and blesses them. The blessing leaves the disciples filled with joy as they watch Jesus ascend, and then they return to Jerusalem, praising God and waiting. Here, the disciples are upbeat, aware, actively waiting, blessing God—unlike the disciples in Acts 1:6.

The end of anything is the beginning of something. For these disciples, the end of what they have known with Jesus no longer produces anxiety: They anticipate the beginning of "something." They connect Jesus' resurrection to his rightful place at God's right hand with his commissioning, blessing, and sending them to wait for the promised power. As God is steadfast, these disciples resolve to fulfill their newly received commission steadfastly. They and Christ set the bar for us today.

Possibilities for your reflection include these:

- an ending or beginning you have experienced and its effect on your life,
- where and how you link the old and the new in your faith,
- your experience(s) of the commissioning and blessing of Jesus for ministry,
- how you are clothed with God's power.

Sending God, clothe me with your power that I may be a steadfast witness wherever you send me. Amen.

Jesus prays in the upper room where he and the disciples gather to share the Passover meal. The disciples have the privilege of overhearing this prayer. All who have read or heard it read since also share in Jesus' words to his Father. Jesus intercedes for his disciples—then, now, and in-between. His trust in God is clear: He leaves the future in God's hands, modeling the behavior his disciples are to imitate.

Using one or more translations of the Bible, count the number of times the word *one* appears and the number of times the words *love* or *loved* appear in these verses. *One* implies unity, coherence, symmetry, harmony, solidarity, unanimity. Love makes unity possible. Love shared does not diminish those who share love. Love shared magnifies, enriches, strengthens the beloved(s) and the love shared. Love shared generates mutuality and reciprocity. Jesus prays fervently for this love and unity to be present in disciples throughout the ages.

Recall how the coming of the Holy Spirit emboldened Jesus' disciples. Their singleness of purpose and shared experience of Jesus are powerful. They remember and live into the words Jesus utters here. The number of Christ-followers explodes because Jesus' disciples are on fire, unified in their mission!

Possibilities for reflection include these:

- a time when someone prayed aloud for me in my presence and its effect,
- when and how I experience the unity of believers,
- how my experience of unity intensifies and sustains love and Christian witness,
- how this scripture is being fulfilled in my life.

God of love and unity, make your love visible through me. Draw me to unite more fully with other believers so that our shared witness may change the world for your glory. Amen.

Creation in All Directions

MAY 9–15, 2016 • BRAD GABRIEL

Scripture Overview: The very nature of the Spirit defies our attempts to explain or control. In the account of the Day of Pentecost in Acts 2, the Holy Spirit gives new life to a dispirited band of disciples. The church is born. Birth imagery is present too in Romans 8 where "all who are led by the Spirit of God are children of God." In John, the Spirit or Advocate's presence will continue to make life possible for the disciples in the absence of Jesus' physical presence. In Psalm 104 the Spirit of God is responsible for the origin and sustenance of all creation. The life-giving power and presence of the Spirit is a gift—unsolicited, unexpected, undeserved. But life in the Spirit is life as God intends, to know a peace that the world cannot give.

Questions and Thoughts for Reflection

- Read Acts 2:1-21. On the day of Pentecost, creation is filled with God's purpose and promise. Where do you see this purpose and promise in your everyday experience?
- Read Psalm 104:24-35b. In what ways can you add your voice to the universal chorus praising the Lord's name?
- Read Romans 8:14-17. Where in your life do you need to trust God more fully? How will this help bring to fruition God's new creation?
- Read John 14:8-17, 25-27. When in your life have you been reminded that God is in control rather than you?

Pastor, St. Mark's United Methodist Church, Memphis, Tennessee

God's grace, freely poured out on us and all creation, births us into new creations. No longer are we slaves to fears and fads, nor do we form circles of exclusion. No longer do we fear the night or worry about the length of our life journey. We have family to walk with us, to carry us when we are unable. They also give us the great gift of trusting that we will carry them when the need comes. No longer do we wander aimlessly, seeking meaning in abstract thoughts, in possessions, or even in the approval of other people. We are heirs of Christ, which means that heaven is our destination. The psalmist reminds us that our present and future are clear; our past is redeemed as well. We walk as free people, joyful as we continue to learn and grow on the way of the Cross.

"O LORD, how manifold are your works! In wisdom you made them all; the earth is full of your creatures." We proclaim the truth that we are not accidents. God brings the entire cosmos into being for a purpose. God's wisdom, beyond our comprehension, fills creation with varieties of fish and fowl, mammals and people beyond count. There are as many ways to show our love of God as there are people and maybe as there are fish and fowl and other creatures. One way rises up above them all: "I will sing to the LORD as long as I live; I will sing praise to my God while I have being." With unrestrained joy for the new creation that continues in all directions, we add our voices to those who came before us and those who come after us, calling out in universal chorus: Praise the Lord!

Lord of all, fill my heart with delight in your works, and fill my heart with joyful praise of goodness. Amen.

God's new creation does not begin in some random, unfocused manner. The new creation shows God's promise and purpose. God promises that all people will be blessed through the descendants of Abraham and Sarah. At Pentecost, God enters creation where those descendants gather to praise God and give thanks. The people who gathered on that day represented the extent of the Roman world. The nations and peoples are named in a grand, rolling account of the world. There, with the nations gathered in the midst of Israel, the new creation begins. God promises that blessings will spread like waves over the entire world beginning with the covenant people.

God's purpose is seen with the new creation beginning in Jerusalem. God's purpose is for a restoration of Eden; for healing of all hurts, reconciling all broken relations, restoring the world. In accord with God's purpose, the waves of the new creation wash over the entire world. Unlike a stone in a lake, the waves that spread out from Jerusalem will reach every person and every place on earth. This is part of the meaning behind the divine promise to Abraham that his children will be as numerous as the stars. All humanity is to be gathered up in the grace-filled waves that move out in ever-widening circles. No one is left out or left behind. As the new creation reaches the entire cosmos, we proclaim with joy, "Everyone who calls on the name of the Lord shall be saved."

The new creation begins not in a vague sometime or somewhere; it begins with purpose. The Holy Spirit begins a new creation here and now, in you, just as God promised.

Gracious God, root me in the long story of the people of faith and set before me a vision of the even greater story to unfold. Amen.

Jesus promises the new creation that begins at Pentecost. We humans usually desire the fulfillment of promises sooner rather than later. Promises are all well and good, but what about today? we ask. Philip bluntly asks Jesus to show him and the others the Father. Exactly what Philip means by that is open to discussion. Possibly he desires to have the promises satisfied according to his timetable, not the divine plan.

Confusing our agendas with God's will is more common than we might like to admit. Jesus offers us the same correction that he offered to Philip. "Believe me that I am in the Father and the Father is in me; but if you do not, then believe me because of the works themselves." In Jesus' works we see the first signs of the new creation that will begin in earnest at Pentecost. Creation obeys him. The hungry receive food. He lifts community restrictions on belonging as lepers are healed, the blind see, and the lame walk. People on the outside are lifted up and welcomed in—from women to children to foreigners. Such works bring forth the first rays of dawn of the new creation promised. Jesus invites us to live by his example and so ride the waves of God's new creation and take part in bringing it to completion.

Jesus gives the disciples another promise. He promises that God's intimate presence, the Holy Spirit, the power that motivated and directed the prophets, sages, and psalmists will come and live in them. Jesus will have returned to the Father, completing his work. We will do even greater works because we reveal the completed story of the Word made flesh in the new creation, thereby giving glory to God.

Jesus, Lord and Savior, allow me to see clearly who you are, allow me to see you clearly in other people, and allow me to trust your promises so completely that I take my part in bringing to fruition God's new creation. Amen.

In additon to the other promises that believers enjoy, Jesus promises the Holy Spirit's presence with us. Our lives do not end, after all, the day we claim the new birth offered through Christ. John Wesley, who began the Methodist revival, taught that such a moment comes when God declares that our just punishment for law-breaking is forgiven. We find ourselves justified, born all over again or from above or anew so that we may be part of God's new creation.

As new creations of God's grace, our past no longer haunts us. We understand that we are free from the soul-crushing burden of thinking that we have to earn God's love. We can start to grow into the new creation ourselves. This is new for the world. This is new for us. We will learn what all the newness means as we journey with Christ on our way.

If we are to learn, then we will want a teacher. Jesus tells us the Holy Spirit will teach us everything we need. The Spirit will teach us who we really are. We will learn both our destination and our purpose on our journey through life. We will learn to live in the new creation birthed at Pentecost. We will learn how to be new creations ourselves, continuing on the journey Jesus began for us. On our journey we will cooperate with the Holy Spirit and grow into spiritually mature people.

Jesus also promises us the luxury of learning because we will know God's peace. God's peace is the heart knowledge that we can do nothing to make God love us less or love us more. With that awareness at our center, we live and love abundantly in holy peace.

God of creation, when I fear the world is out of control, remind me that you remain the source of creation. Your will plays out in your love and compassion for us. May your Spirit quiet our fears, calm our nerves, and settle our minds. Amen.

Perhaps the Spirit's most important lessons emphasize our freedom and our family connections. We may acknowledge our freedom on an intellectual level, but how many of us know people chained by fear? The fear may be as common as an over-concern about what the neighbors will say. Fear of losing status is possibly as real today as it ever has been. How many of us know persons who have compromised their faith in order to be viewed as those who are willing to go along to get along? Paul writes that with the Pentecost gift of the Holy Spirit, we do not have to compromise who we are. The Spirit unleashes the new creation in all directions. Those "led by the Spirit" have a new identity: "children of God."

Our new family joins us on the journey of life. When the new creation begins at Pentecost, the waves that spread out across creation allow us a new means of transportation. Instead of slogging along the footpaths of life, alone, isolated, afraid of threats both real and imagined, we walk boldly as those of the company of saints. As sons and daughters of the Living God, we have family to support us, guard us, and care for us.

The Spirit who leads us into lives of divine adoption comes alongside our spirit as we cry, "Abba! Father!" We become heirs with Christ with whom we share both suffering and glory.

As heirs of the promises of God, we walk freely, slaves to no one and nothing. Our journey may be long or short, but every day is a blessing, every step is a prayer, and every act of mercy a statement of faith. Shadows may mark our journey at times, but we travel as a part of the company of light. The waves of new creation have swept us up in the creating, loving will of God. We have no fear. Our future is secure.

Blessed God, remind me that when I cannot see your face or hear your voice, my sisters and brothers will let me see you in them. Amen.

The new creation spreads out in all directions. The disciples have the breath of God blown into their souls, empowered to bring the good news to everyone. The waves of the spiritual tsunami roll out from the upper room to the Temple; to Judea, Samaria, and to the entire earth. The first disciples, then their students, then the next generation of believers, swept by the tide of the new creation, carry the word to all people.

The waves of a spiritual birth sweep across geography and forward to our time and into time ahead as far as we can see. We become heirs with Christ through the power of the same Holy Spirit that filled those first disciples long ago. Here, though, we encounter a part of the power and love of God that we do not normally consider. Time has no power over God. The new creation sweeps out in a direction that we, from our limited perspective, refer to as "back in time." We hear this truth in the words of the psalmist who responds to the Spirit's presence.

"[All creatures] look to you to give them their food in due season." "When you send forth your spirit, they are created; and you renew the face of the ground." These verses from Psalm 104 show us that the Holy Spirit has no bounds, unlike mere mortals who can only move forward in time. God, unconstrained by our concepts and working theories, occupies all of creation, including all time. When the new creation begins at Pentecost, the waves of that revolution reach as far into the past as they do into the future. This truth allows us to understand that God forgives even our past, setting us free to live as new people.

Holy God, I stand in awe of your grace. You set me free from the sin and aimlessness of now. You direct me to walk with sisters and brothers toward a new future. You even redeem my past, as littered as it may be. I offer my everlasting thanks to you. Amen.

PENTECOST SUNDAY

If you have ever dropped a rock in water, you know what happens. The impact creates changes. Ripples spread out from the point of contact. Many factors determine the size, extent, and duration of the ripples. Imagine what could happen if all the created order were impacted by a reality greater even than creation. How far from the point of impact would the effect be felt? We don't have to imagine. We know. We know because of Pentecost. The reality that entered the world that day is the Holy Spirit.

On the day of Pentecost, the Holy Spirit entered the world in a new way and began a new creation. Greater than the whole of creation, timeless and eternal, powerful enough to spread the skies with the stars and the oceans with countless schools of fish, loving enough to lead us through Exodus and out of Exile, confident enough to come to us as a newborn baby, God comes with infinite love and compassion to birth the new creation. This is the size and force of the reality that entered our world at Pentecost.

We see the ripple effect immediately. The words for wind and breath and Spirit are all the same in the Bible. So the wind that sweeps the disciples out of hiding and into the public is the Holy Spirit, moving them and moving in them. The curse of Babel is reversed. Everyone can understand God's word once more. The new beginning is announced with creative power. The ripples spread from Jerusalem, Samaria, and Judea to the ends of the earth. They spread still today. Spirit-bearing waves sweep away human failing and timidity and wash creation in the baptismal waters of new birth.

Creating God, wash me anew in the power of your Spirit that I may continue in your work of restoring creation. Amen.

Aligned with God

MAY 16–22, 2016 • RACHEL G. HACKENBERG

Scripture Overview: The lessons for Trinity Sunday offer an additional opportunity to consider the work of the Holy Spirit. Romans 5 refers to God, Jesus Christ, and the Holy Spirit. Through their mutual work, the believer experiences peace. In particular, it is through the Holy Spirit that the love of God "has been poured into our hearts" (Rom. 5:5). The lesson from John is another passage in Jesus' "farewell discourse" that mentions the Spirit's role as teacher. Proverbs 8 opens the way to consider the feminine dimension of the Godhead. Psalm 8 suggests that the God-given "glory" of humanity is compatible with suffering. Romans 5:1-5 reinforces this conclusion. To "boast in our hope of sharing the glory of God" (Rom. 5:2) means to "boast in our sufferings" (v. 3). As the Romans lesson from last week suggested of the relationship between the believer and Christ: "We suffer with him so that we may also be glorified with him" (8:17).

Questions and Thoughts for Reflection

- Read Proverbs 8:1-4, 22-31. Where in your life do you struggle to listen to Wisdom? How can you be more open to the understanding Wisdom brings?
- Read Psalm 8. What practices enable you to understand and experience God's love for you in particular?
- Read Romans 5:1-5. How can you attend to your alignment with God in a more purposeful way?
- Read John 16:12-15. While Jesus still had more to give to the world, he left the responsibility of carrying on his mission to the disciples. How can you take on this mission in your daily life?

United Church of Christ minister, author, soccer mom, Shaker Heights, Ohio

Imagine typing words into a word-processing program without any parameters for the alignment of those words on the page. No left justification. No right justification. Not even center justification. In fact, no rules at all to determine where the words begin on the page, whether the lines are evenly spaced, or how much distance falls between the letters of the words. How would we read and comprehend the writing?

Alignment is a simple yet necessary feature of word processing programs; the text must align to the margins and the words with one another. Alignment is also principal in faith. In the opening chapters of Romans, Paul establishes that our alignment with God, our justification, comes by faith—not by circumcision, not by law, not by works. All have sinned and are out of alignment. All are justified and brought into alignment. (See Romans 3:23-24.)

So Paul begins chapter 5 with words to this effect: "Because of our alignment, we know that we are at peace with God. Because of our alignment, we know that we stand in grace through Jesus. Because of our alignment, we look forward to participating in the glory of God." Paul focuses on the required maintenance needed by our alignment with God; just as we attend to the alignment of our documents, our cars, and our backs, so too we must be attentive to living rightly in our alignment with God.

Breathe in as you raise your arms up. Breathe out as you reach your arms down. Feel your spine as you stretch, and pray: Help me align myself with you today, O God, in mind and body and spirit and in the fullness of faith. Amen.

From the highest heavens to the deepest oceans, the psalmist declares, God has aligned creation—given purpose and order to all of life—and God's name is majestic over all! Follow the alignment of creation as the psalm reports: Above and beyond and in all, God reigns with glory that stretches farther than the heavens. Much to his surprise, the psalmist discovers that humanity falls only "a little lower than God," esteemed among all creation. Humanity in turn receives authority over all creatures of the air, earth, and sea. All things are aligned toward God; all things are aligned with one another by God's good wisdom.

When I was a child, I felt determined to pray for the whole earth at bedtime. To accomplish this colossal prayer, I arranged my thanksgiving topographically, beginning in the deepest darkest canyons of the oceans and gradually reaching the peaks of the Himalayas and then beyond to the farthest reaches of the galaxies. "Dear God," I began, "thank you for glowing sea creatures and undiscovered animals at the bottom of the ocean. Thank you for squid and sharks and clown fish and stingrays and dolphins and tuna. Thank you for clams and crabs and sea gulls and sand dunes and alligators and manatees." And then, somewhere around the rising slopes of hills and the edges of deciduous forests, I fell asleep.

The created world is so vast, so complex, so beautiful! We can easily feel small and lost (or fall asleep, actually or metaphorically) amidst it all. Humans live as but one species among many. You and I are each just one among billions of humans. Who are we that God recognizes us among the crowds? Who are we to have purpose in the grand scheme of this universe? And yet we are and we do.

When I feel unnoticed by you, O God, or when I feel aimless, open my heart to see the careful attention and purpose you've given to all creation. Amen.

Listen to Wisdom as she tells the story of God's ordering work at the beginning of time:

What she saw

when there was not yet depth or height or light

What she heard

when God described to the wild water its boundaries

What she smelled

when the dark, rich soil was molded with clay into earth

How she laughed

when fresh springs first gurgled and splashed to form streams

How she thrilled

when she saw the new mountains scrape the tender belly of the sky.

Listen to Wisdom as she tells of her role in those first, holy moments of designing life:

The masterful artistry

with which she speckled the cheetah and Dalmatian and eagle ray

The deft engineering

she brought to the structure of the sequoia and the spider web

The ethereal lullaby

she sang to the Pleiades and whistled through the Black Hills

The joyful dance

with which she skipped across the plains and the tundra

The continual applause

with which she celebrated and delighted God through it all.

Listen to Wisdom as she calls at the crossroads, "See this life! Come with understanding!"

I delight in you, O God! I smile as I recognize you blazing in the noonday sun, scampering with the squirrel, clapping with the trees, and winking with the stars. How delightful you are, O God, in all of life! Amen.

Despite the majesty and design of the created world, there are detractors who dispute God's ways and undermine God's work. Why, in the midst of such a celebratory psalm, does the psalmist choose to admit that God has foes and raucous enemies?

God's order—God's method for creating, empowering, and renewing life—is not impervious to dissent and defiance. The beautifully created alignment of which Wisdom sings in Proverbs 8 can be damaged and imbalanced. The psalmist would be less than truthful if he rejoiced over God's sovereignty but neglected to acknowledge the nagging problem of cruelty and chaos. We see this contradiction daily: the joy of loving relationships and the heartbreak of abusive ones, the breathtaking appearance of a hummingbird and the horror of an oil spill, the joyful release of a foot-stomping dance and the destruction of communities by war and famine.

How will God care for and repair the order of life so deeply injured? In verse 2 the psalmist suggests a most unexpected method of restoration: Where enemies have frustrated God's design, God will further upend all designs by naming the youngest and weakest as God's cornerstone for strength and healing. God will turn familiar orders of power and dominion on their heads. With the coos and giggles of babes, God will silence the noise of chaos. With the wisdom of newborns, God will outsmart the cleverest foes. With the wiggling-not-yet-walking toes of infants, God will stand up a fortress to shelter life from the storms of violence. Though we lament the chaos and fear that our warring world generates, God continually renews life through the least and the least expected.

Calm my fears, majestic God, and remind me again that your ways are not my ways. Help me align myself not to strength but to humility, not to power but to mystery. Amen.

Aligned with God   173

Jesus left unfinished work. The restoration and realignment of all creation to God remained incomplete when Jesus' life on earth ended. Before his death, in his final teaching to the disciples on the fateful night of his arrest, Jesus concedes what must have been difficult for his friends to hear, perhaps difficult also for him to articulate: "There is still much more for me to say, still much more for me to teach, but I cannot say what needs saying and you cannot hear what needs hearing. My time with you is ending, even though our work is not done."

Why couldn't Jesus say everything he wanted to say? Was there not enough time? Were the disciples unprepared to listen? Were they not mature enough in faith? Was the moment too full of all that had already been said, too full of bread and wine and the poignancy of Jesus washing their feet, so that just one more word would have been too much to hold in their hearts? Yes, for these reasons and more, Jesus did not say everything. In the final days of his ministry, Jesus left an ellipsis . . .

. . . and he promised that the Spirit would pick up the unfinished words and whisper them into ears that were ready to hear. The Spirit would continue the incomplete work by empowering Jesus' followers. The Spirit would ignite generations of disciples with dreams of what was still to come in God's healing and glory. Jesus left an ellipsis . . . because the work needed to continue by the Spirit.

Had Jesus stayed, had he said every word and taught everything and healed everyone, there would be no work to continue. There would be no reason for the disciples, and now for us, to be light and yeast and salt to the world. There would be no reason for the Spirit to draw us into God's work of realignment.

I have unfinished work, Jesus. When I am impatient, remind me that the Spirit is faithful in continuing the work and the dreams that are still to come. Amen.

How shall the work continue? How is God working out the healing of the world? When will it be done; when will you and I live consistently in the confidence of our alignment with God; when will the heartaches and chaos be over?

Are we there yet?

When Jesus gave his farewell speech, he knew the disciples listened with increasing worry and fear. How would they know what to do? How would they have the power to do it? Where would they go? What would they say? When would the promised Advocate appear? How would they recognize this Helper?

Jesus reassures, "You will recognize the Spirit because the Spirit will tell my stories. You will know the Spirit's presence because the Spirit will teach you the same lessons I taught you. What is mine is the Spirit's and the Father's. My work is the Spirit's work and the Father's work. If you recognize me—standing before you in flesh and blood, breaking bread and sharing wine with you—then you will recognize the Spirit and the Father."

How shall the work continue? It continues just as it began: by God, in Jesus, and through the Spirit. How will it be done? It will be done by God, in Jesus, through the Spirit. And are we there yet? Friends, we have never left it; even as the work continues, we have always been "there." We may not always feel it or claim it, but we have never been outside of God's grace; we have never left our alignment with God. The Spirit continues to declare this truth to us—we are aligned with God— and Jesus continues to teach us the work of aligning ourselves to one another, neighbor and stranger alike. The work continues, but we are here by grace to do it.

I forget, gracious God, that I cannot leave the bounds of your love. No matter how I bend and twist and turn, my life is aligned within yours. Thank you. Amen.

TRINITY SUNDAY

So then, if we are not out of alignment with God but participants in the work of aligning ourselves with one another and with all creation to the glory of God, let us boast in hope.

Many days—sometimes long stretches of seasons—hope seems out of reach. Daily stresses, overwhelming hardships, the 24-hour news cycle, an acute grief or conflict can tangibly impact our grasp of hope. And when hope seems far away, Paul's assurance can seem trite. Boasting in suffering seems an outrage. Yet Paul's conviction that suffering can produce hope is neither religious cliché nor paternalistic patter.

Backtrack to the second half of verse 2 where our boasting begins in hope. We can have no reason for hope if we do not recognize and experience the sufferings of the world. If our lives were perfect, hope would be pointless. We do not need hope unless we realize that the world is a mess, unless we see the foes and forces and misalignments that cause war and injury among us and within us.

Because we know the keen heartache that comes with opening our eyes to the world's mess, we determine that we must join the work of righting the mess. We join the work that God initiated and Wisdom celebrated, the holy work that the Spirit continues. Because we participate in the work, we are changed.

Because we are changed, we find a renewed perspective of hope that the world too can change, that the ordering of relationships and nature and life can be realigned in beautiful peace.

And through it all, God's love pours over us.

Loving God, call me to honest recognition of the world's hurts and of my own. Call me to work. Call me to change. Call me to hope. Amen.

The Lord Reigns

MAY 23–29, 2016 • KEVIN M. WATSON

Scripture Overview: Who has power? Elijah has no power. He is but a "troubler of Israel." Yet Elijah's prayers summon the power of God. Paul has no power. The churches in Galatia have learned that Paul neglected to teach them to observe the law of Moses. He can only insist that there is one and only one gospel, no matter who preaches it. The centurion of Luke 7 does have power. The centurion himself knows his power, but he also knows its limitations. He is not worthy to have Jesus, the powerless one, enter his home. For this acknowledgment of where real power lies, Jesus demonstrates once again the power of God. The question of who has power finds its most direct answer in Psalm 96: "For great is the LORD, and greatly to be praised."

Questions and Thoughts for Reflection

- Read 1 Kings 18:20-39. List the voices that attempt to pull you off-center and out of the range of God's voice. What can you do to set aside these voices and hear God's voice loudly and clearly?
- Read Psalm 96. How do you proclaim God's salvation daily?
- Read Galatians 1:1-12. What actions does your belief in Jesus encourage you to take?
- Read Luke 7:1-10. Recall a time when you allowed God's authority to influence your decision making.

Assistant Professor of Wesleyan and Methodist Studies, Candler School of Theology, Atlanta, Georgia

Like many, this psalm is tricky. At first glance it may come across as mundane. If we are not careful, we can simply ride the wave of the psalmist's call for songs of praise to the Lord, drawing distinctions between gods that are mere idols and the Lord who "made the heavens."

The psalmist begins, "Sing to the Lord a new song." The familiarity of the opening line may lull those who pray it to sleep. But Psalm 96 called the people of God then and calls the people of God now to awaken. "Tell the nations, 'The Lord rules!'" (CEB).

This countercultural claim calls for our unwavering allegiance to the one God of Abraham, Isaac, and Jacob. And so we sing not only to the God we adore but to the God who presently reigns over all. We proclaim God's salvation day after day because God's reign actually brings salvation.

The God of Israel is to be feared above all other gods, and God's reign continues into the present moment. It was not only the ancient Israelites who needed to remind themselves that the Lord reigns; we need that reminder each day as well. As we face competing claims and discouraging realities, we often wonder who's in charge. Christians need to be regrounded in who is Lord. Our God reigns. The God of Abraham, Isaac, and Jacob, who sent his Son to take on flesh and dwell among us and who continues to seek and save those outside the kingdom of God— that One reigns.

Lord, help me to recognize your reign in the world. May you especially reign in my life. Amen.

If the strong affirmation that God alone reigns interrupts the initial familiarity of Psalm 96, the disruption continues with a further affirmation of God's role as coming judge: "Let all creation rejoice before the LORD, for he comes, he comes to judge the earth. He will judge the world in righteousness and the peoples in his faithfulness" (NIV).

When praying or singing this psalm, the people of God were reminded that there is only one Lord and that despite any appearance to the contrary, God reigns. In many contexts, talk about God as Lord, as one who reigns, or as coming judge, has become infrequent because it can seem offensive or too confrontational. Some people have raised concern about using these themes in a way that distorts the biblical witness to who God is.

We affirm that God reigns and comes to judge. The duties of one who reigns involve the establishment of justice and righteousness. God as righteous judge may sound like bad news or a threat to modern ears. But notice the way the psalmist frames the coming of God: "Let all creation rejoice before the LORD, for he comes, he comes to judge the earth." It is good news, even cause for rejoicing! The establishment of justice brings equity rather than partiality, faithfulness rather than neglect.

The psalmist reminds us that these important parts of the biblical witness testify to who God is and how God is at work in the world. Psalm 96 reminds Christians again and again that God alone is Lord. Our God brings justice and righteousness to the earth, and this is very good news indeed!

God, enable me to grasp more completely who you are, and as I do, bless my offering of songs of praise, worship, and adoration. May the recognition of who you are and what you have done bring me a deep and abiding joy. And may it increase my faith, enabling me to proclaim that you alone are God. Amen.

The Lord Reigns

God often shows up when we least expect it. Samaria, the setting for today's reading, has been in the midst of severe famine. Matters have become so desperate that King Ahab and Obadiah, the manager of his palace, scour the land for enough grass to keep their horses and mules alive. Ahab and Obadiah have split up in their search, and Obadiah bumps into the prophet Elijah.

King Ahab, and even more so his wife, Jezebel, have been systematically killing the prophets of the Lord. Elijah appears and says to Obadiah, "Go tell your master, 'Elijah is here.'" Obadiah, while sympathetic to Elijah and wanting to help, knows that publicly aligning himself with Elijah could cost him his life.

Ahab follows Obadiah's request and goes to meet Elijah. Elijah commands Ahab to summon the people and all of the prophets of Baal and of Asherah for a meeting on Mount Carmel. "So Ahab sent word throughout all Israel and assembled the prophets on Mount Carmel." The face-off: Elijah versus eight-hundred and fifty prophets of Baal and Asherah. Elijah expects God to show up in a big way.

"Elijah went before the people and said, 'How long will you waver between two opinions? If the Lord is God, follow him; but if Baal is God, follow him.' But the people said nothing."

Encounters with God that call for a clear decision, a firm and unwavering commitment to follow God and renounce all competing idolatries, often catch us off guard and make us uncomfortable. They can also be gracious occasions of repentance, a returning to faith in God, the Lord of Israel.

God, prevent our wavering between two opinions. Embolden us to declare that you are God, follow you with every part of our lives, and worship you with our hearts, minds, and actions. Amen.

Elijah calls on the people of Israel to decide between following God or following the prophets of Baal. The showdown begins. Elijah, a brilliant showman, highlights the impotence of the prophets of Baal as they whip themselves into a frenzy and call out to a god who does not act. They call on the name of Baal for four hours to no avail. No matter how frenetic they become or how much they abuse their bodies to get Baal's attention, nothing happens.

Then Elijah takes his turn, all alone. He rebuilds the altar of the Lord, using twelve stones—one for each of the tribes of Israel. He digs a trench. After arranging the sacrifice on the altar, he has the people pour bucket after bucket of water over the meat and the altar until the trench is full of water.

And then Elijah simply prays to the God of Israel. Interestingly, he doesn't ask God to send fire to consume the sacrifice. Instead, he calls for God to make it known that the Lord is God in Israel. He asks God to answer him "so these people will know that you, Lord, are God, and that you are turning their hearts back again." Elijah, though alone, trusts that God will not abandon him and will act.

And God answers Elijah's prayer. God's fire falls, burning up the sacrifice, the wood, stones, soil, and all of the water in the trench. And, more importantly, the people fall before God and cry out, "The Lord—he is God!"

Isn't it amazing what great lengths God will go to in order to turn people's hearts back to God!

Lord, give us undivided hearts. If we have turned away, bring us back to you once again. Help us see and respond to your great love. Amen.

I don't know about you, but when Jesus praises someone's faith, it usually makes me uncomfortable. The faith of the centurion offers an excellent example!

Jesus often uses outsiders as positive examples of the way that people living in the kingdom of God would conduct themselves. In today's passage, Jesus praises the faith of a Roman centurion, a leader in the Roman military who would have commanded a significant number of soldiers.

The centurion, a man of great authority, gives way to the greater authority of Jesus; "I am unworthy, just say the word." While this story raises a number of questions, two aspects come clear. First, Jesus is able and willing to heal the sick. Second, Jesus praises the faith of the centurion and lifts it up as an example for the Israelites to follow.

The centurion believes that Jesus can and will heal his servant. His faith leads him to act by sending people to Jesus with requests for healing; not even in Israel has Jesus witnessed such faith.

Today, this story continues to call forth faith in Jesus Christ, not merely as a good moral teacher but as God in the flesh who brings physical, spiritual, and emotional healing to our lives. We are invited to active faith in Jesus, a faith that expects to encounter God in transformative ways in our lives.

What might active faith look like for you today? What specific concern do you need to bring to God in prayer? What holds you back? In stepping out in faith, may you experience God's active and living presence!

Jesus, help me believe that you are able and willing to bring life and light in the darkness. Give me a trusting and confident faith in you that leads me to follow actively. Amen.

Cheap imitations can entice. I remember buying a pair of sun-glasses in New York City as a child that cost ten dollars and looked like a pair of sunglasses that would have cost at least one hundred dollars if they had been the real thing. I was drawn in by the prospect of owning cool shades I could actually afford. By the end of the trip, the sunglasses were broken and unusable.

Rather than Paul's standard opening of thanksgiving, the letter to the Galatians begins with a stern rebuke to the churches that have allowed themselves to be enticed by a knock-off gospel. Paul writes, "I am astonished that you are so quickly deserting the one who called you to live in the grace of Christ and are turning to a different gospel—which is really no gospel at all" (NIV).

The gospel of Jesus Christ cannot be improved upon—better news is not possible. And there are no shortcuts to the kind of life this gospel demands. The opening verses summarize the gospel that commands Paul's commitment: God raised Jesus; Jesus gave his life for our sins and thereby set us free from the evil age. The gospel in a nutshell. Paul ratchets up what is at stake by saying that those who preach something different than the gospel of Christ, "let them be under God's curse!" (NIV).

Paul asserts that the gospel he preaches is not of human origin but a direct revelation from Jesus Christ himself, which is why he emphasizes so strongly the importance of this gospel rather than its perversion or improvement.

The good news is the best news the world has ever seen or heard. We cannot improve on the gospel of Jesus Christ, and we will answer to God if we water it down.

Jesus, protect me from being enticed by false gospels. Drench my thoughts, words, and actions with the good news of your gospel. Amen.

The first few times I read Galatians, I actually missed how upset Paul is at the beginning of the letter. I breezed right through the sarcasm in verse 6 and the strong language that rejects the possibility of a different gospel being valid in verses 8 and 9. Paul believes that any corruption of the gospel message will cause deterioration in both the message and what following that message looks like.

Look at verse 6 again: "I am astonished that you are so quickly deserting the one who called you by the grace of Christ and are turning to a different gospel." He asserts the true gospel and reminds the Galatians of the authority of his preaching. His gospel is not of mortal but of divine origin.

Paul cares about what the Galatians believe because he knows that belief leads to action. The gospel involves a way of life. If we change the message, the life of a follower of that gospel message will also change.

Did you notice the recurrent theme in this week's readings? Again and again they call for recognition of the uniqueness of God. This God calls people to decide to whom or to what they will give their lives.

When we recognize who God is and what God has done, the only appropriate response is to give ourselves completely to the Lord, to submit to God's reign. What parts of your life are not in sync with God's will?

Perhaps today is the day to confess these areas of disobedience. Ask for God's help in bringing all of yourself into the reign ushered in by the resurrection of Jesus Christ and sustained by the Holy Spirit.

Lord, forgive me of my disobedience and my desire to be lord of my own life. Help me turn completely to you and your will for my life. Lead me to rejoice in the joy and freedom of your salvation. Amen.

Embodying God's Compassion

MAY 30–JUNE 5, 2016 • **HEIDI GROGAN**

Scripture Overview: God intercedes powerfully for God's people. The reading from 1 Kings 17 continues the story of God's protection of Elijah from the wrath of Ahab, but God's protection here extends beyond his prophetic messenger to a non-Israelite widow. Psalm 146 reminds us that God alone may be trusted, for God is the one who cares for the outsider and the powerless, those rejected by human society and neglected by the "normal" standards of the world. In the Gospel lesson, Jesus encounters a woman whose position closely parallels that of the widow of Zarephath. For her also God intercedes, this time in the person of Jesus, whose own power restores the life of her son. Galatians 1:11-24 reminds us that God's intercessions do not always supply the pleasant fulfillments of our needs; sometimes they lead us where we would be happier not to go.

Questions and Thoughts for Reflection

- Read 1 Kings 17:8-24. The woman in the narrative gives to Elijah even though she has next to nothing. How can you demonstrate this kind of hospitality?
- Read Psalm 146. In what ways can you embody compassion and take action to relieve the suffering of others?
- Read Galatians 1:11-24. How can you grow in your willingness to allow God's compassion to humble you? How will this allow you to claim God's authority?
- Read Luke 7:11-17. When in your life have you linked your words with action to bring about change in another's life?

Instructor, Ambrose University College and Carey Theological College, Calgary, Alberta, Canada

In this reading, we meet a woman depleted. She has exhausted her food supplies and as she prepares a last meal for herself and her son, Elijah shows up asking for food and drink—a hard request for her to honor given her circumstances. Yet the Spirit of God calls her to offer hospitality out of her nothingness.

Imagine this scene: a woman sharing her grief with a stranger, protesting that she simply has nothing to offer in this famine time. She is out of resources in all ways. Indeed, she expects death after preparing this final meal for her family. In response to the emotion she surely conveys in her tone and body language, Elijah says, "Do not be afraid."

The widow does as Elijah asks (as God directed), and in a miraculous increase of her sharing, all are sustained. And more, relationships are nurtured. The story indicates that Elijah stays on with the woman and her family. This story resonates with Gospel accounts of fishes and loaves: Sharing when there is "not enough" changes everything.

When we feel depleted, it feels difficult to offer hospitality. To give when our resources are nil, whether they be emotional or physical, seems too much. Yet God often asks us to give out of this place of emptiness, even in our fear or grief. The truest hospitality comes when we have nothing in us to give. God can provide even when we have nothing left—either of basic resources or emotional resiliency.

Help us develop a posture of hospitality, God, living generously even in times of personal famine. May we be amazed at the miracles that follow our sharing from our nothingness. Amen.

Elijah engages a widow who has an edge. She makes it clear that this is not a good time for him to be asking for hospitality. Notice the dynamics of this exchange. He acknowledges a fear she has not yet stated aloud. By personalizing his response, he attends to her emotional reality compassionately, and she does as he asks. Despite the woman's circumstances, Elijah insists that she do her original job: providing hospitality to the stranger. He does not allow her to remain in the victim role. Hospitality brings with it a mutuality. Elijah knows that to receive help the widow needs to contribute via transformative choices. As the story evolves, the meal and oil continue in abundance. This encounter surely alters her worldview of Elijah's God.

And yet when all goes wrong and the widow's son dies, she reverts to a posture of distrust and anger. Without rebutting her accusations or responding to her hostile tone, Elijah takes her son in his arms and prays.

Let us wonder at Elijah's spiritual sensitivity and consider what it means to come alongside people who are thoroughly broken. When people feel out of control and losses seem too great, projecting fear as rage is human. Elijah meets the woman's bitterness straight on. He attends to her physical needs: "There was food every day" (NIV) and to her emotional state, holding close her beloved son in prayers to the God of life. The relief of her physical and emotional crises becomes the means of attending to her spiritual needs and brings her to a clear knowledge of and belief in God.

Perhaps when we speak hope to people and embody God's presence in their despair, they receive in abundance that which was in scarce supply, that which they need to live.

God of mercy, teach us how to come alongside those who despair so that we embody your concern for the broken. Amen.

The psalmist points us to the reliable love of God, which manifests itself in concrete help for people desperate for compassionate aid. We wisely ask ourselves: How does God provide all-encompassing care for those who are broken and who fall between the cracks of support systems?

The statement that leaps to our attention as unique in the psalmist's poetic rhythm comes in verse 8: God "loves the righteous." In the midst of reciting God's acts of compassion on behalf of the oppressed and hurting, the psalmist writes this new and different line: "The LORD loves the righteous."

And who are the righteous? We might assume they are morally perfect people. Instead, we find the answer in the psalm's invitation to embody the compassion of God: Not to behave in ways that disempower the powerless; rather, to see ourselves as God's feet traveling to the places where the shamed hide, God's hands tenderly lifting a chin, God's eyes lovingly seeing a person with distorted self-worth, God's voice advocating for the oppressed. The purposes of the righteous align with those of God's.

With the psalmist, we praise the Lord with all our soul because we know God attends to the cries of those on the margins. When we embody the ways of God in attending to the bowed down, we have reason to praise, for we are loved by this compassionate God.

At the end of the day, let us never pause from praising God whose love has lifted us and restored us when we were bowed down and has empowered us to do likewise.

Loving God, may we stand with you, whose concern is for the bowed down. May we embody your compassion and action to relieve the suffering of the oppressed. Amen.

The psalmist invites us to look to God for support we can count on: "Blessed are those whose help is the God of Jacob" (NIV). The Hebrew word translated "help" implies the strong presence and aid of God in situations of grave vulnerability. Psalm 146 stresses that it is God who takes care of the people in such times, not powerful leaders.

Throughout most of the Old Testament, kings ruled the Jewish community. Their primary job was to ensure the safety and welfare of the people, but often the kings of Israel did not live up to the responsibilities of their position. By the time of the writing of Psalm 146, no king protected Israel: Jerusalem and the temple were destroyed and the people made captives in Babylon. No wonder the psalmist disdains the human princes who cannot save and whose plans come to nothing.

Our world differs greatly from ancient Israel, yet many nations experience conditions of hunger, injustice, emotional pain, refugee vulnerability, economic hardship. Political leadership and social systems of support provide needed help but remain susceptible to changing ideologies and budgets. The marginalized of the world continue to suffer. God, on the other hand, attends to the despairing people of the world—often through the presence of men and women who show up in seemingly hopeless and broken places, embodying God's words of justice advocacy and compassionate action. The psalmist refers to God nine times in verses 6-9, underscoring God's engagement with the oppressed and presence in their suffering.

We receive blessing when we look to God as the source of help. Where today do we need wise leadership translated into concrete compassionate action?

God, we thank you for being our strength. Give us wise leaders who have compassion for people who need protection and help. Amen.

Paul, an advocate for inclusion of the Gentiles, now finds himself going toe-to-toe with leaders who question his apostolic authority. He counters their accusations in a very personal way—by insisting his authority comes from Christ who met him at the margins with grace. Paul calls his accusers to look with him to the action of God in his life.

In the face of Paul's murderous actions to destroy the Christian church, God moves with compassion. This remarkable grace transforms him and establishes the credibility of the gospel he preaches. Paul's life, claimed by God's grace, becomes a living testament to the extension of God's grace to the Gentiles. Paul's response to God's compassionate heart supports his authority as an apostle.

The authority Paul claims for his gospel comes not from any human endorsement but from a deep connection with God. God included Paul, and now Paul becomes a messenger of inclusion. No demand for earthly credentials will undermine these divine credentials.

Will we be able to say with Paul, "They glorified God because of me"? Only if our gospel rests in a strong sense of being grasped by God, especially in our places of woundedness. When our words and actions destroy and hurt, can we allow God's compassion to humble us and, in that humility, to include those the establishment would reject? If so, we, like Paul, will be messengers of grace who embody a divine authority whose love includes those on the margins.

May we fully realize that God does not marginalize us in our brokenness. This realization gives authority and credibility to our lived gospel.

Dear God, may we base our authority on you and your grace.
Give us a gospel worth sharing. Amen.

The grief of a mother in Nain evokes an emotional and physical response from Jesus. The widow loses her only son. She also loses her security and will live in poverty. Jesus shows the onlookers the heart of God.

Consider the scene. Two groups meet at the city gate: Jesus and his crowd of disciples and the widow's community. Both groups note that "the Lord" had compassion. This is the first time Luke refers to Jesus as "Lord," and he uses the word in relation to Jesus' compassion.

The Greek word for this compassion literally implies a gut reaction to the situation of the one who suffers. Jesus has such compassion for the widow that in his gut he empathizes with her pain.

Luke stresses compassion as having two distinct aspects: Jesus' heart is moved, and then he acts. Without both aspects, the encounter becomes mere pity, which diminishes the person in need. Jesus first comforts the woman with words: "Do not weep." Then he offers physical help: the son rises and speaks.

Our words and actions can restore life. The tears that move Jesus can give us pause to consider that Jesus consistently models the way compassion orients right action. We embody the character of Jesus when we feel moved emotionally to initiate concrete responses.

Will we allow ourselves to experience such a compassionate encounter? Can we bring our grief and fear to the gate of our life as it once was, and can we imagine Jesus' heart going out to us? If we can, then inevitably we will do likewise.

God of compassion, may we meet people at the gates of their grief and embody your care. May they experience life restored as our hearts go out to them and as we offer aid through word and action. Amen.

Embodying God's Compassion 191

Jesus restores a young man to his mother and community. He moves in close, touching the bier that carries the son. His action causes the bearers to stop, to stand still. We can then imagine Jesus leaning in close, whispering, "Young man, I say to you, rise." Consider the pause before the dead man sits up and speaks. What were his first words and to whom? This episode invites us into a world of wonder.

Can we identify with the son in our need for restoration from places of death and darkness, places where we feel powerless to move? Can we feel the warmth of the divine hand where we lie lifeless; hear the strong words whispered into the deep places of our soul to arise, to sit up, and to return to our families and lives? Can we imagine speaking from that transformational experience? What would we say?

In what ways do we identify with those in the gathered community who witness God's presence with people we love, people who experience places of deadness in their lives? We grieve our helplessness to restore them. Are we like the bearers of the bier, carrying our loved ones to the gate at the borders of our community? Let us sense God's presence coming toward us. Let us stop and stand still as words of life are spoken.

Maybe it's when we are able to still ourselves and hear Christ's words of life that the narrative in verse 17 comes to life in our time. We can only tell if we have heard; we can only share if we have had an experience of Christ's presence in our lives. We are the channels through which the news of Christ will spread throughout our community—yes, and even throughout the world.

God, we thank you for reminding us that Jesus brings life from death, that he heals our grief and insecurity as well as that of all humanity. Amen.

Exuberant Joy, Confident Faithfulness

JUNE 6–12, 2016 • THOMAS R. HAWKINS

Scripture Overview: In the story of Naboth's vineyard, Ahab and Jezebel act with unbelievable treachery against an innocent man. Only when Elijah confronts Ahab does Ahab recognize his sin against God. Psalm 5 powerfully recalls that only God may truly be called king and that the true king will not finally tolerate the wickedness of humankind. Both these passages remind us that the relationship between an individual and others reveals something powerful about the individual's relationship with God. The Gospel and epistle readings support the belief that an individual's relationship with God reveals something powerful about that individual's relationships with human beings. Paul attempts to deal with the boundaries some have attempted to reinforce between Jews and Gentiles. Luke's version of the woman who anoints Jesus with oil presents us with a Pharisee who does not understand that relationship to God involves social relationships as well. Jesus insists that the love of God requires loving generosity among human beings.

Questions and Thoughts for Reflection

- Read 1 Kings 21:1-21a. What power imbalances do you recognize in our society? How do these compare to the power balance in God's economy?
- Read Psalm 5:1-8. How would your days be different if you spent time with God early in the day?
- Read Galatians 2:15-21. What external markers do you allow to define you?
- Read Luke 7:36–8:3. Where do you discover joy in your life? How does this joy foster courage in discipleship?

Assistant Chair and Professor, The School of Technology, Eastern Illinois University; copastor, First Presbyterian Church, Charleston, Illinois

All four Gospels include stories about a woman who anoints Jesus during a meal. Three Gospels describe this anointing as happening in Jerusalem before Jesus' arrest as a foreshadowing of his passion and resurrection: The woman prophetically anoints Jesus for burial as well as for enthronement as king. Luke instead places it in Jesus' Galilean ministry where it describes the exuberant, extravagant joy that erupts when Jesus' grace-filled presence transforms someone's life.

Luke describes this unnamed woman as a sinner. In Jesus' time, sin was as much a social as it was a moral one. When Jesus reaches across the boundaries that have excluded her and accepts her, she knows herself as forgiven.

The woman then responds to this forgiveness with extravagant joy that overflows into a bold act of love. An unexpected role reversal occurs. The unnamed woman arrives as an uninvited, unwanted guest in Simon's house, but she suddenly takes on the role of the banquet's host. Simon, the official host, should have ensured that Jesus' feet were washed. Yet she, rather than Simon, performs this humble act of service, washing Jesus' feet with her tears and covering them with her kisses.

Sometimes we best proclaim our love of Jesus by our humble service to the marginalized ones he loves and forgives. In washing their feet, we wash his feet. Her joy in receiving Jesus' forgiveness empowered her to act courageously. In the same way, our most courageous acts of ministry arise from exuberant joy rather than a sense of duty or obligation.

Lord God, may my ministry to others arise from the joy of your presence and not from a sense duty or obligation. May my humble service to others boldly proclaim my love for you. Amen.

This story concludes with a description of several other women who follow Jesus. They too live generously and gratefully in response to Jesus' healing and forgiveness. Like the Twelve, they are faithful disciples of Jesus.

Luke portrays these women as models of discipleship, especially the woman who washes Jesus' feet with her tears. Her actions stand in sharp contrast to Simon's. As the story unfolds, Simon moves from mild curiosity about Jesus to doubt and then finally to silence. Luke clearly is describing the progression of some well-connected, high-status believers who were initially attracted to Jesus but later refuse to follow him. Simon labels the woman a "sinner," but he is the one who falls short. He does not see Jesus or the woman for who they really are. He reduces people outside his circle of acceptability and respectability to labels: sinner, prophet, teacher.

Simon is the ultimate insider. He writes the rules that turn others into social outcasts. Consequently, he can never experience the transformation that comes in response to Jesus' offer of grace and acceptance. Trusting in his own goodness, he simply doesn't know he needs forgiveness.

Do we sometimes see the label and not the person? Do we note the fault instead of the unhealed wound or need that lies hidden beneath it?

Do we fail to find joy in our discipleship because we believe God has already made us insiders at the heavenly banquet and that we can determine who else may have a seat at the table? How often have we forgotten that those who are forgiven little, love little as well?

Save us, Lord, from the temptation to label others rather than to call them by name, to find fault with others rather than to understand the wounds they carry within their hearts. Amen.

King Ahab covets the vineyard next to his palace. He approaches its owner, Naboth, with an offer that he cannot refuse. But Naboth does refuse. He knows that his land is a gift from God, not a commodity to be bought and sold. God has allotted this plot of land to Naboth's family. Selling it to the king would violate God's commandments. Naboth even states his refusal as a religious oath.

Seeing Ahab's distress, Queen Jezebel decides to obtain the vineyard for her husband through a cynical and ruthless manipulation of Israel's religious laws and institutions. She involves the elders in orchestrating an accusation of blasphemy against Naboth, a crime that carries the penalty of death. Jezebel even arranges for two witnesses to speak against Naboth because Mosaic law demands two witnesses in cases involving the death penalty. Naboth, the one person who has shown genuine faithfulness to God, is stoned to death for blasphemy.

Ahab and Jezebel, meanwhile, have wrapped their abuse of power in a cloak of religiosity and obedience to God's law. For the writers of Israel's history, these two characters become larger than life in their representation of an oppressive social order that disrespects faithfulness to God and justice to neighbor.

Examples of powerful people who manipulate religious values and institutions for their own selfish ends litter the annals of history. Unfortunately, religious leaders, like the elders in our story, are often complicit in this hijacking of religious faith out of concern for their own status, power, or influence. The story of Naboth's vineyard reminds us to be ever alert to ways that human greed and sin can corrupt the spheres of church and state.

O God, may we cherish all we possess as gifts from you rather than commodities at our disposal. Keep us alert to the ways powerful people may manipulate genuine piety for their own ends, thus defeating your purposes for our world. Amen.

Israel's royal ideology demands that its kings deliver the needy from oppression and defend the poor from violence. Jezebel and Ahab do not simply neglect this responsibility; they intentionally repudiate it by murdering Naboth and taking his vineyard.

Ahab's previous transgressions involve the worship of foreign gods and the persecution of the prophet Elijah. Now he and Jezebel corrupt the very basis of God's covenant with Israel. They place their own desires above God's demand for equity and justice.

Ahab wants to turn Naboth's vineyard into a vegetable garden. Why a vegetable garden? In Deuteronomy 11:8-12 Moses contrasts the freedom and plenty of the Promised Land with Egypt's vegetable gardens, which slaves water and maintain. The prophets and psalms repeatedly use the image of vine or vineyard to symbolize Israel as God's chosen people. By digging up a vineyard and planting a vegetable garden, Ahab signals his desire to turn Israel into another arbitrary, unjust, oppressive kingdom like Egypt. No wonder Elijah, the representative of Israel's covenant traditions, prophesies so vehemently against Ahab and Jezebel. The Sinai covenant demands that the people live in relationships of equity and justice. Israel is not to become a kingdom like Egypt where the powerful enslave and exploit the weak.

Elijah's message is particularly relevant in an era of corporate greed and political irresponsibility. What power imbalances exist in our world that encourage the powerful to exploit the weak? Who ultimately are the "takers" and the "makers" in our global economy? in God's economy?

You, O Lord, satisfy our needs, not our greed. Help us live as signs and instruments of your coming kingdom's justice and righteousness. Amen.

Naboth's widow and children could have written Psalm 5. The psalmist praises God as the one who takes no delight in evil, greed, dishonesty, or treachery. The psalmist's God is the arbiter of justice and the strength of the oppressed. We can imagine Naboth's survivors praying this psalm of lament, pleading for God to execute divine justice on Ahab and Jezebel.

Verse 3 refers twice to the psalmist's coming before God in the morning. This reference suggests a particular context for the psalm. In Exodus 29:38-42, God instructs Moses to institute daily morning and evening sacrifices. Our psalmist has perhaps spent the night in the Temple as an act of devotion and prayer. Now awakened by the rising sun, he asks God to answer a personal plea for deliverance.

The reference to prayer in the morning challenges us to start each day with God. The psalmist's first thought in the morning is of prayer and relationship. Mine is usually, *What e-mail arrived since last night?* Or, *What's for breakfast?* Caught up in the busyness of the day, I later realize that I have done everything *except* spend time in prayer.

Psalm 5 reminds us that our morning and evening sacrifice is the offering of our praise and prayer to God. We are invited to sacrifice our own time and agendas in order to bring our praise and prayer before God. How different would each day be if, like the psalmist, we anticipated "early in the morning" spending time with God? How might our day change if early in the morning we looked at the shape of our day and asked for God's guidance? Or if we anticipated the day's rough spots and surrendered them to God? What might change for us if our first prayer in the morning were this: *[fill in the blank with your prayer]*   ?

Lead me, O Lord, in your righteousness . . . ; make your way straight before me. Amen.

Marketing consultants tell companies that they must "brand" their products. Otherwise they won't stand out from the other businesses around them. Branding employs external markers to distinguish a product from its competitors.

During the Babylonian Exile, Judean refugees, surrounded by Mesopotamian religions, struggled to maintain their identity as God's people. One solution came in reemphasizing external boundary markers that had earlier allowed their ancestors to maintain an identity distinct from the Canaanites around them: purity codes, sabbath keeping, and circumcision.

Although Christians labeled these external markers as "works of the law," first-century Jews did not typically experience these external markers as ways to win God's approval. Because they were God's people, God's love was already theirs.

External markers can lead to an attitude of exclusivity or become a substitute for the inner reality of faith, however. This is the crux of Paul's confrontation with Peter at Antioch, which he summarizes here. Peter has set aside purity codes in order to eat with Gentile Christians. But then he breaks table fellowship when Jewish Christians arrive. For Paul, these Jewish-Christian purity codes no longer establish the identity of God's people. Internal, ethical markers such as the fruit of the Spirit now define a person as Christian.

We Christians have sometimes reverted to our own "works of the law" and used external markers such as not dancing or going to movies as ways to define who is Christian. Paul challenges us to let a self based on external markers of religious identity be crucified with Christ so that Christ, who embodies self-sacrificing love, may live within us.

Lord, may I be crucified with Christ so that Christ may live in me and so that my life will bear the fruit of love. Amen.

One bedrock principle of the Protestant Reformation was justification by faith. We are not justified by meritorious works but by our faith in Jesus Christ. However, this principle depends upon a particular translation of the Greek text.

The Greek in Galatians 2:16-17 has no preposition between the words *faith* and *Jesus Christ*. To connect them, translators must insert an English preposition. But which one? Since the Greek text uses the genitive case, the preposition "of" seems the most logical choice. Most Greek genitives, in fact, are translated in just this way. Verse 16 would then say that we are justified through the "faith [or faithfulness] of Jesus Christ" rather than our "faith in Jesus Christ."

Does this word choice from "in" to "of" matter? Yes. Saying that we are justified by the faithfulness *of* Jesus places the focus on what he did for us rather than on what we can do for ourselves to make ourselves whole. What matters is God's sheer grace—a love we cannot earn and do not deserve—not the acceptance of a certain formula of belief about Jesus or the good deeds we can perform.

If we are saved by Christ's faithfulness to God, even to his dying on the cross for us, then our response to this astounding grace is to embrace a cross-shaped faithfulness of our own. When we act in faithfulness to God's promise, which is that God always brings new life out of death and healing to a broken creation, then we continue Jesus' own work of healing and reconciliation.

Gracious God, Jesus' faithfulness to your promises broke the power of sin and reconciled the world to you and to itself. May we embrace your Son's cross-shaped faithfulness and trust in the grace and love we know through him. Amen.

Noise, Doubt, Grace, and Healing

JUNE 13–19, 2016 • EMILY REEVES GRAMMER

Scripture Overview: The acknowledgment and service of God powerfully threatens the way the world generally does its business. Precisely because he has done the Lord's bidding in killing all the prophets of Baal, Elijah must flee from Jezebel's wrath. Utterly discouraged by the limitations of his own resources, Elijah proposes that he be allowed to die. God's response comes, not in the form of words of encouragement but in the form of nurture, God's own presence, and finally in the form of yet another summons to work. The psalmist portrays the human need of God's presence and the human cry in the face of God's apparent absence. The words of Galatians call for liberation from anthropological boundaries of race, class, and gender. The Gospel lection poses a threat to the status quo. For the man possessed of demons, the arrival of Jesus Christ means freedom and the opportunity to serve.

Questions and Thoughts for Reflection

- Read 1 Kings 19:1-15a. We live in a noisy world. How do you enable yourself to hear God's whispers that come in the silence?
- Read Psalm 42. What triggers your doubt? How can you use these experiences to lead you closer to God?
- Read Galatians 3:23-29. What do you perceive to be your primary identity?
- Read Luke 8:26-39. How can we resist the familiar "devils" of our existence to find the radical freedom that Christ offers?

Associate pastor, City Road Chapel United Methodist Church, Madison, Tennessee

I have two children under the age of four. I often spend my days in a cacophony of shouts, wild laughter, and shrieking tantrums. I frequently find myself competing with the noise in order to make myself heard. But as a first-grade teacher, I learned a marvelous trick in communicating with young children. I get the children's attention, and then I drop my voice to a whisper. They stop what they're doing (usually), draw near to me, and listen intently. They like whispering and "telling secrets."

Elijah has been caught in the noise, both literally and figuratively. He has raised the ire of Ahab and Jezebel through his truth-telling prophecy. He fears for his life. Exhausted, he is ready to give up. In the midst of this "noise," the word of the Lord comes to him and directs him to stand on a mountain and wait for the Lord to pass by. While he waits, he hears more noise. A great wind, "splitting mountains and breaking rocks in pieces." An earthquake. A fire. This level of noise must have created sheer sensory overload for Elijah. It also highlights by contrast the depth of the silence that follows. The silence draws Elijah in, and then he hears the whisper, "What are you doing here, Elijah?"

We live in the noise. Our lives are noisy with television, radio, smart phones, the expectation of instant e-mail response, and more. Our lives are also figuratively noisy with stress, fear, and broken relationships dominating our attention. God speaks to us in a whisper, but sometimes that whisper speaks louder than the noise. Sometimes the contrast of God's silence jars us out of the noisy grind. Are we hearing the silence? Are we hearing the whisper?

Whispering Lord, help us find our words and your will for us. Amen.

Many of us feel perpetually overwhelmed by financial difficulties, relationship problems, health issues, and more. All of these can weigh on us, leaving an impression in our souls. When I am driving from place to place, my brain will frequently bring forward a laundry list of concerns and issues—both my own and the world's. They marinate and soak into my soul, and even if I forget the details as my attention is redirected, I feel the weight of them. Something nags at me, and I feel troubled. We sense unrest in our lives, and often we can't quite pin it down.

The psalmist asks twice: "Why are you cast down, O my soul, and why are you disquieted within me?" The downcast and disquieted soul is not a uniquely modern problem, although the sources of that despair may be new in each age. We don't know the specific troubles that burdened the psalmist, but we can identify with that sense of disquiet that rolls over life like a fog. That feeling of unease is as instinctual and basic as the hunger and thirst the psalmist describes in verse 1.

However, the psalmist doesn't leave us without hope. We can reassure ourselves, even as we hear the psalmist reassuring himself, that we "shall again praise him, my help and my God." We may not know when this feeling will lift. We may not know if our circumstances will change or whether our attitudes will shift around those circumstances. Once again, the psalmist offers no specifics. The soul who suffers and waits on God, however, will not be disappointed.

Our help and our God, we pray that you will remove the weight of disquiet from our souls. We long for a time when we feel the joy of praising you once again. Amen.

The issue of doubt remains ever present as the shadow side of belief. Even the most stalwart believers can find themselves in situations that generate doubt about God's existence or the extent of God's goodness and concern with humanity. Our psalmist, struggling with unknown issues that cause extreme duress, does not doubt God's existence. However, he believes that God has forsaken him: "I say to God, my rock, 'Why have you forgotten me? Why must I walk about mournfully because the enemy oppresses me?'"

If we are honest with ourselves, we can probably name one or two times when the thought that God no longer cares about us fills our minds. I am usually stricken with such ideas when I consider situations that seem too horrific for a loving God: abused and hurt children, political injustice and oppression, economic policies that value profit more than people. I cannot reconcile the activity of a gracious God with these evils in our world. Each of us has our own list of triggers for doubt. If we don't have them, we probably aren't paying attention to the manifold ways humans can hurt one another.

But we have the example of the psalmist who doubts God's care for him, and then in the same breath urges all to renew hope in God. The tears the psalmist has been eating will neither sustain nor nourish (Ps. 42:3). We will experience seasons of doubt, dryness, hunger, and thirst for God. But we will also revel in the harvest of grace and mercy. We do ourselves a service by remembering that all things grow in their season.

Gracious God, heed our hunger and thirst for you, abate our doubt, and give us seasons of praise and joy. Amen.

The central issue of the early Christian church centered on identity. Before Christianity emerged as distinct from Judaism, the question of observation of Jewish law was largely null. Jesus and his followers, observant Jews, occasionally made exceptions to the law to make a point, but they were reared and steeped in contemporary Jewish culture.

However, Paul was one of a wave of missionaries who brought the gospel to new lands. Through his activity, Gentiles will experience conversion and baptism into the body of Christ. The questions begin: Do the Gentiles require circumcision? Should the Gentiles observe Jewish law, including dietary and sabbath regulations? A single, urgent issue lies at the root of this quandary: Are the Gentiles, along with God's people Israel, heirs to God's promises? And at what cost?

Paul makes his point succinctly, writing to the church at Galatia: "In Christ Jesus you are all children of God through faith." Within the body of Christ, there may be difference and distinction, but identity cannot be disputed. "Christian" becomes the foremost marker of identity among those who are baptized into Christ. Jew, Gentile, male, female, slave, free—all are important varieties of human experience. But they no longer serve as the defining characteristic of those in the body.

In the Christian church of our time, we continue to struggle with issues of identity. What comes first: liberal or conservative, rich or poor, black or white, male or female? What defines us? Our faith and membership in the body of Christ becomes our identity; all the rest comes behind—not unimportant but not the central fact.

God of grace and truth, allow us to see our membership in Christ's body as the central fact of our existence. Amen.

In this portion of Galatians, Paul layers his discussion of "the law"—the guidelines laid out for observant Jewish practice in the Hebrew Bible—with his understanding of traditional Greek education. The word *disciplinarian* is a translation of the Greek word *paidagogos*, from which we get a word like *pedagogy*. A *paidagogos* was a special kind of slave in upper-class Grecian families. This slave guarded the activities and behaviors of the family's boys. The boys went nowhere without their *paidagogos*, a chaperone and moral instructor in one. However, when the young men emerged from boyhood, they left the *paidagogos* behind. Society and families expected grown men to have absorbed their childhood lessons in morality and proper behavior. They no longer needed the external guidance of the *paidagogos*.

Paul extends this metaphor of the *paidagogos*. "But now that faith has come, we are no longer subject to a disciplinarian." Paul then goes on to deconstruct the various differences in identity that the believers have allowed to divide them: national origin, ethnicity, socioeconomic status, gender.

In our time, parents serve in the role of the *paidagogos*. All of us have parents. Many of us also have parents in faith—those people who played a strong role in bringing us to where we are in our spiritual journeys. Perhaps our beliefs have diverged from those faith parents. Perhaps, through our maturity in faith, we have come to different conclusions than those we were taught. The blessing of being in Christ is that we are free to experience faith for ourselves—unmediated by a *paidagogos*.

Eternal God, we pray that we will experience the fullness of freedom we are promised through faith in Christ. Amen.

I've heard an old saying that rings true: "Sometimes you prefer the devil you know to the devil you don't." When I was a young seminarian, I counseled with a woman in my congregation who was physically and emotionally abused by her husband. She wanted a change, and so we set about making the plans that could free her and her sons from this situation. Yet, she continually fell back into the cycle of violence that characterizes such relationships. When I finally asked her what was keeping her in her marriage, she responded, "At least I know what's going to happen. If I leave, I have no idea what will happen to me or my family." She preferred the devil she knew.

In today's passage, we read a genuine and life-giving exchange between Jesus and the demoniac. But then we witness a troubling response from the demoniac's community members who ask "Jesus to leave them; for they were seized with great fear." The swineherds are upset because the hogs into which Jesus sends the demons are a huge loss. Losing them into the water probably means the loss of livelihood for the better part of a year, and the people of the region have an established social order. The demoniac clearly resided on the bottom and outside of the order. Now that Jesus has healed him, they feel unsure of his fit in their structure. They prefer the devil they know.

The introduction of the gospel into our lives and our world continues to cause upheaval and resentment. Although Jesus Christ brings freedom and healing, he also asks us to rethink the ways we interact. Many of us will prefer the devil we know to the radical freedom Christ offers.

Healing Lord, give us courage to embrace the freedom the gospel brings us. Amen.

To fully grasp this story's meaning, we must understand the place of the pig in the author's time and culture. Even the most cursory look at Jewish dietary law brings to light the awareness of swine's uncleanliness. In Deuteronomy, the law states that "the pig, because it divides the hoof but does not chew the cud, is unclean for you" (14:8). For the Jews who traveled with Jesus at the time, the Gerasene swineherds' reliance on raising hogs could mark them as people with whom the disciples would not share table fellowship.

However, the author of Luke writes for a largely Gentile audience—people not bound by the dietary restrictions of Jewish followers of Jesus. This major sticking point for the early church plays out in the subtext of the healing story through the idea of cleanliness versus uncleanliness.

The demoniac's place among the dead marks him as a pariah in his community as well. (Consider how we would receive someone who lived in a cemetery in our time.) Yet Jesus comes to him and heals him despite his unclean status. Jesus then sends the legion of demons into the swine who rush into the water. Jesus saves even those who live among what is unclean.

The reality that Jesus willingly ventures into unclean circumstances to heal unclean people offers us enormous hope. After all, we live with legions of voices and influences pulling us in every direction. Many of them are unclean as well. We may not recognize them as demons, but some of us are as tormented as the demoniac. But no situation lies beyond Jesus' ability to heal, redeem, and save. The powers of sin and death can never defeat the surpassing power of Christ to bring wholeness.

Triumphant Lord, we thank you for your healing power. Grant us your peace. Amen.

Learning from What We Would Avoid

JUNE 20–26, 2016 • ROBERT P. FUGARINO

Scripture Overview: The passing of a great leader of God's people gives rise to a crisis of sorts, for only the work of the Spirit of God can supply a newly empowered person around whom the people may rally. That God does not abandon the people and the fruit of the work of the Spirit may be seen in the authorization of Elisha to fill the void left by the departure of Elijah. Psalm 77 is a cry of distress from one in trouble, but the bulk of the verses have to do with the psalmist's meditation on the goodness of God, especially on God's saving deeds in the past. Galatians 5 is an important statement on the work of the Spirit. Freedom in Christ involves obligations to Christ and to others. The memory of Elijah is raised in the Gospel passage. However, unlike Elijah, Jesus rebukes his followers and invites further resistance by a series of statements concerning the nature of discipleship.

Questions and Thoughts for Reflection

- Read 2 Kings 2:1-2, 6-14. How can you let go of what limits you? How will this release allow you to recognize God's care and faithfulness?

- Read Psalm 77:1-2, 11-20. Do you identify with the psalmist? What moments in your life has your soul refused to be comforted?

- Read Galatians 5:1, 13-25. How do you avoid becoming "enslaved to sin"?

- Read Luke 9:51-62. What can you learn from Jesus' anger? How does anger deepen your love for God and for others?

Ordained minister in the Christian Church, working with Park Hill Christian Church, Kansas City, Missouri

Often we do not control the most important matters in life. Consider Elisha. The great Elijah calls him to follow, and he does. Elisha leaves his home and serves Elijah. And here we pick up the story at the end of their time together. The time for Elijah to leave has come. Elijah asks his protégé what he can do for him before he leaves.

Elisha responds, "Give me a double portion of your spirit." Although not father and son, Elisha asks Elijah to consider him as Elijah's rightful heir, to receive his master's call and ministry and power from on high. It is a natural request. It seems to be what the entire apprenticeship has been building toward. Surely Elisha has done all he can to prepare himself to take over.

Yet Elijah comes back to him saying, in essence, that this request lies outside his power to grant. It resides beyond his control and *far beyond* Elisha's control. It is something only God can give.

Mildly put, being limited stinks. We can do all the little steps of technique perfectly and still see the jump shot clang off the rim of the basket instead of falling through. We can do everything in our power and still not receive the love of the person sitting across the dinner table from us.

Yet in the end, Elisha sees what he needs to see and receives what he needs to receive. In this way we are all Elisha. Our power and control remain limited, but God is still good and God's care provides what we can't provide for ourselves.

Allow me, God, to recognize my limits but not be frozen in despair because of them. Amen.

I remember moving across the country during a difficult time in my life. As I packed up the kitchen, I—how to say it—*accidentally* broke a plate or two. (wink, nudge.) It felt good. Why?

I remember a couple, both in their eighties and married for decades. The husband had Parkinson's, and now he couldn't speak or move. However, they'd never spoken about his end-of-life desires or the funeral or much of anything related to the illness. Why?

One reason: Even the best transitions create stress and challenging situations. Transition equals stress, and that's hard because life is always in motion, always transitioning from one situation to the next.

Here in Second Kings we note a transition, a passing of the torch from Elijah to Elisha, from one generation to the next. Time and again Elijah tells his understudy to leave him, and Elisha refuses. So they walk together and cross the River Jordan. Everyone—Elijah, Elisha, the company of prophets, God—acknowledges the importance of this transition point. I'm pretty sure Elisha feels tense.

Like our world, the world of Kings was a brutal place. Elijah served as God's mouthpiece in it by speaking truth to power. Now he is leaving; will the world swallow up the witness? Will Elisha be able to carry the holy things into a new day?

Will we?

Yes, because God remains engaged and faithful not just for the days of Elijah but for the days of Elisha as well. Yes, because Matthew reminds us that the risen Jesus said, "I am with you always, to the end of the age" (28:20). Yes, because we are God's.

Give me eyes, Lord, to see the transitions of life—be they happy or sad—as opportunities to be honest before you about both my hopes and my fears. Amen.

The Psalms are a big deal. They're strewn throughout the New Testament. Jesus quotes Psalm 22 from the cross. Monks chant them in chapels. You can't overstate their importance in Judeo-Christian spirituality.

But for most of my Christian life I didn't encounter them very much. When I did, it wasn't this one. I'd hear the quiet confidence of Psalm 23 or Psalm 121's recognition of protection or the joy of Psalm 150. Psalm 77? Nope.

This is a dark psalm. We hear the darkness most clearly in verses 3-10, the verses omitted in our reading. (Commentators note that verse 4 sounds like a description of depression and verses 9 and 10 sound like a challenge to the heart of biblical faith.) Nonetheless, the first two verses capture the tone. The psalmist cries out for help, and nothing is happening.

In a melancholy way, this can be helpful even before the happy turn begins in verse 13. Why? Because real life has lots of moments that sound like verses 1 and 2; and if God heals and saves the real world, we need to ponder the dark moments as well as to dance in the light ones.

I imagine a man in despair stammering out something like verses 1 and 2 as he considers doing something drastic. I imagine the parents of a teenager shot dead in the street shrieking those words when they see the unthinkable. When has your soul refused to be comforted? Can you speak of that time aloud? Can you admit to that lack of comfort? The psalmist does.

And I imagine Mary singing these verses as a sad song while she walks the garden path to a certain tomb on a Sunday morning long ago. How could she not? But a new song was beginning.

Lord, our lives include darkness as well as light. Help us not to pretend this away, even as we seek to be filled completely by the life of your resurrection. Amen.

During my life I have usually employed the Psalms as personal devotional prayers. But the Psalms primarily function as the songbook of God's people. When the community gathers, the members share them.

Psalm 77 breaks into two sections. In the first (verses 1-10) the psalmist seems alone, in distress, and meditating upon the pitfalls of his own life. But in the second (verses 11-20), his perspective appears to shift. The psalmist meditates on the story of God, the Exodus, and how God can bring life from certain death.

During the first section, I picture a person in a worship service with head in hands. On the movie screen of her mind she replays all the emotions and events that have brought her to this moment of need and sees no relief.

Then, as the second section begins, she lowers her hands, opens her eyes, and sees that she is not alone. She stands in the middle of her community. They sing and speak and toast the good news of God with food and drink. She realizes that life is more than her situation; the song expands beyond her, offering more to meditate upon. And this "more-ness" creates space for her to dare to move forward and receive comfort at last.

At some point we all look at our lives, cry to God for comfort, and sense nothing in response. Psalm 77 reminds us that it isn't just about us. In such times we have more to meditate upon: God's story written in the language of Christ's life. Other people around us believe when we cannot and, in doing so, they offer us the space to be made new.

God, even in yourself you form a community of three, a Trinity. Help me remember I am not alone. You are with me, as are others. Amen.

I hate forks in the road. I don't care if it is a highway interchange or an intersection out in the country. Even if I know exactly where I am going, at the fork I face that moment of unpleasant wondering: *Will I choose the wrong path and get lost?*

I hate the forks because I hate to blow it.

Christian faith is built on the primacy of God's love, faithfulness, and grace in Jesus Christ. This serves as the foundation for Galatians too. It appears that after Paul built a community based upon becoming children of God through "the faithfulness of Christ Jesus," others came through teaching other "essential" aspects—circumcision, for instance.

This letter expresses Paul's "NO!" to this particular aspect, but that doesn't mean we can't blow it. Despite the fact that everything rests on God's grace, we do not lose our freedom to choose the wrong path at the fork in the road.

This is a dynamic tension for Paul. As he states in the first verse, "For freedom Christ has set us free. Stand firm, therefore, and do not submit again to a yoke of slavery." Paul uses the rest of the passage to describe the options and real choices that confront people of faith.

This gives us pause. Being gracefully adopted into God's family through Christ is not the end of the story. It is the beginning of a story that does not guarantee our good decisions. We are not puppets in God's hand. We can still blow it.

Yet Paul says "we live by the Spirit" of God, so we need not fear the road's forks. And even when we realize that we've made the wrong choice, we recall that when everyone chose to put Jesus on the cross, God still turned it into a resurrection.

Lord, help me to affirm that your grace powers all and that my freedom really matters. Amen.

When a bad mood spreads we often think nothing good can come of it, and usually we're right. But sometimes important—if uncomfortable—growth can only come from something as foul as a bad mood. A biblical commentator suggested that this passage may embody that very growth.

Jesus turns his face to Jerusalem—which means death—and that can make anyone sour and angry. Then, seeing Jesus focused on Jerusalem, a Samaritan village refuses to welcome him. Maybe this refusal comes for ancient reasons of ethnic and religious bias. Or maybe Jesus' focus has caused him to disappoint them in some way. Anyway, this rejection turns the disciples nasty. James and John suggest destroying the village. This gets Jesus even angrier. He rebukes them before they all move on to another village.

Then three potential followers come up to Jesus looking to sign on with him and his movement. In response, Jesus allows the ugly mood to flow their way. His stern words and harsh manner make this an unpopular text with preachers and Christians in general.

Jesus forces each of the potential followers into a necessary crisis. He forces each to wrestle with whether or not Jesus and the rule of God he embodies are first in their lives. Is God, well, God? Or does some other god remain their god? The demands of discipleship and following Jesus are great.

Our growth in the life of faith includes facing these questions for ourselves, but we rarely will unless our backs are pushed up against a wall. Sometimes it will take nothing less than a holy wildfire of bad moods to get us to take a serious look at what makes us fit for the kingdom of God.

Lord, help me to see even the hard times as opportunities to grow. Amen.

Jesus got angry. This has always made sense to me intellectually, especially when I ponder the Incarnation, the confession that, in Jesus, God is truly and fully one of us. However, emotionally I don't often grasp this fact. On that level I prefer to deny anger. I equate anger with sin, so I have Jesus speak all his lines in the Gospels with a kind, even tone. The Story does not allow this.

Jesus was angry when he turned over the tables in the Temple, tussled with the Pharisees, and took the disciples to task for repeatedly missing his point. He clearly exhibits anger here.

Jesus rebukes his disciples James and John for wanting to call down fire on the Samaritan village that has rejected them. Why?

Well, even chapter 9 presents plenty of reasons. At the beginning of the chapter he instructs his disciples on how to deal with rejection. They are to shake the dust from their feet and move on, not call in an air strike.

A few verses later, Jesus stands a little child beside him and notes that whoever receives the child receives him and the one who sent him (God). He does this because the disciples pointlessly argue over who is his greatest disciple.

So, of course Jesus is angry. He sets his face toward Jerusalem and the cross and his community remains off-track.

What can we learn from Jesus' anger? From our own? What is the basis of our anger? In what ways does our anger reflect sin? righteousness? How does it deepen our love for God and others? How has God's love in Christ called us forward by using challenge, confrontation, and even anger?

Holy One, may I learn from Christ not only through happiness but through anger as well. Amen.

The Disciple's Journey

JUNE 27–JULY 3, 2016 • CHANEQUA WALKER-BARNES

Scripture Overview: The passage in 2 Kings 5:1-14 portrays the arrogance of the leprous Naaman and the faithfulness of Naaman's anonymous servants. Because of the trust expressed by these unnamed menials and because of the power vested in Yahweh's prophet, Elisha, Naaman's body is renewed. Psalm 30 expresses God's help in suffering. The epistle lection reminds us that the gospel's radical invasion of human life is linked to nothing less than a cosmic change, initiated by God. The authority of the Luke passage lies in its larger declarations: Jesus' call for prayer on the part of those who undertake his mission. The Lord who sends out the laborers is also the Lord who is in charge of the harvest. The mission is tough, but its absolute importance motivates those who are sent. Their joy flows not from their success but from their identification with Jesus and his people.

Questions and Thoughts for Reflection

- Read 2 Kings 5:1-14. Where in your life have you recognized God's quiet blessings? How have these allowed you to experience prayer in new ways?

- Read Psalm 30. The psalmist praises God even in times of God's seeming absence. How do you continue to praise and glorify God in difficult moments?

- Read Galatians 6:1-16. Paul reminds us that accountability is an important aspect of Christian community. How do you avoid growing weary of working and seeing no change?

- Read Luke 10:1-11, 16-20. What do you need to let go of in your life to lean into the arms of Christ? How will this allow you to move beyond your comfort zones?

Assistant Professor of Pastoral Care and Counseling, McAfee School of Theology, Mercer University, Atlanta, Georgia

Naaman is a great man, a powerful and wealthy military commander. But he has leprosy. While his disease does not disable him, it must be distressing nonetheless. The slave girl, by contrast, is a nobody, so unimportant that she remains unnamed. She is a young prisoner of war, an Israelite who has been kidnapped and enslaved by the Arameans. And she serves in Naaman's household.

For all the power of Naaman and the kings of Aram and Israel, they remain ignorant of a simple fact that this young woman knows: A great healer resides in Israel. The king of Israel seemingly knows nothing of Elisha's presence. When Naaman comes to him, the king tears his clothes in anguish, terrified that his being asked to do the impossible signals a pretext for Aramean attack.

Naaman could easily have dismissed the girl's report. She is young, a slave, and a foreigner. Even more, her people are the enemy of Naaman's people. Even if she knew what she was talking about, she would have no reason to use her knowledge to benefit Naaman. Fortunately for Naaman, the enslaved girl not only knew about God's work in the world—she willingly shared that knowledge with her captor. And Naaman listened.

Many of us would be less receptive. The church does a poor job of listening to young people. We limit their participation in worship and sequester them in spaces where they cannot be heard. This passage invites us to approach matters differently— to assume that young people know God in ways the church needs to hear about, to begin doing ministry *with* young people instead of ministry *to* them.

Jesus, help us welcome the young ones among us, to hear the messages that you send through them, and to cultivate them as leaders of the church. Amen.

There's an old joke about a faithful disciple who is drowning in a flood. As the water rises, he prays, "God, I believe in you and I know that you're going to save me!" Several vessels come and offer help: first a rowboat, then a yacht, and finally a rescue helicopter. He rejects each of them, saying, "God is going to save me!" After he drowns, he faces God in heaven and asks, "God, why didn't you save me?" God responds, "I sent you a rowboat, a yacht, and a helicopter! What else did you expect?"

In today's passage, Naaman is the man of faith who almost misses out on his blessing because it doesn't come in the way he expects. He has finally tracked down the great prophet that he first heard of from his slave girl. He seemingly expects a grand gesture from the prophet that will reveal God's power in a mighty way. He cannot hide his disappointment when Elisha tells him to go take a bath. "Are you kidding me? I came all this way and brought all this treasure for this?"

When have we prayed for a sign or miracle from God, only to experience disappointment or unsureness when it arrived? Perhaps we asked God to give us a sign to affirm a decision or to deliver us from a financial or health burden. We wanted to receive some flashy token so we could brag to others. And all we received was an inner sense of peace over our decision, a referral to a good physician, or an overdue payment that finally came. Our passage today reminds us that those quiet blessings are just as much God's work as the flashy works of power.

Lord, attune our ears and eyes to the quiet ways that you work in our lives everyday, and instill within us an ever-present spirit of thankfulness. Amen.

After her death in 1997, one of Mother Teresa's spiritual directors revealed letters in which she described a decades-long "dark night of the soul," a period during which she felt that God had abandoned her. She even spoke of envying the poor people to whom she ministered because they seemed to possess a passion for God and a surety of God's presence that she desired.

The psalmist in today's passage is well-acquainted with the anguish that comes from God's absence. The psalmist has recovered from a serious illness, one that almost cost his life. Before his illness, he felt confident of God's presence. But at the height of his suffering, he too felt that God had abandoned him.

It is hard when we suffer from a serious illness or hardship. When we no longer feel God's presence with us in our suffering, our distress can turn to despair. The pain of God's silence is especially agonizing if it follows an experience of divine communion, a period when we have heard God's voice or felt God's presence in a palpable way. We can easily begin to doubt our faith. Are we deluding ourselves about the strength of our faith? Have we sinned and lost God's favor? Will we ever feel close to God again?

The psalm offers no answer to these questions. But it does assure us that our doubts are a normal part of the journey of faith and provide a model of faithful discipleship in the midst of doubt. Even when God is silent, the psalmist refuses to be. He continues to praise God for the grace and favor that he knows God will manifest in his life. And so should we.

Gracious God, we thank you for being the one who not only welcomes our cries but who hears and responds to them. Bolster our faith in the midst of our suffering and doubt, so that we may continue to magnify your name. Amen.

Many young people in America view the modern church as judgmental, insensitive, and hypocritical. The popular perception of Christians is a finger-wagging crowd that believes discipleship involves following rules and castigating people for breaking them. Our text today tells us that this perception is nothing new. The beliefs of missionaries who upheld circumcision and Torah law as necessary for full covenant membership in the body of Christ are fracturing the churches in Galatia. Paul writes this letter to refute the claims of that group. He tells them and us that salvation comes not through our actions but through the redemptive work of Jesus Christ on the cross.

Many people take the message of freedom in Paul's epistle to justify a laissez-faire attitude about sin and discipline. They believe that it is never the church's role to pass judgment and that Christians may do whatever they want as long as their behavior does not harm anyone else. Our choices, they argue, are between God and ourselves because, after all, only God knows our heart.

Paul refutes that idea too. Christians, he says, are supposed to hold each other accountable, not with an attitude of judgment and insensitivity but with a spirit of gentleness. We cannot simply look the other way. Nor do we confront another with the in-your-face style so popular today. Rather, we assume a posture of mutual admonition and responsibility. We approach one another in a way that fulfills the law of Christ who lived among us so he could better understand our burdens and show us what real love looks like.

Merciful God, may we love our sisters and brothers in Christ to the extent that we are willing to restore them to you when they fall. And grant us the wisdom and compassion to do so in a spirit of gentleness. Amen.

Have you ever noticed that every superhero movie or TV show includes a moment when the villain nearly defeats the hero? It usually turns out that the villain has been playing the long game. While the hero has been going about his or her usual routine, the villain has been planning, acquiring resources, and mustering support. The villain has anticipated every move, including possible failure and has backup plans, escape plans, and even comeback plans. The villain's in it for the long haul.

When it comes to being the light of Christ in the world, Christians must also learn to play the long game. We cannot weary of doing what is right. But that's hard. We may weary of giving to the poor when we see the same faces begging for handouts everyday. We have difficulty forgiving the friend who makes the same mistakes over and over.

It is hard not to grow weary of working to eliminate injustice when our efforts seem to produce hostility with no meaningful change. It is even hard not to grow weary of gathering in community each week to worship God when we have so many other obligations pulling on our time. We weary of doing what is right when it grows uncomfortable, when it does not result in immediate reward, when it goes against the grain of society, or when it requires sacrifice.

In this letter to the members of the church in Galatia who may have realized that Jesus' return might not occur in their lifetime, Paul reminds us that we cannot grow weary. We must learn to play the long game because the enemies of God certainly are.

Come, Lord Jesus. Fill us with your loving power so that we do not grow weary of working to establish your kingdom here on earth, as it is in heaven. Amen.

The seventy disciples must have felt terrified. Without warning, it seems, Jesus sends them into the world to minister. In some ways, it is what they have desired. Surely some of them have been thinking, *I want to be like Jesus. I want to do the things that he is doing.* But it is one thing to have those thoughts and another thing entirely to act on them. Now the time to act has come. They can no longer sit in the background, watching Jesus teach and do works of power. It's their turn to step up. As if that were not enough pressure, Jesus adds a catch: Carry nothing.

We would have a hard time following Jesus' direction today. In our daily lives, our focus on schedules, plans, and material possessions leaves little space to hear how God wants to use us that day. Or for mission trips, we send out reconnaissance teams to study the mission field and figure out its needs. Then we plan for months, accumulating supplies that will meet any need that the mission team might have or encounter. While necessary for many mission endeavors, imagine the possibility of engaging the mission field and following Jesus' direction: Carry nothing.

Carry nothing. These words invite us into the moment, to lean into the arms of Jesus who supplies our needs. Carry nothing. It reminds us that our power does not come from possessions or planning but from our faith and trust in the Son of God who holds all power in his hand.

Lord of love and light, free us from the entrapments of material possessions and dependence on our own efforts that keep us from leaning into your abundant grace and power. Help us to love and trust you fully and to carry that love into the world. Amen.

Our readings this week have taken us through the disciple's journey, a journey that begins with conversion, proceeds through deepening discipleship, and culminates in ministry to the world. We began with the story of a powerful military commander who, at the prompting of an unnamed slave girl, embarked on a journey in a search of a prophet whom he did not know, laden with treasure to pay for his healing. The passage in Luke inverts the narrative. This time, it is the followers of Jesus who are unnamed. They are the ones being sent on a journey, but they carry nothing of material value. And rather than going out in search of Jesus, they are being sent *by* Jesus to proclaim the gospel and to heal the sick. Whether welcome or unwelcome they speak of the nearness of the kingdom. Their words come to the hearers as salvation or judgment.

Just as Naaman had little reason to believe the word of the slave girl, as readers we have little reason to expect much from this group. But against all odds, they are successful. They return victorious, testifying to God's power. Their obedience prompts Jesus to pronounce this apocalyptic vision in which he affirms their authority over the power of the enemy. And he announces the biggest reason for celebration: Their names are inscribed in heaven.

Jesus invites us to embark on the disciple's journey: to take the next step and move beyond our comfort zones. He affirms the critical nature and importance of our work. It's tough work, but our faith can overthrow the powers of the enemy—even the demons will submit. Then we too will rejoice that our name is written in heaven.

Thank you, Father, for inviting us to be part of your family. Bless us with the power of faith that allows us to overthrow the enemy. May all that we do be for your glory and for the welfare of your people. Amen.

A Fruitfulness Measure

JULY 4–10, 2016 • JUAN HUERTAS

Scripture Overview: Amos appears to have lost all hope that the people would realize the serious nature of their sin and renounce it. Because Amos has now come to terms with this melancholy reality, he also understands that God's judgment must inevitably come. Psalm 82 proclaims the supreme rule of the God of Israel: those who forfeit loyalty to the true God will only have their lives dominated by false and destructive gods of their own creation. Colossians emphasizes the crucial place within the Christian life of the qualities of faith, love, and hope. In an ironic twist, the parable of the good Samaritan makes an outsider the one who is "good." We then can place ourselves in the ditch as the victim at the mercy of the very outsider who has been rejected.

Questions and Thoughts for Reflection

- Read Psalm 82. In what ways are you guilty of ignoring the plight of those who need God most?
- Read Amos 7:7-17. Who are the prophets in your path? To whom are you paying attention?
- Read Colossians 1:1-8. How can you bear witness to God's love today? Tell someone about their impact on your life and God's kingdom.
- Read Luke 10:25-37. Where are the front porches in your life that allow you to get to know others?

Pastor, Grace United Methodist Church, Shreveport, Louisiana, spiritual director and retreat leader

At times we have trouble discerning a course of action. We get caught up in our daily living and focus on what is best for us. At other times we purposely ignore the needs around us. After all, paying attention might force us to take action: take a stand or make a sacrifice.

Other times we purposely turn our face because we no longer feel compassion or because we cannot be agents of God's love in the world. At these times, we are so far from living justly that we are now—through commission or omission—part of the problem, an agent of the forces of wickedness as the psalmist so aptly tells us.

The psalmist notes that God calls this reality to our attention. Even within the divine council, God calls to accountability those under God's lordship. It turns out that God reminds us of the expected fruits: justice, compassion, salvation, and deliverance.

What would happen if we stepped back and asked if our way of life favored those who oppress the poor and needy? What if we stepped back to take stock of our life and to assess the ways we live up to God's calling on our lives? In what ways do we live up to the standards and measures that God has set for us?

This week we have an opportunity to pay attention. Let us look around and keep God's standard before us. Our simple consciousness will afford multiple opportunities to be agents of God's love, bearing fruit in the way that we attend to the least, the last, and the lost.

God of justice, you open our eyes to care for those whom we choose to forget. By the power of your Holy Spirit shine a light on our path that we become agents of your loving-kindness, bearing the fruit of justice and peace in the world. Amen.

My spouse and I look around at a house filled with boxes. It has been a busy time, and soon we recognize that to settle into a rhythm in this new place we need not only to begin unpacking but to make a home. One way to make a new place seem like home comes in decorating the walls. Soon pictures, shelves, and other items lean against the wall, waiting for my wife to begin the process of hanging.

Before my wife begins making holes in the wall, she uses a laser level to make sure that all our pictures hang straight. As soon as the laser hit the wall, we discover that our wall is not plumb. We can hang the pictures straight, but they will never look straight on the wall.

Without a measure how do we know that our lives are just? How do we know that, although our lives *look* just, truthfully our souls are a bit crooked, not having been transformed?

Before Amos can report on the state of the nation of Israel, he needs a standard. The standard comes to him in a vision. Visions seem hyperbolic or the stuff of sci-fi. We tend not to view our world in this way. Yet here the plumb line becomes the way that God measures the justice and faithfulness of the people. It provides an image to pave the way for Israel to return to a fruitful way of life.

In our lives it is good to know the standard, the plumb line, by which God measures us, our actions and thoughts of justice. Accountability to our growth in God's love is not easy, but God's call to fruitfulness on behalf of the kingdom demands that we live into God's care for those who need it most. Let us not ignore the vision that, like a laser level, restores us to righteousness.

God, open us to visions that help us see our future in you. May we respond to the ways those visions help us redirect our lives toward justice, peace, and love. Amen.

Recently my five-year-old son came home with a note from the teacher. Apparently he had consistently disobeyed the rules, and he had received a red mark related to his behavior for the day. I knew this rule-breaking required some action on my part. I believed that a conversation would provide an opportunity for better results the next day. My son's response to my questions about his poor behavior was immediate: "I don't know what you are talking about." He proceeded to explain that the teacher was probably in the wrong.

Amos comes to relay word that both he and God condemn the people's behavior. Speaking for God, Amos states, "I will rise against the house of Jeroboam with the sword." The king, Jeroboam, and his priest Amaziah respond defensively to God's chastisement. Self-centeredness and aversion to accountability keep them from accepting God's call to wholeness. When called on the carpet, Amaziah, like a five-year-old, attempts to discredit the prophet and asks him to leave. That request seals the future: Sin puts an end to Jeroboam's fruitful reign.

Often we have the opportunity to change our hearts and lives. Friends, loved ones, and sometimes even strangers remind us of God's standard, of our own commitments. But we must pay attention and be willing to hear and obey. Like the people of Israel, we need to acknowledge that our rule-breaking days are over. The consequence for lack of obedience for Israel and for us is dire: exile.

I pray that you pay attention to the voices that cry out around you. Do not dismiss them; pay attention and look around! Opportunities for just and righteous living abound; the prophet's voice is calling you back. Listen!

God of new life, help us see the ways that we have not lived up to our call. May we be willing to redirect our lives as we pay attention to the unlikely prophets around us. Amen.

There seems to be an abundance of fruitfulness talk in the church today, although many feel uncomfortable with it. It seems too businesslike (we can easily substitute fruitfulness for profits) and not faithful enough. Yet, comfortable or uncomfortable, stories of fruitfulness and its importance in our lives with God fill the scriptures. So what creates the difference between our call to fruitfulness and our success-obsessed culture? The author of Colossians helps us differentiate between an obsession with success and the call to fruitfulness.

The author begins with a strong commendation of the local congregation. He commends their faith in Christ and their love of one another and then makes the link to the growth and expansion of the gospel.

Our encounter with the good news of Jesus Christ provides the starting point to our call to be fruitful. We see this fruitfulness in the community of believers, in the way they relate to one another, in the way they engage the community around them, and in the way others speak of them.

A call to fruitfulness in the kingdom is made known through our witness. Imagine us becoming a people who call our faith communities to put into practice the spiritual disciplines of justice, reconciliation, forgiveness, and love. Then those disciplines attract the attention of a world that lacks loving ways. Our reputation becomes the standard by which people measure God's identity.

Fruitfulness seems impossible, but we have the Spirit of God given to us through our encounter with the gospel of Jesus. We have all we need to witness to God's love in the world.

In the midst of a success-obsessed culture, loving God, help us commit to true fruitfulness by our witness in everyday life. May we be both doers and proclaimers of the importance of fruitfulness in our world today. Amen.

In my church office I have a large whiteboard where I record calendar items, scripture passages, facility needs, and anything else that requires my attention. Often I tell those who enter my office and ask me about the board that it gives a hint of what our congregation is currently doing or dreaming about.

When things are going well, the board can serve as a source of celebration: We realize accomplishments, dreams becoming realities, errands finished. But the board can also become a source of frustration, a record of things that are *not* accomplished, ongoing initiatives, and seemingly endless ministry.

The whiteboard of the Colossians seems to be filled with edge-to-edge success. The gospel has been bearing fruit among them since they first heard it. In these verses the author moves into a time of intercession for the congregation. He desires that they be filled with the knowledge of God's will, spiritual wisdom, understanding, and strength. They share in the inheritance of the saints and have been rescued from the power of darkness.

Sometimes in our spiritual lives we feel alone. We see no end in sight to the whiteboard demands. Are we heading the right way? Are these the matters to which God calls us?

Today's scripture reminds us that even when we do not know it, people lift us up. People pray, intercede, and celebrate. Sometimes those who receive ministry walk away praising God. At other times our witness inspires those on the sideline; in short, people know and notice even when we don't realize it.

We, with the Colossians, acknowledge our transfer "into the kingdom of [God's] beloved Son" where we receive redemption and forgiveness of sins.

Dear God, when we feel discouraged, help us remember that we are held in prayer. Move us to pray for others, for their witness, for their ministry, and for their inspiration. Thank you for those who let us know and pray for us. Amen.

A recent study notes that those in American culture work more than ever, taking no vacations. Many workers do not even receive paid sick leave. We work very hard, trying to achieve, to succeed, and to bear fruit that, in the end, will spoil.

Often we approach our lives with God in similar ways. We work at it, going down the spiritual checklist, hoping that the work paves the way for our salvation. Yet no matter how hard we try, the question remains: Am I doing enough?

Like today's "legal expert" we want to check in and see where we stand. We want an evaluation of our progress; we want to make sure we are in line for the reward. Like every faithful and learned person of his day, the legal expert knows what the law requires in order to live into the promise of eternity: love God and love neighbor.

Jesus' call is ours: Go and do it! Immediately our minds race to Sunday school classes, Bible studies, and small-group accountability meetings. Why do we still feel like we are not doing enough, like there has to be a more complex answer? Is this all that you require, Jesus?

Let us take time today to consider what we understand to be our call of discipleship. Loving God and neighbor must move from being a checklist item, a sign of our constant temptation to earn our salvation. Instead we remember that this love is the fruit of our encounter with God's love for us. Now we have an opportunity to introduce others to this gift of grace.

God, we hunger to know where we stand. May we resist the temptation to earn our salvation. Instead, may we by your Spirit share the love we have been given. Amen.

One of the great memories of my childhood is sitting on the front porch of my grandparents' house. My grandmother's stories of her life and encounters with her neighbors amazed me. The front porch provided a space for neighbors to get to know one another. They would walk by, greet each other, and share stories. Sometimes they would speak to one another from one porch to the other: Someone was sick; sugar was needed; a double shift at work kept someone out late. Neighbors were part of your life, part of your family.

In yesterday's meditation we found ourselves making sure that we fulfilled the requirements to enter into God's kingdom. We came questioning, and Jesus reminded us that we knew the requirements; we just had to go do it!

Now we desire reassurance and wonder who our neighbor is. Obviously the legal expert and many of us need a porch!

Jesus challenges us to a standard higher than mere intellectual assent. He asks us to look beyond our prejudices and stereotypes and to act as loving, compassionate, and just people in the world. Belief as intellectual assent does not replace our continued action that leads to transformation.

As an adult I have realized that my grandmother did not necessarily like all her neighbors. Personalities clashed, gossip spread, and feelings got hurt. In the end, though, her neighbors were part and parcel of her identity; the porch provided a place to practice the way of love daily. Heavenly fruit indeed! May we do likewise.

Living God, help us open our hearts to those who live alongside us. May we build porches of transformation as we love the stranger as we love ourselves. Amen.

The Better Part

JULY 11–17, 2016 • NATALYA CHERRY

Scripture Overview: In the Amos passage, the vision of judgment is followed by a statement of God's impending justice. Psalm 52 is addressed to some anonymous tyrant who, out of love for evil, has worked against God. But God will not allow such tyranny to go unchecked and will ultimately vindicate those who have lived faithful lives. The Colossians hymn heightens the connection between the cosmic Christ and the church, his earthly body. The familiar complaint of Martha directed against her sister, Mary, constitutes the Gospel passage. When placed in its larger context, the passage is balanced by the parable of the good Samaritan, which suggests that listening without doing is an empty exercise. The story of Martha and Mary maintains that doing without listening is equally futile.

Questions and Thoughts for Reflection

- Read Amos 8:1-12. When have you simply gone through the motions of a relationship with God?
- Read Psalm 52. What enemies do you face, and in what or whom do you place your trust?
- Read Colossians 1:15-28. How do you respond to the concepts of mystery and revelation?
- Read Luke 10:38-42. Do you identify more with Mary or Martha in this passage? How difficult is it for you to choose the better part?

Full-time student pursuing a PhD in Systematic Theology, Southern Methodist University, Dallas, Texas; ordained United Methodist minister

The better part." What is it? Mary chooses stillness while Martha chooses busyness. Mary chooses to listen to Jesus' words while Martha chooses to tell him what she requires to provide proper hospitality. Preachers who think Martha gets a bad rap usually emphasize the latter interpretation.

During my ordination process to become a minister in The United Methodist Church, the bishop (the person who oversees clergy within a region) included a letter to candidates' physicians for our mandatory physical examinations that declared that pastoral ministry demands at least sixty highly stressful hours per week. Thus I am acutely aware of the hypocrisy of clergy as we use this passage to call church members to stillness. Yet here we are: I'm choosing to pause from demanding doctoral studies and family care, as are you from the busy demands on your time, in order to be still and to linger together at the feet of Jesus as we listen to this passage.

Why? What is "the better part" that Mary has chosen, and what are the consequences for Martha of not having chosen it? The Bible readings for this week offer us several insights if we who practice these daily *disciplines* (a word that we could easily mistake for Martha's busy work) remain still enough to pay attention.

The same bishop who had considered sixty highly stressful hours per week an acceptable description of ministry was scheduled to meet with area clergy for a spiritual retreat. Upon arrival, we discovered that stress-related health issues precipitated the bishop's absence. Thankfully, the bishop recovered and now balances activity and stillness, even while serving in retirement.

Reflect on how high a priority it is for you to seek, find, and choose "the better part."

Why does the first leg of our journey in search of "the better part" take us back to the earliest minor prophet of Israel? Most people today recognize Amos's words because of Martin Luther King Jr.'s oft-repeated call to "Let justice roll down like waters, and righteousness like an ever-flowing stream" (Amos 5:24). We've heard Jesus and Martin Luther King; what can Amos still say to us?

After offering numerous unheeded admonitions throughout the first seven chapters to "seek good and not evil, that you may live" (5:14) and having described prophetic visions through which God has urged the people to turn from their ways, Amos now seems to envision a picnic, perfect for a July day in the United States! But why does the association of "summer fruit" with the "end" sound like bad news? The New International Version translates these two Hebrew words in a way that helps us recognize the wordplay. The Lord shows Amos a basket of ripe fruit, then tells him that "the time is ripe for my people." God is fed up—not with summer fruit but with the empty worship eked out impatiently by God's people as they long to get back to business and calculate the greatest possible gain at the expense of those who have the least.

Amos's words expose our hypocrisy. How easily we forget that King's prophetic cause at the time of his death was the Poor People's Campaign, seeking not mere handouts but the end of systemic poverty. How often do we eke out our worship "hour" and rush back to earning and spending? Even our innocent efforts at bargains on purchases often exploit the poor and unwittingly feed corporate greed. Perhaps God's command to "be silent!" will offer us time for contemplative reflection.

God of justice, I confess that my bargaining ends cannot justify unholy means. Do not pass me by, but give me a hunger for justice that transforms my appetite. Amen.

In this passage—which itself seems like the worse part, not the better—the people finally get what they want. God promises that they who have impatiently waited for worship and sabbath observance to be over will see it ended altogether so that they may return to their busy lives. Actually, what they want does not turn out to be a change for the better. God may seem angry and vengeful in this passage, when in reality God plans to grant the wish of the impatient in Israel. The result of worship that merely goes through the motions while minds remain fixed elsewhere is that the light of the faithful goes out, and darkness prevails.

To the people who have focused solely on crops and currency God promises a famine worse than the kind that destroys the crops. It is not a depletion of water or grain that is coming, but a total lack "of hearing the words of the LORD," which turns out to have been "the better part" all along. Too busy to have appreciated this better part, God's people will not know where to turn when they soon find themselves in circumstances unfamiliar to them.

It is hard to imagine what the threat of trembling earth, mourning, and darkness actually denoted for the first hearers of these words in Israel. But it is not hard for us who read these words now to look at the most recent natural disaster, act of terrorism, or systemic violence in our midst and recall the feeling of desperation and helplessness that it engenders. Sadly, we can also remember our own instances of going through the motions in worship, of relief that the preacher didn't "get too wordy" and interfere with our plans for the rest of the day. What if, rather than too wordy, there were no words at all?

Speak your words, Lord. Amen.

Now we know that the better part involves hearing the words of the Lord. Even before Amos identified that component of the better part, David relied on its reality and revealed another key component: being rooted in God. Perhaps David composed this psalm as he "inquired of the LORD" multiple times about his course of action as King Saul, green with envy, pursued him. (See 1 Samuel 20–23.)

The green to which David refers in this psalm is far brighter than the shade of envy and belongs to a more hopeful plant than the "summer fruits" of Amos, which will signify the "end" for many of David's descendants. David flees for his life through the wilderness. "But," he declares, "I am like a green olive tree in the house of God." Even as he stays on the move, he remains rooted in God's love. If a tree planted in a house seems odd, it helps to remember that the tabernacle had a dirt floor.

I am currently studying a unique feature of the grammar of Christian belief that understands belief as movement "into" God. Much as we may imagine an olive tree needing to be uprooted and replanted in order to be "in the house of God," David and any of us seeking the better part must be willing to be uprooted from wherever we have placed our trust and sink our roots deep into soil that accesses the living waters of God's steadfast love. Where I live in drought-stricken Texas, trees' roots are visible through brown lawns; they break underground pipes in search of water. David vows to put down roots among God's people in worship, where he will stretch his limbs to point to God's name.

Steadily flow your streams of mercy, O God. Help us root in your rich soil and believe into you. Amen.

As I prepare these words for our journey in search of the better part, the images visible on screens and newspaper pages report interracial violence in the Midwestern United States and terrifying persecution of Christians and other perceived infidels by a new militant group in the Middle East. One result is hateful comments on social media from people who do not understand their power or privilege, touching off rifts among friends, family, and strangers as we seek to make sense of these incomprehensible realities.

The image of the invisible God, on the other hand, calls us to reconciliation. This passage amounts to a wondrous hymn and clear teaching on the matter. Its message carries above the cacophony of false teaching that suggested that Christ, by virtue of his coming in lowly flesh, was less than sufficient for salvation. On the contrary, the apostle declares, it is by means of his fleshly body that the One who is before and above all created things has transformed minds and deeds from lowliness to holiness, rooted and grounded in faith and hope.

Both fleshly bodies and minds and deeds lie at the center of the swirling media storm surrounding me now, and I am reminded of the audience Amos addressed. Cameras zoom in on looting in the Midwest, and screens display statistics about possible international intervention, dividing family and friends over issues, detracting attention from systemic mistreatment of individuals based on skin color or creed.

The heart of the matter is that it pleased God to reconcile all things and everyone by the peace of Christ. Any moment wasted busily blaming or bickering detracts from the power of Christ and the purpose of peace.

Reconciling God, as images of bad news swirl around us, make more visible your image in us. Through our faithful, hopeful words, slow down the busy to see and know your reconciling love. Amen.

Now we come to the final component of the better part: the mystery revealed. What is the mystery? The words of the Lord have come and gone, but now the Word of God has come and has revealed what neither David nor Amos knew. The Word became flesh in Christ, and now we fleshly creatures entrust ourselves into his hands. That those who are in Christ have Christ in us seems mysterious indeed—what does it all mean? The apostle's words about riches and hope of glory are better than we can imagine and certainly welcome! But wait . . . there's more: "warning everyone" seems far less exciting, and being "mature" doesn't sound much better.

Yet back at the beginning of the apostle's description of his mission and this mystery, he rejoices! "I am now rejoicing in my sufferings." Suffering? How can the better part involve suffering? Christ suffered, and if we are in Christ and Christ is in us, all that is in Christ is in us, including the willingness to suffer with and for those who suffer. The apostle is willing to suffer for the persecuted body's sake.

Today many within the body of Christ find themselves in a position to choose whether they will suffer with those in need in order for them to gain the hope of glory. Recently, children seeking a better part of life than the deadly danger they have endured in Central America poured across the US border into Texas and other border states at unprecedented rates. Tempers flared on both sides of the immigration debate. While little has been revealed about the mystery of how to end the suffering of children worldwide, the sacrificial choices local church members make to help these children encourage hope. Only through such efforts can we expect to "present everyone mature in Christ."

Christ in us, reveal to us how to rejoice in suffering with those who suffer. Amen.

We end our journey where it began, in Bethany with Mary's choice of the better part and Martha's choice of the busy part. Now we know what Mary has chosen: the words of the Lord, a rootedness in God, and reception of the revealed mystery of Christ in us.

Do we also now know the consequences for Martha of not having chosen the better part? We sense that more urgent than her guests' hunger is the end of the famine of hearing the words of the Lord that takes place in her presence. We see her bustling around with the tiring work of hospitality rather than planting herself at the feet of the One who already has and gives living water. We hear the absurdity of her question, "Do you not care?" The mystery that troubles her has been revealed already—God's care for the universe evidenced in the sending of the only begotten Son for eternal life.

John's Gospel offers evidence suggesting that Martha eventually chooses the better part, at least as robustly as Mary does in Luke. When John 11 describes Jesus' arrival at Bethany after Mary and Martha's brother Lazarus has died, Martha greets Jesus first, shows faith in his ability to do the impossible, and declares, "Lord, I believe that you are the Messiah, the Son of God, the one coming into the world" (11:27). Believing into God, as the phrase translates literally from both Greek and Latin, she steps into the place at Jesus' feet that Mary occupied alone in Luke's Gospel. Together with them at his feet, we remember what he said then in their house as we look forward to the Resurrection, the consummation of "the better part that can never be taken away from" any of us.

Lord, rooted in you we acknowledge your care. We choose the better part and believe into you! Amen.

Intimacy with God

JULY 18–24, 2016 • STEVEN LOTTERING

Scripture Overview: The Hosea passage implies that the relationship between God and Israel is similar to a marriage that has been ruined by an unfaithful spouse. Yahweh has been scorned, and judgment is at hand. However, the prophet implants a reminder that Yahweh's final word is not destruction but redemption. Psalm 85 reveals a community of God's people who are suspended between the "already" and the "not yet." Colossians reminds the readers that no other force or personality may compete with Christ, for Christ and only Christ embodies "the whole fullness of deity." Faith and action are one. Luke's Gospel directs the disciples' attention to their real needs, as well as reminding them of the only one who can fulfill those needs.

Questions and Thoughts for Reflection

- Read Hosea 1:2-10. Do you truly believe that nothing is beyond God's redemptive love? How does that affect the way you live?
- Read Psalm 85. How do you respond to God's forgiving, redemptive love? When have you experienced the healing and wholeness of that love?
- Read Colossians 2:6-19. How is your life rooted and established in Christ? What fills your life?
- Read Luke 11:1-13. How much do you trust God to provide for all you really need?

Ordained minister in the Methodist Church of Southern Africa, currently serving in Cape Town

God calls Hosea to provide a lived-out parable of God's rela-tionship with the people of Israel. Hosea's life dramatically illustrates an intimate relationship that is broken. The people of Israel have abandoned their relationship with God, but God doesn't give up—God desires to draw them back into the place of intimate relationship again.

The people of Israel are not only estranged from God—they are divided among themselves. Hosea's place in history comes at the time of the divided kingdom of Israel (1:1). Hosea's actions become a prophetic call to restored relationship, and they demon-strate God's unrelenting love and forgiveness. Hosea marries a prostitute, and the names of their three children offer clues about God's relationship with Israel. Jezreel recalls a bloody massacre from the past, but the next two names describe a horrifying and current reality: Not Pitied and Not My People. God's patience is coming to an end. Israel's unfaithfulness to the covenant relation-ship with God surfaces as the Israelites flirt with Baal worship.

It appears that the consequences of such infidelity will cause a permanent rift between God and Israel, but in verse 10 we catch a glimmer of the promise that God will not abandon them completely. Though Israel is unfaithful, God remains faithful; "In the place where it was said to them, 'You are not my people,' it shall be said to them, 'Children of the living God.'"

God invites us into an intimate relationship within God's family. We may choose to turn from that intimate embrace, to embrace all sorts of things that at first seem to offer untold plea-sures. God's invitation does not expire, and our positive response draws us once again into the life-giving, loving embrace that leads to healing and wholeness.

Gracious and loving God, we hear your call to return to you, and we thank you for reminding us that only in your embrace do we find true life. Amen.

Broken relationships affect all those around us, but God holds out the divine possibility of healing that brokenness. Relationships can be mended, intimacy restored. "The number of the people of Israel shall be like the sand of the sea, which can be neither measured nor numbered; and in the place where it was said to them, 'You are not my people,' it shall be said to them, 'Children of the living God.'"

The parable Jesus tells years later of the son who leaves his father's house and squanders his inheritance echoes Hosea's lived-out parable. Upon the young man's return, he does not count on the intimacy he knew as son. But his father welcomes him back into the family with an intimate embrace. (See Luke 15:11-32.)

In Jesus' parable the elder brother resents the sinner's welcome and embrace. We too may believe that some people lie beyond God's intimate embrace that offers healing and wholeness. We may believe, like the elder brother, that the sinner does not deserve mercy and grace. But through Hosea's life, through Jesus' love, God shows us that nothing lies outside the scope of God's redemptive love.

Like the prodigal son, we may feel unworthy of restoration to that place of intimacy. But God is calling us, like God called the people of Israel through Hosea, to return to that place of intimacy. God never gives up on us but will embrace us each time we fail and will work with us to rebuild what was broken.

Sin has consequences, some far-reaching, but not as far-reaching as God's redemptive love. We cannot escape the consequences of our actions; but when we open ourselves to God's redemptive love, the result may surprise us.

Thank you, merciful God, for your unfailing, redemptive love that heals and restores. Amen.

God has forgiven, and God will forgive again. The psalmist recalls God's past pardon and asks God to "restore us again," to "show us your steadfast love." God forgives but forgiveness requires a response of acceptance. When accepted, the gift of forgiveness leads to reconciliation, to peace.

In his book *No Future without Forgiveness*, Desmond Tutu offers the illustration of a person who sits in a dark, stuffy room with windows closed and curtains drawn. Outside the sun shines, and a fresh breeze blows. To allow the light to flood in and the air to flow, the person has to open the curtains and the window. Forgiveness leads to reconciliation when the person to whom it is offered responds to the confession and accepts the forgiveness.

God's love and forgiveness, like light and air, are available, but we have to say yes to experience it. God speaks peace to those who turn their hearts to God. Where God's steadfast love and our faithful obedience to that love meet, "righteousness and peace will kiss each other."

Sin separates; intimacy is broken, but it can be restored. As we respond to God's steadfast love by acknowledging our role in the brokenness (confession) and accepting God's healing and transforming love, we find healing and wholeness, salvation and shalom.

We experience God's restoration. But then by virtue of our human nature, we fail in our faithfulness to God and cry out with the psalmist, "Restore us again!" Our healing, wholeness, salvation, and shalom comes from right relationship with God.

Thank you, Lord, that "while we still were sinners Christ died for us" (Rom. 5:8). Your forgiveness invites our repentance and restoration to healing and wholeness, salvation and shalom. Amen.

The whole body receives nourishment and grows through a life lived in intimate relationship with Christ. Three images within today's passage illustrate our union with Christ. The first is of a tree with its roots deep in the soil: "rooted . . . in him." The tree draws its nourishment through the roots, which also anchor the tree—the deeper the roots the stronger the tree. Christ is the source of our nourishment and our strength.

The second image brings to mind the foundation upon which we build a house: "built up in him." The house is only as strong as its foundation, just as a tree is only as strong as its root system. Our lives are only as strong as the foundation on which we build them.

The third is of the head: "holding fast to the head." The head serves as the center of control. Christ is the head and under his supreme authority we flourish and grow. In Christ, "the whole fullness of deity dwells bodily."

It's not about what we do or don't do, about making and keeping rules. What matters in our living is our rootedness in Christ and our bearing in mind that Christ is both our foundation and our head. Christ frees us to live the fullness of life God intends for us—free from the power of sin, free from bondage to rules, free from debt to God, free from the power of "rulers and authorities" other than Christ, "the head of every ruler and authority." Free from condemnation, free to live and grow in relationship with Christ. Free to combine our faith with our action. Intimacy with Christ sets us free! That very thought fills us with thanksgiving.

Gracious and loving God, thank you for the fullness of life in union with Christ. Amen.

There's a story told of a lecturer who brings a see-through bucket to class one day. He proceeds to fill it with large rocks and then asks the students if they think the bucket is full. Most of the students think it is. He then proceeds to add smaller stones that fill in the gaps among the big rocks. He asks the class members if the bucket is now full. Fewer answer positively this time. The lecturer then pours in fine sand that closes the gaps between the rocks and stones. He then asks if the bucket is full. The students feel reluctant to answer. The lecturer then pours water into the bucket filling any remaining gaps and asks, "Is it full now?" The students all believe it to be full—they can't imagine how he can fit anything more in—but few are willing to say so. The lecturer then asks what lesson they can learn from this exercise. One student yells out, "You can always fit more stuff in!" "No," the lecturer responds. "The lesson is this: What you put in first determines what you can add later."

What fills your life? What "more" are you trying to add?

Today's reading indicates that many who wanted to fill their lives with anything other than Christ heavily influenced the church at Colossae. The writer emphasizes that "In [Christ] the whole fullness of deity dwells bodily, and you have come to fullness in him."

Christ is filled with God, and we are filled with Christ. As long as we remain rooted and established in Christ, all we need will fill us. Christ is the one who should fill our lives first—in Christ our lives are fulfilled.

Lord, help us to put you first in our lives. Amen.

Many of us have repeated the prayer Jesus taught so often that we have lost the sense of intimacy that the words convey. Familiarity breeds contempt, and we can easily allow familiarity to overshadow intimacy.

Jesus begins by teaching his disciples to address God the way he does: as Father. So the prayer opens with relationship. We are, first and foremost, members of God's family, and our relationship with God entails a relationship with all God's children and all creation. It sets the tone for everything else.

God, our divine parent, invites us into an intimate relationship through Christ, but this intimacy is not the familiarity of being a best buddy. Jesus teaches us to say, "Hallowed be your name." When we say, "Hallowed be your name," we acknowledge that we can't limit God. We can't put God in a box. We are not defining or seeking to control God. We let God be God. True intimacy doesn't seek control. True intimacy changes us, and so we pray, "Your kingdom come"—not as a future event but here and now. When we participate in God's reign, we become more like God; God's life begins to shape our lives and our world.

The prayer goes on to list requests: "give us," "forgive us," "do not bring us." Jesus defines the disciples' needs and directs them to the one who can fulfill those needs. All the requests emphasize the notion that we are not simply in a one-on-one relationship with God—we are in relationship with all of God's family. Life with God leads us to life with others.

Pray the Lord's Prayer slowly, focusing on each thought. Rather than simply speaking the prayer to God, consider what God is saying to you through this prayer.

Prayer brings us into a close relationship with God. Our relationship with God is closer even than that of a friend whom we awaken at midnight for a favor. The friend may respond because we nag, because we test the friendship; God responds simply because we ask. God answers because God loves us more than any parent could love a child.

Most parents provide for their children's basic needs as best they can. Jesus reminds us that if we, who are imperfect, give good gifts to our children, how much more will God, the Divine Parent, give the Holy Spirit to those who ask?

Jesus tells us to ask, search, knock. He encourages our seeking, our *spiritual desire* for more. Notice that Jesus does not mention God's giving us whatever our hearts desire. Jesus says, "Ask, and it will be given you." God gives God's self in intimate relationship to all who ask.

The disciples come upon Jesus in prayer and then ask that he teach them how to pray. Jesus offers the model prayer and then a parable of the unfriendly neighbor. The great value of prayer resides in the generosity of the loving and listening Father who both hears and responds to our petitions.

When our lives are rooted and established in Christ and we live in union with him, that intimate relationship transforms our lives. We trust that God is near and will provide for us. God's Spirit empowers us to do all and be all that we are meant to be.

For those who knock, the door will be opened.

Thank you, Lord, that you enter into an intimate relationship with us and that you transform us with your love. Amen.

Transforming Mercies

JULY 25–31, 2016 • SUE ENGLE

Scripture Overview: The Hosea passage portrays the agony of God, who is torn between the demands of judgment and of grace. When justice and grace are weighed in God's balances, grace always prevails. Psalm 107's language applies to many experiences of alienation. Lostness, hunger, thirst, and weariness characterize the condition of those cut off from God; yet if they seem abandoned, they are not. God has guided them out of the desert and back to their homes once again. The freedom to live in goodness is the subject of Colossians. The passage points readers beyond "things that are on earth" to "things that are above." Freedom from greed is the focus of Luke 12:13-21, a text that addresses the difficult issue of how the Christian is to deny the temptations of materialism while living in a very material world. The farmer is not condemned because he worked to produce a bumper crop, but his demise is viewed as tragic because he wrongly believed that his bulging barns would be his salvation.

Questions and Thoughts for Reflection

- Read Hosea 11:1-11. God's constant love, mercy, and grace allow for transformation. What would it be like if our systems employed a justice designed to transform?

- Read Psalm 107:1-9, 43. From what captivity has God redeemed you?

- Read Colossians 3:1-11. What do you need to take away from your life in order to clothe yourself with the practices that reflect the image of God?

- Read Luke 12:13-21. How can you feel more satisfied with what you have? How will this allow you to share more with others?

Resource Director, Paducah District, Memphis Conference of The United Methodist Church

Many a parent has been driven to such a moment of recitation by a rebellious child. "I was there when you took your first step, threw your first ball, and played at your first recital! I have told you time and time again how important it is to avoid these problems. I have rescued you from harm, and I have been there whenever you called. Why will you not do as you have been taught?"

How comforting to encounter through Hosea a parent just like us. One who has dealt with rebellion, has grieved over loss, has endured the hard times when deeply loved children choose to turn away and reject the love that brought them life. No matter how bleak the circumstances, God is with us. God understands our hearts and our hurts; God will give us grace to endure.

God too has grieved over God's stiff-necked children. If ever a parenting plan, a book, a program existed that would produce obedient, faithful kids, surely God would have used it. That we, who have been rebellious and faithless over and over again, are still loved and acceptable to God is a mercy that encourages us to be merciful. After all, if we depend on God's mercy to belong to the family, why would we withhold mercy from those who belong to ours?

The sting of disappointment and rejection are made easier by the comfort of God who knows the pain. We have a safe place to share our hurts. God understands them and is already redeeming them. Our glorious God knows us and our actions. God loves us unconditionally!

God, thank you for forgiveness and unconditional love, new every morning. Help me to forgive and love unconditionally in response. May your mercy to me become my mercy to others. Amen.

Our vision of God as judge, dispenser of punishment, often conflicts with our view of God as Father, dispensing grace with mercy new every morning. We often create God in our own image, shaped by our experiences, to be either a divine Santa Claus waiting to fulfill all of our wishes or a stern grandfather who is unforgiving and unkind.

Our God is just, expecting obedience and faithfulness, and is also the Abba Father who exemplifies mercy and loves us even when we are at our worst. God disciplines and calls the children of God to obedience and to follow even when the following is unpleasant, painful, or against our nature. God also pours out transforming mercies daily to make such obedience possible. In the wholeness of God, discipline comes less as punishment and more as a calling us home. Even in exile, God's plan includes a homecoming.

Transformative justice centers in a purpose far beyond punishment, separation, or rejection. It is centered in the wholeness that leads to true freedom, the freedom to follow without fear. Perfect love drives out fear, not because there is never discipline but because the discipline never drives out love. God's love, experienced in mercy and grace, is never conditional or situational. That constant allows transformation to take place.

What could the world be like if our systems employed a justice designed to transform? What would our churches be like if individuals experienced unconditional love and a discipline designed to help them move on to perfection? What would our families be like if we understood justice and mercy as partners in wholeness?

Heavenly Father, help me to see justice and mercy as partners that move me to holiness of heart and life. Amen.

My husband served in the navy for many years. After a deployment, the families would gather at the pier to welcome the ship and the sailors home. If the sailor for whom you waited was unavailable, you would go to a holding area to wait for release to visit the ship. My husband worked as an engineer and was often long delayed in coming to claim his family from holding. How long that time seemed to drag as I waited to be reunited and "redeemed" from holding. By the time my husband arrived I was extremely glad to see him and to be free!

The redeemed know what captivity feels like. They understand the waiting, hoping, praying for someone to come and free them. They have lived the overwhelming joy of having a deep hunger or thirst satisfied. Their depth of gratitude and thanksgiving has transformed them. People reside in captivity to all kinds of things: drugs, prison, abuse, cultural limitations, poverty, prejudice, traditions, and more. Freedom from such bondage—true redemption—is life changing.

These verses open and close with praise for God's steadfast love that redeems. As Christians we have been redeemed through our Lord and Savior Jesus Christ. We sometimes forget that we too have been held captive in some way and have forgotten the joy we felt in our redemption. We begin to view freedom as a right not a gift. Perhaps that becomes a form of bondage in itself: forgetting that we have been blessed with freedom from bondage and are a means of grace for others. That mission relieves us of the burden of judgment and condemnation of others.

God, redeem us from those things that hold us captive. Help us to find freedom in your reign. In our freedom, may we never forget how blessed we are. We have much to celebrate; help us to be gracious and joyful always. Amen.

In the hymn "Come, Thou Fount of Every Blessing," the author mentions raising an Ebenezer. In First Samuel, Samuel uses a stone he calls Ebenezer to commemorate the Israelites' victory over the Philistines (7:12). Today we no longer raise Ebenezers to mark those places where we have encountered God's faithful love, but perhaps we should. In our busy lives, days fly past without notice, and we seldom stop long enough to recognize and remember God's activity at work in and through us to others. We may feel important and productive, but does our lack of reflection indicate wisdom?

The psalmist reminds us that wise people carefully consider the Lord's faithful love. God brought us life, gave us gifts and talents, helps us produce and provide. The Holy Spirit is at work in us, but we often fail to notice or to give thanks. Many prayers are answered without appreciation or attention. The busyness that claims our attention keeps us from living lives of gratitude and hinders our faith from growing as we see God at work.

Paying attention to God and the love that God pours out on us and through us to the community we serve keeps us focused. Like Peter walking on the water, the storm and the waves seem pretty frightening when we stop looking at Jesus. As a church we easily forget our calling and spend time instead trying to keep people happy and satisfied: an impossible task. Remembering who God is and how God calls us to serve is more than wise; it is faithful. God's love enables us to become children of God. We are worth a few Ebenezers that remind us of who we are and whose we are. Where would you raise an Ebenezer to celebrate God's work in your life?

Almighty God, give us the vision to see you at work in us and to give thanks. Amen.

Paul, a person of action, tells us to put to death sinful actions, to set aside harmful behavior, to take off the old nature, and to put on these spiritual practices that identify us as people raised with Christ. Only the power of the Holy Spirit makes these actions possible, and Paul invites us to participate actively in the transformation. God's love reaches us wherever we are, but it moves us on to become more like Jesus.

Gender, race, class, and culture become inconsequential to those who are in Christ. John Wesley talked about God's love shared with us through grace and expressed in a variety of ways. Prevenient grace is the love that acts before our awareness of God. Convicting and justifying grace is that which helps us see that apart from God we are lost and hopeless. Sanctifying and perfecting grace create the opportunity to move from divisions, prejudices, and behaviors that cause harm toward unity, love, and holiness of heart and life.

While our lives are "hidden with Christ in God" and what we shall be has not yet been revealed, Paul challenges us to become a different kind of community in particular ways. He invites us to "put to death" external negative behaviors that others may witness. And he goes a step further to note that even our emotions (that are not seen) be set aside. We strip off the old self and its practices and clothe ourselves with the new self. That "spiritual clothing" helps us live together in love with Christ at the center. That love is how the world knows that we follow Jesus. What practices do we need to strip away in order to clothe ourselves with those virtues and practices that reflect the image of our Creator?

Eternal God, create in me the desire to be transformed in Christ. Help me to surrender my will to yours and to follow you faithfully into the world. Amen.

Entering into someone else's argument seldom leads to a good end. No matter how reasonable the side presented might be, it is never the whole story. We fail to see the "other side" as adding any validity to the big picture. In this case, a man wants Jesus to force his brother to share the family inheritance. Sharing seems like a good principle; but without the details, it is hard to discern whether the brother who won't share is in the right or in the wrong. Jesus wisely sidesteps that invitation, asking why anyone would think he held the deciding vote.

Jesus then moves on to address the issue of greed. We have no idea who is guilty of this particular sin, the brother who won't share or the brother who demands a share. Jesus makes it clear that the sin of greed is not in possessing things but in being possessed by them. Both brothers may be guilty of this sin. Perhaps the one with the inheritance had little, while the one who did not receive the inheritance had much. Regardless of who was in the "right," the sin of greed is Jesus' concern. He warns the brothers to "Take care! Be on your guard."

Greed never seems as obvious to us as it does to others. We have good reasons for our desires and wants. The culture around us encourages us to gather as much as we can.

Creating moments of reflection that allow us to consider whether we truly need the "next thing" may save us from being possessed by our stuff. Praying before we head out to shop may change how we view our needs. Our possessions neither define us nor secure our future.

Dear God, may I desire you more than anything I can possess. Make me a generous giver rather than a greedy consumer. Fill me with a hunger for things that are eternal. Amen.

Acertain man who has a bumper crop decides to build bigger barns to hold it all. In 1973, the average house in the United States was 1600 square feet. By 2010, it had increased 1000 square feet to 2610. At the same time, the family size decreased about one person; from 3.42 to 2.65. So we own bigger houses to hold more stuff!

Jesus poses this question: Who is going to get all that stuff when we die? It may be that we no longer think about who gets our stuff; we may believe that for now we need it. Most of our possessions are disposable; we don't anticipate having them all of our lives anyway. Computers, phones, furniture—everything is temporary. How do those of us with a mind-set of disposability and dispensability respond to God's question? Do we, like the farmer with the bumper crop, equate possessions with security? How do we secure our future?

If we have more than we need, might we share it with others? Generosity grows our faith. Blessing others when we have been blessed extends the transforming mercies from us to others. Building bigger barns, bigger houses for temporary goods seems to limit the love, even within ourselves. May we affirm the belief that life is God's gift.

Why does God choose to limit God's self in meeting needs through partnership with us? Free will presents a serious risk in that we often choose poorly. Transforming mercies give us the opportunity to make better choices each day. Today may be the day that we decide we have enough, and we will share with others who do not.

O God, may I choose to be satisfied with what I have and share with those in need. May I give with joy! Amen.

God Is Great

AUGUST 1–7, 2016 • L. JOSEPH ROSAS III

Scripture Overview: The lesson from Isaiah and the psalm call the people of God to "Hear!" The message has to do with sacrifices and burnt offerings: God does not want them! The sacrificial system had come to be understood as a means of attempting to manipulate God for self-centered purposes, and the texts therefore call for worship that is God-centered. The Gospel lesson also calls the people of God to decision. Our use of financial resources is inextricably linked to our conviction that the future and our destiny lie ultimately with God. What we believe about the future affects how we live in the present. This affirmation is precisely the message of Hebrews. The entrusting of one's life and future to God is "the reality of things hoped for, the proof of things not seen." For those who trust in God's reign, "God is not ashamed to be called their God."

Questions and Thoughts for Reflection

- Read Isaiah 1:1, 10-20. In what ways can you let go of a self-centered focus in worship?
- Read Psalm 50:1-8, 22-23. What are your antidotes to worry? How do they allow you to deal with anxieties in your life?
- Read Hebrews 11:1-3, 8-16. What allows you to focus on the awe and wonder of being held in God's grace?
- Read Luke 12:32-40. Where do you see God at work in your life? How is this awareness a part of having your "lamp lit"?

Associate chaplain, Baptist Hospital, Memphis, Tennessee

The apostle Paul frequently begins his letters with reminders of God's grace and mercy (Galatians being the exception). No matter how severe his word of warning or rebuke, he fosters a continual awareness of God's love and forgiveness.

The words of today's reading challenge Judah through harsh words of rebuke and condemnation, language frequently reserved for those not part of God's covenant people. God sees the forms of religious observance everywhere, yet the people fail to know and acknowledge God. Isaiah describes them as "a sinful nation, people laden with iniquity" (Isa. 1:4).

Verse 10 likens the people of Judah to Sodom and Gomorrah—biblical shorthand for bad, really bad, bad to the bone! Numerous Bible references list sexual immorality as among the sins associated with Sodom and Gomorrah. But the context here and in Ezekiel 16:49 indicates that the sins are deeper and broader than sexual immorality: "This was the guilt of your sister Sodom: she and her daughters had pride, excess of food, and prosperous ease, but did not aid the poor and needy."

Religious observance, proper décor, and liturgical form are poor substitutes for moral clarity that includes compassion for the poor, the powerless, and the least. Does this sound familiar?

In a consumer-driven economy we tend to think that worship is about us, appealing to our tastes and meeting our needs. However, worship divorced from the demand for justice for all God's children rings empty and hollow. Are we doomed?

Isaiah (like Paul) provides a hint of hope in verse 1. Isaiah's name means "Yahweh will save." In other words, even with the bleakest of judgments, there is a reminder of God's grace and mercy. God intends to deliver!

God of justice, hope, and mercy, grant us a glimpse of divine love that compels our loving and faithful response to all those we encounter who are in need. Amen.

Enough! A popular worship video a few years ago titled *Me Church* carried the tagline "where it's all about you." The video promises would-be attenders that the church service won't start until they arrive, they won't have to give but they can know what others do, a car wash and wax—even an oil change, Super Bowl tickets, and a pony (in the backyard).

But are these really worshipers? Are we? If our only motivation is what we get out of the service, then maybe not! Jesus said that God seeks those who worship God "in spirit and in truth" (John 4:23). Worshiping "in spirit" includes the realization that God is spiritual. Therefore we must be attuned to God's will and work in the world. As Christians, worshiping "in truth" surely includes the idea of our lives conforming to the character and teachings of God revealed in the person and work of Jesus.

God complains about Judah's worship practices, expressing no delight in sacrifice, offerings, incense, or solemn assemblies. Yet the levitical code prescribes these religious practices. How can God be so critical when the people attempt to follow God's will? They indeed follow a form revealed by God, and they worship according to a semblance of truth. But they are not in sync with God's spirit or God's truth. They have forgotten that the fruit of authentic worship is faithful living. Worship calls them and us to repentance, ceasing evil to learn good, to seek justice, rescue the oppressed, and defend the widow. In other words, the measure of worship does not hinge on acquired information but on transformation by God.

In worship, we are not the audience. God is! Instead of focusing on where we want God to bless us today, may we be vehicles of God's blessing to others.

God, forgive our self-centered focus. May we remember to worship you in accordance with the Holy Spirit who expresses your truth this day. Amen.

In these verses, the psalmist steps aside and God comes to testify against the people. As in Isaiah's time, worship has become a time to glorify self. The people misunderstand sacrifice; they are not walking the talk. Worshiping God rightly requires more than a perfunctory expression. It involves genuine engagement of the whole person. God has less interest in what we have to offer that is external to ourselves (sacrifices, gifts, the forms of observance). God seeks *us*.

The people have forgotten God, so God as judge tells them to "mark this." God calls for a renewal of commitment and states that the offering that pleases God comes through the sacrifice of thanksgiving. When we praise God we declare our awe at who God is in God's being, wisdom, power, and holiness. Through thanksgiving we acknowledge God's specific acts of blessing and benefit visited upon us as God's children.

In Philippians 4:6-7, Paul prescribes an antidote for worry and anxiety. He tells us to bring our prayers and specific requests before God. He also encourages us to mix this with thanksgiving. Why? Because taking time to be thankful lessens the load of our burden. Our anxieties don't seem as large when compared to the manifold grace of God experienced in our life. And the refrain in Paul's exhortation in Philippians 4:7 is that the peace of God will guard our hearts and minds through Christ Jesus.

As a pastor I have observed families going through the most difficult circumstances imaginable with a calm dignity and quiet certainty that can only be explained as God's peace that passes understanding. Invariably, this peace grows out of a sense of gratitude for the sustaining power of God—the salvation of God.

God, may we count and name our many blessings received at your hands. Amen.

How does God communicate with you? I have had a few "mountaintop" experiences on retreat or after a time of intense prayer, meditation, and holy conversation. But most of us encounter God in our daily routine. We would have the good sense to pay attention to a burning bush. But to hear God's voice in the daily round of life presents a greater challenge. The problem arises not with a lack of God's speaking but with our inability to listen.

The author of Hebrews looks to the past to affirm the faith of the ancestors and then encourages that same faith in the present generation. Abraham listens to God, and God continues speaking despite Abraham's doubt. He obeys God's call and believes God's promises. The particulars that surround his dramatic encounters with God occur amidst the mundane and ordinary daily grind.

How often and in how many different ways does God come to us through our circumstances, the wise counsel of others, impressions of the still small voice of the Spirit within our hearts? If we feel too harried and hurried to stop and listen, we miss the encounter.

Abraham hears God in the midst of the ordinary and believes. This simple yet bold response of faith and belief in the promise of God regardless of the circumstances is what God credits as righteous standing in Abraham's behalf.

The writer of Hebrews points to the singular focus of Abraham's faith when observing that he "obeyed," "stayed," and "received" both the promise and the power of God. At the end of his life he still looked forward to the ultimate fulfillment of God's promise.

Dear God, in the daily routine of life may I hear and do your will. Amen.

We are called to believe in God, and Abraham is the quint-essential exemplar of such faith. He believed God's promises related to an as-yet-undisclosed land, an unborn heir, and an unfulfilled promise of blessing.

The writer of Hebrews refers to faith as both "assurance" and "conviction." Assurance is foundational. As the Benedictine monk Anselm said, "I believe in order that I may understand."

We would prefer it the other way around. We want to understand clearly in order that we might believe. Thomas refused to believe until he received evidence. Jesus did not rebuke him, but he did commend the faith of future generations who would believe without seeing.

Faith provides support like the foundation of a building. We may not see it, but the foundation determines the safety and durability of the edifice. We are not alone in bearing witness to this unseen but substantial foundation. A great cloud of witnesses has gone before.

Faith is also like an established conviction. An engagement ring serves as a token of a promise. The promise: At some point in the future the couple will come together in holy matrimony. But neither the beauty of the stone nor the quality of the ring determines the integrity of the promise. No, it is the character of the one making the promise that is decisive.

We, as children of God, can have "conviction of things not seen" because we know the character and integrity of the One in whom we have believed. God keeps God's promises. We have the record of other witnesses, and daily we experience the sense of awe and wonder at being alive, held in the unseen reality of God's providence, perseverance, and grace.

O God, may I see with eyes of faith the foundation of the faithful and the certainty of unseen presence in my life today. Amen.

Messages of fear fill our world: fear of violence, disease, financial ruin, or simply being out of fashion. Often the message of the faith community gets lost in our fear of a contrary culture, an angry God, or a disappointing self.

How refreshingly different are Jesus' words: "Do not be afraid"—a simple yet profound declaration of God's never-failing love. Do we sometimes feel overwhelmed by a culture increasingly indifferent to our faith? Yes, but Jesus identifies with the "little flock." God does not panic at the signs of institutional decline, the growing numbers of those called the "nones" (not identifying with any organized religion) and "dones" (alumni of the church who aren't going back). Nor should we.

We do not remain oblivious to the concerns, fears, and doubts of those around us. Rather, we take seriously the promise given by Jesus: "It is your Father's good pleasure to give you the kingdom." We do not create this kingdom nor are we to preserve our feeble efforts at kingdom building. Jesus and the Father (by the Holy Spirit) bring about the kingdom—the righteous rule of God. We look to see where God is at work building the kingdom and join in the process.

Naturally we fear, which is why Jesus reassures us. We don't feel guilty over our fears; we acknowledge the reality that God has already anticipated them. We therefore have no need to live under their power. Jesus reminds us that God is at work. God intends and is able to bring about God's kingdom. God will do it in God's time and way. In the meantime we are "the little flock" under God's protection.

Father, the One who builds the kingdom, show me where you are at work in my world and give me the willingness to join you in the task. Amen.

Jesus instructs his disciples to "sell your possessions and give alms" and goes on to observe that "where your treasure is, there your heart will be also." Speculation abounds as to what the end of the age might look like and what kind of return we might expect from our Savior.

Jesus shifts the focus when talking to the disciples. They allow the times and seasons to distract them, asking when Jesus will restore the kingdom. Jesus insists that we live in the moment in readiness.

"Be dressed for action" does not constitute a fashion statement; Jesus speaks of our spiritual preparation for the kingdom of God. Paul says we are to "clothe [ourselves] with compassion, kindness, humility, meekness, and patience" (Col. 3:12)—not speculate about the Omega point of history. We don't need more prophetic information. We need spiritual transformation into the image of Christ so that we can live on behalf of others.

Jesus also encourages us to "have [our] lamps lit." Light enables us and others to see; the lamp is not an end in itself. "Your word is a lamp to my feet and a light to my path" (Ps. 119:105). A lamp for the feet directs us to the next step and illumining the path gives us enough light to continue the journey.

We dress for action and have our lamps lit not so we can escape the situation around us but so others can see. Jesus said, "Let your light shine before others, so that they may see your good works and give glory to your Father in heaven" (Matt. 5:16).

Christian clergyman, writer, and radio evangelist, Theodore Epp stated, "We should live as if Christ died yesterday, rose today and is coming tomorrow." In other words, be ready!

Father, may we be so clothed in your grace and reflective of your light that others will see Jesus in us. Amen.

Shocked into Change

AUGUST 8–14, 2016 • MANDY HACKLAND

Scripture Overview: Isaiah 5:1-7 and Psalm 80:8-19 employ similar images to represent the people of God—a vine or a vineyard. The image clearly communicates the careful commitment of God to God's people. Unfortunately, the people do not respond in kind, so God must destroy the vineyard. The people plead for restoration, and their future life will depend not on their repentance but on God's repentance! Jesus issues a radical call for human repentance in Luke. God will bear the burden of human disobedience, and God's gracious turning to humankind makes life possible. Hebrews shows that the story of God's people does contain outstanding episodes and exemplars of faith and suggests that God never gives up on calling us to follow, to run the difficult race that leads to life.

Questions and Thoughts for Reflection

* Read Isaiah 5:1-7. What fruit are you growing—wild grapes or sweet ones? How can God redeem you?
* Read Psalm 80:1-2, 8-19. How do you recognize God's love and presence?
* Read Hebrews 11:29–12:2. Think of a cirumstance when your faith in God was all you could rely on.
* Read Luke 12:49-56. Where do you recognize the urgency of the kingdom of God? How does this awareness affect your daily actions?

Longtime Christ-follower, church small-group coordinator, author, Johannesburg, South Africa

Walk with me through the vineyard. We stroll between the vines in the early morning sunlight. The vintager has worked hard, caring for this land that he loves, doing all he can to encourage a good harvest. Do you feel a sense of satisfaction, peace, and contentment as all seems well with the world?

Come closer and look for the grapes. Cup a small cluster in your hands. In the midst of this tranquil scene you make a disturbing discovery: rather than tasty edible fruit, the foliage masks wild grapes. The wild fruit will not ripen and produce a sweet crop.

God, the vintager, chose fertile land cleared of stones to plant the choice vines of the people of Israel. With such care, God expects a high yield of grapes for good wine—not a failed vineyard. Like the grapes, the Israelites seem to be doing okay; externally, all looks well. But in reality they have turned their backs on God; they yield only inedible sour fruit. So God asks, "What more was there to do for my vineyard that I have not done?"

We have to ask ourselves if we differ from the Israelites. As the green leaves concealed the sorry state of the fruit, so we too conceal whatever is wrong in our personal, inner worlds. That may be a situation beyond our control—an illness or retrenchment. Or we may have turned our back on God and refused to acknowledge what we know deep inside—that we are sadly imperfect.

Do we as choice vines of God's choosing, whom God protects with a watchtower, ignore God's clarion call, God's lovesong for the vineyard? What more must God do to redeem us?

Abba, make me aware of your Spirit's movement in my life. Let nothing come between us so that I can bear fruit for you. Amen.

The vintager sings of the vineyard as a place that is dearly loved. He has done everything possible to produce a sweet crop, but the vineyard produces only wild grapes.

God speaks to the people in referring to "my" vineyard. Imagine them in the marketplace listening to Isaiah as he speaks for God. The vintager needs their help—what more could he have done? Surely now they will pay attention.

The hedge and the wall come as a surprise. Planting a hedge, plant by plant, and building a wall, stone by stone, represent a labor of love to protect the vines and the crop, but God states that the hedge will be removed and the wall torn down. These acts of love and care on behalf of the vineyard will vanish and the vineyard given over to briars and thorns.

Not only will the vintager expose the land completely, he plans to stop working it altogether. Even the clouds will not rain on it! Water, the essence of life, will be withheld. What tender life can survive in such circumstances? The vineyard will become a desert land without hope of fruitfulness.

Suddenly, the listeners realize that God's vineyard is Israel, and they are the vines. They have been cared for and protected; but they have disappointed God, producing a sour, shriveled crop instead of the plump fruit that the vintager had nurtured and expected. They find themselves outside God's tender, loving care and protection. Does this shock them? How do they react?

What is your reaction as you consider that you too are part of God's vineyard? How does God's love and protection encourage your growth?

> *Lord, forgive me for not appreciating and valuing your care and cultivation. I submit myself again to your loving care. May I be a fruitful vine. Amen.*

Luke's Gospel begins with a glorious account of Jesus' birth. The angels bring a message of peace on earth. So Jesus' question comes as a shock: "Do you think I have come to bring peace to the earth?" Yes, of course that's what we think. But Jesus goes on to state that his coming will bring division—and not just among strangers but within families, the fabric of community.

We may experience broken relationships as some choose to follow Christ and others choose to reject him. It becomes challenging as these close relationships become more difficult and even toxic. Relationships between friends can end, intentionally or gradually. Colleagues require respect. But what happens in a family? As Christ-followers we do not cut ties with family members. The Bible tells us to honor our parents, to love one another. What a challenge! How do we love when others repeatedly reject and provoke us?

Jesus experienced opposition within his family. (See Matthew 12:46-50.) Scripture does not reveal what happened when the family members met again. Jesus loved with God's love and remained unswayed by arguments or differing opinions. He continues to love his family.

Can we love with God's love those family members who oppose our faith, even though we do not agree with them? When we become a channel of God's love, we continue to touch other people's lives. We may be the only channel available to them.

Jesus never said following him would be easy, and he offers the only solution—his love! How will you let Jesus' love flow through you to difficult people you encounter?

I believe I can do all things in your name, so here I am, Lord. Help me love as you love. Amen.

With his disciples, Jesus has addressed the issues of preparation and readiness and has made it clear that there is no peace without conflict. He wishes the fire that both destroys and refines were already kindled!

Now Jesus turns to the huge crowd that surrounds him—and begins to talk about the weather! The people know that the rain comes from the Mediterranean in the west and that the hot dry weather comes on the winds from the south. They must wonder where Jesus is going with this topic!

Suddenly two words thunder across the hillside: "You hypocrites!" And Jesus turns his comments on the weather into a rebuke for the people's failure to recognize the "present time." Jesus chastises the crowd for their ability to read the signs related to weather while being unable to interpret the current times. They can predict rain and heat but cannot see signs of the coming judgment. With the kingdom at hand, the end is near.

Do those words thunder across the hillside to us as well? Are we aware of the signs of our present time? We all have areas of knowledge to which we give attention. Are we attending to some lesser areas to the neglect of a more important focus? When we stand at the crossroad of kingdom nearness and judgment, how will we discern appropriate action?

The kingdom is at hand; can we sense the urgency?

What signs of the present time do you see? What do these signs demand of you, and how will you interpret them?

The magnificent words *by faith* ring down through the ages. That was all it took. *By faith* in God the Israelites crossed the Red Sea on dry land. Who took the first step? Was it an elderly priest—wise in the ways of God? Or a young boy with the faith of a child, trusting and eager to get going? Yahweh had gotten them this far, and there was no turning back. So the first one took the first step—and then another and another. Slowly others began to follow until the multitude crossed safely—by faith.

How ridiculous the Israelites would have looked as they marched round and round Jericho blowing their trumpets. What must the townspeople have thought? And then the walls fell down—*by faith* in God.

By faith Rahab the prostitute offered hospitality to the spies from Israel. She did not perish because she sided with the God of Israel. Each instance above contrasts the faith of Israel with the unbelief of the adversaries.

And we know the names and stories of so many more faithful men and women. Through their amazing deeds, suffering, and perseverance they became the people of faith God created them to be. What made them persevere and not give up?

As those in battle and the martyrs lay dying, having fought the final battle, what were their thoughts about God at that moment? What did they think when they realized that God's promises had not been fulfilled? Had God let them down? They probably died as they had lived—by faith in God. They depended on the faithfulness of God, whose plan unfolded to reach its full glory in Christ. We can do likewise.

Lord God, strengthen and deepen my faith. I want to be the person you created me to be. Amen.

The writer of Hebrews now focuses on the men and women of the fledgling church and tells them, "You can also live faithfully!" I suspect they listened, nodding wisely, as the letter was read to them and each name was mentioned. They knew about these giants of faith—great men and women. But I suspect they sat up in astonishment when the letter writer said, "You too!"

"Lay aside every weight, . . . Run with perseverance!" Once again the words trumpet through the generations; we hear the challenge as clearly as those early Christians. We run, looking to Jesus, the embodiment of faithfulness, who leads the race.

What is your biggest hindrance to persevering in your relationship with God? Where do you need to cut the ties to things that ensnare you and hold you back? Will you be the first to step into the dry riverbed with the water impossibly piled up on either side? Will you march around your Jericho if that's what it takes?

Jesus has crossed the finish line. He endured the shame of the cross for the sake of joy. We stay focused on Jesus because he has walked the path ahead of us, and he did it willingly.

And what a reward: the salvation of humankind! By faith, even his own faith in his Father God, he accomplished it.

By faith we too can finish the race—and persevere!

Lord, may I cut myself free from things that ensnare me and persevere as I follow only you. Amen.

The psalmist refers to God as Shepherd but also acknowledges God's majesty and power on the throne. As in our reading from Isaiah, Israel is likened to a flourishing vine that God brought out of Egypt and planted in Israel. The Israelites spread out from Lebanon in the north to the mountains in the south, from the Mediterranean Sea in the west to the Euphrates in the east. They exerted great influence in the area. But now the psalmist cries out to God to save the people. God has removed divine protection, which leads to vulnerability. The people understand that God is angry, and they express concern for their safety. They want God back in their lives.

God's absence is painful. The psalmist acknowledges that there is no hope of life without God. He implores God to "turn," to "restore" the people. Despite the many instances of unfaithfulness, the psalmist pledges that the people will "not turn away" (NIV) from God.

I wondered if the people would turn back to God if God granted their request and once again blessed them with divine presence. Or would they run back to God with delight because God moved back into their lives, just as children do when they receive a gift for which they yearn? Would they worship God because of compliance or because they loved God?

The complaining is over. The psalmist acknowledges God as Lord of all. When God's face shines, the psalmist knows that all is well. And the people know that they are saved, back where they belong—in God's hands.

Father, may I worship you because you first loved me. Amen.

Faith or Fear—Our Choice

AUGUST 15–21, 2016 • JAMES E. MAGAW SR.

Scripture Overview: The Luke text portrays the healing that Jesus has just performed as a call to decision, a call to "repentance and changed lives." Hebrews proclaims to the readers that they "have come . . . to the city of the living God, the heavenly Jerusalem . . . and to Jesus, the mediator of a new covenant." For Luke, Jesus and his wonderful works signal the accessibility of God's transforming power and thus signal also the time for repentance. The accessibility of God's transforming power is evident in the lessons from Jeremiah and the psalm, although Jeremiah has no choice! And amid opposition from the wicked, the psalmist affirms what Jeremiah had been told by God—that his life from its very beginning has belonged to God.

Questions and Thoughts for Reflection

- Read Jeremiah 1:4-10. God offers light to a world covered in darkness. Where do you see God's light in your life? How can you offer this light to others?

- Read Psalm 71:1-6. When in your life have you turned to God for refuge? How did trust in God help the situation?

- Read Hebrews 12:18-29. We belong to a kingdom that cannot be shaken. How does that realization help during difficult times?

- Read Luke 13:10-17. How do the limitations we experience turn us to the power and grace of God?

Retired clergyperson, active at Gay Street United Methodist Church, Mount Vernon, Ohio

A friend of mine once said, "You can pray or you can worry, but you cannot do both at the same time." We might likewise say, "You can have faith or you can be afraid, but you cannot do both at the same time." Centuries after Jeremiah's time, First John would record, "There is no fear in love, but perfect love casts out fear" (4:18).

Jeremiah's prophetic ministry took place during the forty years before Jerusalem and Judah were attacked and conquered, when many survivors were exiled to Babylon. It was a fearful time. Judah's kings made desperate alliances trying to save the nation and refused to trust in God's protection.

God calls Jeremiah to keep Israel on God's path. Jeremiah is fearful and tries to refuse. It does not work. It never works.

Since God calls the prophet to speak God's words and not his own, Jeremiah has no choice. He has to trust the one who calls him. He speaks what has been given. Jeremiah's prophetic attempts do not save his nation and people from attack, defeat, and exile, but he keeps the light of faith burning through years of defeat and darkness.

As I write these words, the daily news coming from Afghanistan, Syria, and Ukraine could make us fear for the future. By the time you read this, the names of the countries may differ, but the stories will be much the same.

Our world is a dark place. God offers light. We whose lives have been illuminated by God's light must offer it boldly to others, never fearing the outcome.

We know who holds the future.

The whole world is in your hands, O God. Even as your words spoke all things into being, your Word will be the last word. Keep us praying through the darkness until your eternal light prevails. Amen.

Self-preservation is both a natural human instinct and a grave spiritual danger. If we never move beyond measuring every action and relationship by how much is in it for us, this behavior becomes self-aggrandizement. Multiplying our own power, wealth, and reputation becomes the purpose of our life. It becomes the prison that shuts us away from the richness of human relationships.

If we choose to remain stuck in this infantile phase of life, yet claim allegiance to some form of religious faith, it is a religion whose little god loves no one but us. An old story tells about a man who said his prayers diligently every night for his family: "God bless us four, no more. Amen." One wonders whether he could have made room for grandchildren.

Many people in Jeremiah's time believed that their God took interest only in them and their welfare. Other people, other nations were on their own. "We have our God; let them find their own." However, God calls Jeremiah to be a prophet to the nations, not to Judah only. A little god is for little, self-centered people. That is not the God who drafts Jeremiah and tells him not to be afraid. When we try to limit the love of God to people like us, then we see others as a threat to us, as less than us, and as enemies to be eliminated.

Six centuries after this great prophet's call, Jesus reaffirms Jeremiah's message, reminding us that God loves the whole world and gave the Son so no one needs to perish. The borders of God's family and reign encompass all and within the borders we find no place for fear.

God, whose love is always expanding, stretch our minds and hearts, enlarge our neighborhoods, and prepare us to live in the vastness of your love. Amen.

Note the cries for protection from the enemy in this psalm: "Deliver me . . . . rescue me . . . . save me." We might add, "Save me from allowing my trust to be shaken when others oppose me."

I have seen many laypersons, as well as ordained ministers, who give themselves to a life of Christian service with great enthusiasm, only to drop out after a few years. For a while we called that burnout. Simply put, they discovered people who seriously disagreed with them, even opposed them, sometimes within their own church! Because the reality in which they had to do ministry did not match their ideal, they gave up. Because they had to endure some failure and loss, they quit.

An authentic call from God remains valid no matter how many set themselves against us. Psalm 71 may give the impression that enemies constantly surround God's servants. That has not been my experience. In fact, I give thanks for hundreds of people who have supported and encouraged my ministry. At the same time, we all will find opposition, perhaps even from those we perceived as cooperative.

One way to deal with being attacked is first to do what the psalmist does: Turn to God and put our trust where it belongs. That keeps us from losing our bearings. Next we listen to our opponent and seek to be reconciled. After we have done our best to restore harmony, even if that effort fails, we return to the work God has called us to do. Our God is a refuge but does not want us to cower when there is work to be done. We press ahead, singing God's praise continually.

O God, take us in when we are bruised, make us strong to love those who hurt us, keep us on course to continue your work. Amen.

So many things are changing and impermanent in our world that we look for something that is certain and unchanging. Perhaps that is why we like to speak of God as eternal. Yet the ways we talk about God and the descriptions we use for God do change. Even among religious people, when we begin to define our God, the theological arguments can turn ugly.

The Jesus who was "gentle and humble in heart" (Matt. 11:29) announced the arrival of God's new realm. God had not changed, but a shift in understanding God's work in the world occurred. Hebrews 12 rejects the notion of a deity who rules by fear and intimidation and replaces that notion with a gathered community marked by celebration and acceptance. The best word I can suggest for this new reality is *homecoming*.

The rural church of my childhood and youth celebrated annual homecomings. At that time, I didn't get it. Former pastors and members who had left the community returned for the day. All the adults had a good time, but it mystified me. The potluck dinner was the highlight. You see, I had never left home. Homecomings have value only if someone has gone away, returns, and finds someone there to welcome her or him.

The letter to the Hebrews speaks of the living God, a heavenly Jerusalem, and a festal gathering. For those of us who know the church as a foretaste of heaven, any gathering of God's people is a homecoming. All are welcome, especially those who have gone away from home. All are welcoming, especially those who have experienced grace, forgiveness, and inclusion in the family. Here resides the certainty that will keep us in peace in the face of every fearful event.

God of profound mystery and perfect love, make us into one great family where no one goes unloved or is afraid. Amen.

Apocalyptic language such as this tends to divide the Christian community. It need not do so. Written in times when it was dangerous to be a follower of Christ, such symbolic language is meant to encourage us to be true to the faith and to trust in God. When the penalty for such loyalty is death, being faithful is not easy; but these writings show that it is possible.

Verse 26 speaks of God shaking "not only the earth but also the heaven." This most likely refers to Exodus 19, where Moses attempted to impress on his people the grandeur of God's covenant with them, and Mount Sinai shook violently. Haggai 2:6 expands this passage by including the shaking of the heavens.

Hebrews 12:28 makes the crucial point: "Therefore, since we are receiving a kingdom that cannot be shaken, let us give thanks." We all experience a lot of shaking. It can be caused by economic recessions, wars, natural disasters, accidents, and human cruelty. Everything we think we possess or can count on can be taken from us, including property, money, power, prestige, and the people we love.

What I have just stated is not easy to hear. In my household, when a violent television show comes on, one family member is apt to say, "This isn't a bedtime story." So we don't watch it. Yet, in real life, many things can happen and will happen that are not "bedtime stories."

We are mortals who live fragile lives. But this message from Hebrews assures us that we belong to a kingdom that cannot be shaken. By God's grace, we shall endure.

Holy One who shakes the earth, you also restore its order. In our fear, give us confidence; in our grief, strength; in our heartbreak, hope; and in the darkness that often returns, be to us the light that never goes out. Amen.

Pain not only hurts, but it colors our view of the world; it slows us down and changes the way we participate in life.

I have been troubled with occasional lower back pain for years—the kind that hurts fiercely, that darkens my disposition and will not leave for days. I have known a few people who have had to live with such pain constantly for years but found the grace to rise above it. One of them was my boss. In spite of his pain, he had a bright spirit and an irrepressible sense of humor. If someone had told either of us, "You are set free from your ailment," you can bet that we would have stood up and praised God.

I have benefited greatly from contemporary science and technology and respect the many ways they enhance our health. Yet, when mainstream medical methods fail us, and someone with less orthodox methods offers relief, most of us do not bother asking for credentials. So it is with the woman in this story in Luke. For eighteen years she has endured pain and the limitations it places on her life. Thank God, this woman meets a man so close to the source of life that he can change her life.

Healing, whether it comes from the latest scientific methods or from unconventional sources, remains a mystery. However healing comes, we rejoice in it and give thanks. When we experience pain of any kind, we turn to the Giver of Life, and in one way or another, we find healing. We do not always get the life we want, but we receive strength to love the life we get.

Source of life and love, we understand so little of the mysteries of life that we do not know how to pray sometimes. But we do trust in your grace and strength to lead us to tomorrow. Amen.

When visiting relatives, I went to the public library to do some work. I failed to notice a sign that restricted parking and pulled into a parking space provided for those with accessibility needs. The envelope left under my windshield wiper made me an offer I couldn't refuse: a hundred-dollar fine. The incident caused me considerable distress. The police did not know that I have tried hard to keep all the rules since I was a child. Had they known, I suspect it would not have changed the fine.

Rules are important. They give order to our lives and to our world. People who habitually break laws bring pain to themselves and others. To avoid chaos and live in harmony, we need to agree on rules that guide our lives.

Now comes the "however." In the story told in Luke 13, Jesus heals a woman (a good thing) on the sabbath (which violated religious laws forbidding work on the sabbath). He does not accidentally overlook a "no parking" sign. Jesus deliberately challenges those who love rules more than they love people. He follows Jeremiah in doing what God called him to do even if it means earning the enmity of some.

Jesus' critics are indignant, but he calls them hypocrites. When good needs to be done, God favors doing what will give health and life. So Jesus said, and so he did.

A wise teacher told me that we break the law in two ways. Criminals break it by falling below its requirements. People like Jesus break the law by doing more than it requires. His purpose rises above unthinking obedience to the law to fulfilling the law—and we are his followers.

Thank you, God, for parents, teachers, pastors, and friends who have helped us understand the rules of life. Help us now, as friends of Jesus, to rise above the law and do what love compels and requires us to do. Amen.

God on the Margins

AUGUST 22–28, 2016 • MIRA CONKLIN

Scripture Overview: The admonition in Hebrews 13 "to show hospitality to strangers" is vividly illustrated by Jesus' advice to guests and hosts in Luke 14. In the topsy-turvy world of divine hospitality, everybody is family. Radical hospitality makes sense only in light of the conviction that God rules the world and therefore adequate repayment for our efforts is simply our relatedness to God and our conformity to what God intends. The texts from Jeremiah and the psalm call the people of God back to commitment to God alone, rather than to the gods of the nations and their values. God is no doubt still lamenting our failure to listen but is also, no doubt, still inviting us to take our humble place at a table that promises exaltation on a scale the world cannot even imagine.

Questions and Thoughts for Reflection

- Read Jeremiah 2:4-13. To whom or where do you go to fill your cup with living water?
- Read Psalm 81:1, 10-16. What shape does God's bread and honey take in your life? Where are you being invited to open your mouth and to name the gift as sacred?
- Read Hebrews 13:1-8, 15-16. How do you offer hospitality to those closest to you?
- Read Luke 14:1, 7-14. When have you been blessed by a party of misfits? How can you extend the table?

Graduate of Garrett-Evangelical Theological Seminary; active at Salt and Light Lutheran Church; part of the Leaven Community, a nonprofit rooted in Spirit and community organizing; Portland, Oregon

From the moment the people of Israel struck a covenant with God, they began looking elsewhere for their sustenance. The prophet Jeremiah points out this reality and invites God's people to turn back to God, over and over again. Jeremiah questions the source of Israel's security and identity, and his inquiry continues to be relevant today: Why do you think power will give you peace and security? Why do you rely on your country's laws or leaders to tell you how to live or how to relate to others?

Our laws draw lines telling us who is in and who is out, who deserves care and love, who can move freely, who is redeemable, and who is beyond repair. We have lost our way and cling to the faulty map. And yet, the living water can seep from the painful lines: the borders that separate or that we risk death to cross, the wrinkles formed by years of worry or grief, the fences between our yards.

Life hands us endless loss and suffering and so we turn to productivity, screens, and substances to dull the pain. Do we trust that God provides peace and direction? All that we need is within us and between us, and yet we fear the quiet and struggle to listen. And still the water flows.

I suspect I will keep turning to the cracked cisterns, seeking fulfillment and peace in an orderly house and balanced days, in a secure savings account. But the rushing water will find me anyway. And so I keep my eyes open and take note when I'm looking in the wrong place. I take deep breaths. I knock on my neighbor's door. I bring along my cup, prepared for the cracks, and for the flowing streams.

God, help us gently release our grip on expectations and to-do lists, and open our hearts to your flowing water. Amen.

My husband and I felt a clear call to leave our church positions, come out of our Egypt of isolation, and live in a neighborhood-based community. We wanted to find the place that could become our long-term home; a place where we could sink our roots deep, investing in relationships with those on the margins, discover what the Spirit was up to among our neighbors, share meals, participate in spiritual practices, and work with our neighbors to create a vibrant community. We moved into an existing intentional community in a nearby city and began our search. What we didn't expect was that in two-and-a-half years, our call to stability and connection would lead us through six moves, one failed community attempt, and a couple of broken hearts.

At times, my husband's and my singular focus on the end product meant we failed to recognize God's faithfulness along the way and even lamented the loss of our previous lives of tidy isolation. We loved the glorious image of ourselves as successful leaders of new ministries so much that we forgot about our daily call to seek God and to value God's activity in our midst. God provided us with a "fertile land" where we could "eat its fruit and rich produce," although it took a while to recognize the bounty.

People with whom we could practice the way of being to which we felt called surrounded us, and we realized that our call was not to *start* a new community but to *create* community and to be the church. The picture of community had become our idol, and we had traded intimacy with God for it. But we give thanks to God for unending opportunities to release our idols' grip and fill our open hands with living water.

God of abundance, help us receive the great love you have for us. May we hold it in our hearts and pour it out freely for others, wherever we are in our journeys with you. Amen.

The psalms, like the music of our great spiritual songwriters, give poetry and rhythm to the history of God active in the world. The cadence of the psalm serves as the reminder of God's constant presence and activity to our ears and voices. The psalmist here also points the people of Israel to where ancestors have fallen short, and how, in spite of their persistent straying, God faithfully provides. We consider the history that has gotten us this far, lumps and all, so we can celebrate God's continued presence and ask for wisdom in the present and future. We work individually to overcome shame and guilt and to practice forgiveness, but we recall that the psalms served as a community choir event, not simply as thoughtful introspection.

Facing a shrinking institutional church, faithful disciples will not sit by and lament about how no one worships God anymore but will instead walk courageously into the neighborhood. It may surprise us to find God even where there are no steeples.

Our monastic mothers and fathers have shown us how to live in community, to follow a rule of life, to balance the inward and the outward, to give sacrificially—yet we keep seeking another way. We participate in systems of inequality and injustice. We know intellectually that financial success, achievement, or being well-liked does not lead the way to wheat and honey, but we keep plodding down that path. Another way calls to us, inviting us to take a bite of fresh-baked bread and a spoonful of honey. Sweet, nourishing, satisfying. If we open our mouths, we may be surprised to see that intentionally remembering God's story in new spaces will re-create the church.

God, help us to take what you offer, to savor it, to let it feed us and strengthen us for the journey ahead. Amen.

The story of entertaining angels points to a God who shows up in all bodies, especially in the unlikely ones. Jesus taught that when his disciples cared for the most vulnerable, they were caring for him. Likewise, this passage calls us to pay attention to the marginalized, as well as to the leaders. But what if the marginalized *are* our leaders? What if we looked to those in prison as teachers on grace? What if immigrants detained at the border or arrested in front of their children are the ones to teach us about liberation? What if those who suffer because of current laws are the ones to teach us about collective power that brings real change?

Strangers first taught me about the power of stories, organizing, and justice. While in seminary, I attended a meeting where undocumented Mexican women on strike from a tortilla factory shared the details of injustice in their workplace—low wages, no benefits, seniority structures ignored. Their raised sleeves displayed burns caused by operating machines without adequate safety equipment. I visited them later on the picket line, and we huddled around a heater in a blanket tent, sipping steaming hot chocolate. We stood outside in the snow, chanting, then praying. One woman was so moved by the Spirit that she fell on the frozen ground, flakes collecting on her back. These women were my first teachers in the immigrant rights movement. They are still my leaders.

Mutual love requires holding space for others to be fully who they are and to make effort to be fully who we are. It means acknowledging privilege and allowing Jesus to show up and lead us through the unlikeliest people. Is not this our Christian vocation?

God, give us courage to seek you out in the unlikely places and in the unlikely people, and help us open our ears to your leadership through them. Amen.

God on the Margins

Practicing hospitality—being a selfless host, providing a place of comfort and safety—is foundational to our ancestral heritage. God's word, "I will never leave you or forsake you," provides a beautiful reminder of an ongoing safekeeping by the host of creation. Hospitality begins with people with whom we spend the most time: our family members, good friends, next-door neighbors. Keeping vows to those to whom we have committed our love is an offering of hospitality in the form of safety and trust that allows new fruits to emerge: new children, shared responsibility, and tales of adventure. We not only provide the space for others' safety and comfort, but we find ourselves increasingly able to be vulnerable, entrusting our own safety and care to the ones we love.

But it doesn't end with those only in our midst. Many a disciple has understood Hebrews 13:2 as an ominous warning: "You'd better be good to whoever crosses your path"—it may just be an angel . . . or maybe even Jesus! And if you ignore Jesus or treat him badly, that would be awful. And this may well prove to be true. But if that is our motivation for being good to one another, then we will surely fall short of satisfaction because we will never know the richness of God's presence for its own sake.

The truth is, we don't have to imagine "what if that was an angel" because Jesus is already present within each of us and is especially present among the "least of these" or those pushed to the margins. The extension of hospitality is not simply sitting and waiting for whoever comes along but is an invitation to see how many angels—currently unknown by us—we can trust our lives with.

God, help us to go out seeking the angels in our world. Give us eyes to see Jesus in the face of each one we meet. Amen.

Proper channels can obstruct kingdom work. While they can provide the needed skeleton for ministry development, they can also be a spiderweb of hierarchical committees that drain the passion from those who felt the initial call to action. In churches whose identity is defined by how closely disciples follow the proper channels, those who jump right into action are scolded. Perhaps the emphasis on rule-following that keeps our national borders "secure" also leads us to keep our church buildings locked up. Unfortunately this often prevents us from forming relationships with the marginalized in our midst.

Jesus didn't disregard norms of behavior but reversed the polarity of channels that were exclusive or not in line with the character of God's kingdom. In Luke's account, proper channels determine the seating order of all banquet guests. The more important (that is, wealthy, powerful) one was, the closer to the host the guest would sit. Reversing the polarity meant that those with wealth and power weren't to assume they were the most important in the room. Jesus invites the privileged to come alongside the poorest and most powerless in the room. The reverse polarity is strengthened further when Jesus instructs the host, "Do not invite your friends or your brothers or your relatives or your rich neighbors. . . . [Instead,] invite the poor, the crippled, the lame, and the blind." Jesus turns on its head the unofficial rule of law: Be kind to those who can repay you with the same kindness. We too are invited, despite the proper channels in our contexts, to align ourselves with the marginalized and to focus time and energy on deepening relationships with them because there the heart of God beats loudest. As we rest in this heartbeat, we will know our blessedness.

God, help us stay faithful to your path. Amen.

Wwhat an interesting picture of the kingdom of God as a party of misfits! God welcomes all to the table to share in nourishment, conversation, and friendship. I envision laughter and moving stories and at times discomfort for some at the recognition of their privilege and assumption. But perhaps this party isn't a one-time deal. What if in our every interaction, we host an upside-down banquet? What if in every moment we intentionally create space for others to be who they are, especially those pushed to the margins? A place of honor includes having a voice at the decision-making table of politics, organizations, and faith communities. It also includes shaping how we live. In our daily lives will we set out place mats in our hearts and minds? Will we make time for conversation? Will we seek out those who suffer, even when it makes us uncomfortable?

Our blessing comes in glimpses of the kingdom itself through a deeper understanding of God and perhaps an experience *of* God in relationship to the other. The blessing comes in letting go, opening the heart, and creating more space for each of us to be who we are. Our acknowledgment of the divine spark in others is often accompanied by a humble recognition that we are not the most important persons in the room. This moment can be painful, but it moves us to reconciliation with God.

Each time we think of ourselves too highly or underrate ourselves, we can return to the just-rightness of God's grace and love. We then hear the invitation: "Friend, move up higher." At the resurrection table of the righteous, we will take our place.

God, we are grateful for the generous welcome you offer. Help us to value ourselves and others as you value us. We welcome your blessing. Amen.

The Decisions of Discipleship

AUGUST 29–SEPTEMBER 4, 2016 • KEN A. RAMSEY

Scripture Overview: The Gospel lesson stresses the cost of discipleship. One of the costs involves family, but the implication is that there are compensations as well as costs. Belonging to God affects the way in which one belongs to others. Traditional patterns, kinship and otherwise, are transformed. This insight lies at the heart of Paul's letter to Philemon concerning Philemon's slave, Onesimus. Without directly requesting that Philemon set Onesimus free, Paul clearly suggests that the ties that bind persons as brothers and sisters in Christ transform traditional social patterns, including slavery. Both Jeremiah 18 and Psalm 139 affirm our belongingness to God, individually and corporately.

Questions and Thoughts for Reflection

- Read Jeremiah 18:1-11. How has the "word of the Lord" come to you? What obstacles prevent you from placing yourself entirely in God's hands?

- Read Psalm 139:1-6, 13-18. How does your life evidence God's handiwork?

- Read Philemon 1-21. What person or group needs your advocacy in the name of Christ?

- Read Luke 14:25-33. How have you counted the cost of following Jesus?

Senior pastor, Bridgeport United Methodist Church, Bridgeport, West Virginia

The word of the Lord comes to Jeremiah at a crucial time in the life of his people. They live in the ever-lengthening shadow of the Babylonian empire, which looms as a serious threat. In a very short time the Babylonians will overtake, conquer, and scatter Jeremiah's people. Into this grave situation God speaks to the prophet about the impending circumstances of the people.

In life's darkest scenarios, our Lord has decided to speak. As with Jeremiah, this word will address the particulars of our life situation. The first and most important decision of discipleship is God's decision. "The word of the LORD came . . . " is in and of itself a phrase full of promise and hope. God has chosen to initiate the contact. In the midst of our lives, when chaos threatens to overwhelm and conquer us, the word of the Lord comes. In the midst of our questions, our doubts, and our fears of the future, the word of the Lord comes. It may come as a word of challenge or a word of comfort. It may come as a word of direction or a word of discipline. It may come as a word that checks us or a word that consoles us. As in this scripture, the word may contain specific instructions. So we express gratitude and give thanks because the word of the Lord came.

When I first moved away from home, my father's phone bill had to be the highest of anyone in the area. I couldn't afford to call home, so he called me almost every night. More than once I said to my dad, "I've been waiting to hear from you." His voice was the voice I needed and longed to hear.

You may be waiting to hear from God. Whatever your current life situation, you may rest assured that God has made the decision to offer the word that you need to meet your every need.

Lord, I am grateful that you speak the word I need, even when life renders me speechless. Amen.

Jeremiah responds to the Lord and goes to the potter's house. There he witnesses the work of the potter as he shapes and molds the clay. As is often the case, the clay sometimes doesn't take shape as intended, so the potter begins again. He fashions the clay and works with it until the vessel he intends emerges.

We do not always see ourselves as malleable clay. We want to control matters for ourselves, be in charge of our own destiny. We desire to manipulate and plan our agendas in a way that best suits our own needs. If, however, we see ourselves as clay, it means that we consciously decide to allow another to shape who we are. This decision, though difficult, ultimately leads to a life that is fashioned according to God's way and will. This choice also has implications for the future. Refusing God's way can lead to destructive outcomes. Turning away from evil and toward God can bring about the emergence of a new beginning. The Potter's hands hold authority over all of life. Will we decide to place ourselves in these hands?

My mother patiently pitched the baseball to me as I tried to learn to hit. I found the bat heavy and unmanageable. She would pitch. I would miss. My father, home early from work, watched this and then moved behind me. He put his hands over mine, and we held the bat together. The ball came, and with new strength and accuracy the bat moved toward the ball. I was on target for the first time. If I had known the difference my father's hands could make, I would have asked for his help much sooner.

In the hands of the Potter, our lives can take shape in ways we never thought possible. The realities of life may leave us scarred or marred, but the Potter does not give up on us. The Potter creates a new beginning and molds us into new vessels for use for a great purpose.

Gracious God, I place myself in your hands today. Make and mold my life for your use. Amen.

Jesus speaks to a large crowd whose overly enthusiastic zeal may prevent them from seeing the serious nature of what following him requires. This journey toward Jerusalem does not parade to the castle; it processes to the cross. Following Jesus is no easy path, so the word of teaching cannot be easy either.

In Jesus' time, the word *hate* did not carry today's meaning of an angry outburst. It meant simply to turn away from or to release from something. He is not instructing the people to quit loving and caring for family, but he does want them to understand clearly that following him can bring to light competing loyalties. In the face of the complexities of relationships that clamor for our attention, following Jesus must remain primary. The decision to place our relationship with Jesus above all other networks and allegiances is never easy. We will find that the primacy of that relationship with Jesus can actually help define our other life commitments.

As a teen, when my parents asked me to do something I often said, "I have some other things to do first." Needless to say, my parents did not find this an acceptable answer. They would quickly inform me that their instruction was first and foremost, and the other things would have to wait.

Jesus asks us to decide whether he can be the primary allegiance in our life. It is a timely word of challenge for a frantically paced culture. We want to have and do it all. However, genuine discipleship is not an afterthought; it is a way of life.

Lord God, give me the courage and strength to follow Jesus and place him first in my life. Amen.

Most of us were taught not to start something that we could not finish. Being able to invest the time, resources, and energy necessary to bring a project to completion is part of deciding to undertake the work. Jesus brings this example to light in talking about what it takes to be his disciple. In essence, he says, "Seriously consider whether you are up to the task." He uses stories of a builder and a king; both stories have the same thrust of meaning: before you start, make sure you can finish.

The decision to follow through entirely on our commitment is essential for the disciple. Walking the way of the Savior will require that we be "all in" and bring to completion what we have started. If we are honest, this is no easy decision. When we read Jesus' words we wonder if anyone can faithfully follow.

I had a math teacher once who gave us an extremely difficult problem. He instructed us to use all the resources available to solve it. We looked in our books. We consulted one another. No one could do it. Finally he told us that we had not used all the resources available. When we protested that we had, he said, "You did not ask me to help you." That very room contained all the help we needed.

We may feel inadequate to be disciples. However, the greatest resource for bringing to completion what we have started is Jesus himself. If we will follow wholeheartedly, he will show us the way to follow through. As we count the cost, let us never forget the One whom we can count on the most to see us through to the finish.

God, show me the way to follow through entirely on my commitment to Christ. Amen.

Being in relationship and conversation with someone who knows you well is a life-giving scenario. You do not have to hide or pretend. An air of confidence and understanding surrounds your interactions in a way that you cannot fully explain but only experience. Such is the atmosphere conveyed in this beloved psalm. The psalmist addresses God, recognizing God's knowledge of his entire being. This affirmation of faith, seasoned with praise, can overcome the darkness of guilt and failure in any life.

The decision to enter into conversation with God is another indispensable element of growing in our discipleship. The psalm invites us to encounter and experience the God of the psalmist: a God who searches the depths of who we are and accompanies us at every turn. The terrain of life may change and the topography of our journey will vary, but God is there. When we decide to cultivate this kind of relationship with the Lord, we discover more and more who God is. We will discover at a deeper level our own identity as well, finding in this intimate connection the ability to live in a genuine and authentic way.

As I returned home one day, my young son came swooping around the corner dressed as Batman. It momentarily startled me. Noting my surprise, he said, "Ah, Dad, it's not really Batman. Look underneath, and you'll see it's just me."

God looks underneath it all, and God knows the real you. God loves the real you and wants you to love the real you each day. In dialogue with God we come to this tremendous realization that sets us free to live for Christ each day.

Living and loving God, dwell within me today and reveal yourself in new ways as I journey in your presence. Amen.

When something is made well it shows. The craftsmanship and the quality are evident. We notice the attention to detail from the earliest moments of the design right up to the finished product—a wondrous work to behold. The psalmist makes this proclamation concerning the Lord. He sees and celebrates the way God has fashioned his life from the very beginning into an awesome creation. The psalmist's language points to one who can take various threads and weave them into a masterpiece of his or her own making and purpose. This heartfelt acknowledgment of God moves the psalmist from realization to exclamation!

While visiting in the home of an older couple, I commented on the layout of their beautiful home. "Who designed this for you?" I asked. "Well," the wife smiled, "we not only designed it, we built it, and now we live in it. This is our dream." From the moment they conceived the idea to the moment they moved in and occupied the space, this was their home.

To acknowledge that all we are and hope to be rests entirely in God's hands signals a decision of discipleship that can lead to humble and reverent living. To relinquish ourselves to the One who made us will transform who we are and the purpose for our lives. God designed us, built us, and desires to live within us. This holy recognition of the One who knitted us together in the beginning can lead us to a holy response in life. We begin to see our lives as God's valued handiwork. God invested the entirety of God's self in each one of us. Our very being is stamped "Handcrafted by the Almighty." Now we have the blessed privilege of living out that designation every day.

Lord, you made me. You understand me. You value me. I praise you today. Amen.

It is glorious to witness people putting into action what they believe. I find it convincing beyond measure to see someone back up words with action. This short letter provides just such a view. We see firsthand that Paul the preacher of the faith is also Paul the practitioner of the faith. Paul writes to his friend Philemon and appeals openly to him to receive the slave Onesimus back not as a slave but as a brother. To speak up and advocate on behalf of a slave and plead for a Christian response that differs from the one culture would dictate seems nothing short of revolutionary. At every level, Paul embodies the essence of the gospel of Jesus Christ as he writes this passionate letter to Philemon.

At this point, the decisions of discipleship come together. When we decide to speak and act on behalf of those who have been marginalized and maligned; those who have been systematically excluded and exited from our culture; those who are left out, left behind, and left alone, we are deciding to live out our discipleship. We become living reflections of the Christ who reflected God's love to all.

The letter to Philemon contains the pattern of this kind of radical discipleship. The decision to speak and act for those who have little or no voice involves interceding on their behalf in prayer and in practice, intervening to seek change in attitudes and actions, and intersecting all those involved with the gospel of Jesus Christ. An intersection always takes the shape of a cross. Paul lived the cross and called on Philemon to do the same. Now the call comes to us.

Lord God, move in my life so that my faith in you will make me bold to speak and act in love for all people. Amen.

The Many Faces of God

SEPTEMBER 5–11, 2016 • LINDA DOUTY MISCHKE

Scripture Overview: The apparent message of Jeremiah 4:11-12, 22-28 is total despair, but verse 27 offers a soft note of grace. God's redemptive purposes for the people will not ultimately be thwarted. Psalm 14 suggests that foolishness and perversity characterize all humanity, but God can gather from among sinful humankind a community of people who will find their refuge in God. In First Timothy, the writer points to his own life as an example of God's ability to reclaim and redeem persons. Luke 15 suggests how far God is willing to go to reclaim the lost. The parables of the lost sheep and the lost coin portray God as remarkably and even recklessly active in pursuit of wayward persons.

Questions and Thoughts for Reflection

- Read Jeremiah 4:11-12, 22-28. When have you made a mess of things and suffered the consequences? What invitation surfaced from that situation?

- Read Psalm 14. How do you feel when you are out of touch with God's call? What practices or disciplines do you employ to recognize God's faithfulness?

- Read 1 Timothy 1:12-17. What can you do today that will show mercy and compassion to another?

- Read Luke 15:1-10. When have you felt God pursuing you? How did this feel like a gracious invitation rather than condemnation?

Author, spiritual director, and retreat leader; member of St. John's United Methodist Church, Memphis, Tennessee

An armed invasion from the north constitutes a "hot wind" that will breathe down the Israelites' necks. The people of Jerusalem and Judah exist in an atmosphere of constant threat, violence, and revenge. In their honest struggle to relate to Yahweh, they understandably wonder how God fits into this dismal picture. The prophet Jeremiah has plenty to say about that.

In the poignant poetry of the prophetic tradition, Jeremiah expresses this oncoming destruction as God's judgment against the foolish, faithless people. In the language of their culture, God's justice is understood in terms of reward and punishment. The prophet says in effect, "You brought this situation on yourselves through your sinful ways." He lets the Israelites know that their lack of harmony with God's purposes will lead to painful consequences.

Not surprisingly, they experience God through the filter of their own imagination and cultural understanding. In a world where kings routinely wielded power through vengeance and retribution, they assumed that the heavenly King operated the same way. We often follow a similar line of reasoning. We make a mess of things through our own willfulness and pay the price, wondering where God was in our story.

But there's another side to the story. Through years of God's revelation, especially through Jesus, we have come to a different experience of the divine nature. Certainly God wants to put things right, to be the harbinger of justice. Rather than the "furious God in the sky" that humans often depict, we understand that God metes out justice not through overt punishment but through grace that invites us to replace judgment with love.

When have you made a mess of things and suffered the consequences? Imagine it not as God's punishment but as an invitation to move into harmony with God's purposes.

This psalm presents a gloomy view of humankind—a picture of "fools" who fail to acknowledge God's reality and presence. It describes the foolishness of a life out of step with God's purposes: perverse conduct with no accountability, a dearth of wisdom, and blatant disregard for the poor. The psalmist minces no words in cataloging the deeds of a life lived without the moral compass provided by divine guidance.

In their limited understanding of God's nature, the Israelites apparently believe that being loved by God means God will favor them over others. But the concluding verses of Psalm 14 state unequivocally that God stands with the righteous and the poor. "The LORD is their refuge."

This psalm offers a mirror to reflect the inconsistencies in our own lives. As functioning adults, we succumb to the need for self-sufficiency, control of our lives with limited regard for the welfare of others or God's will in our attitudes and actions. Truth be told, we often exist in a state of "functional atheism"—a belief that it all depends on us. Actually, our hope lies in divine faithfulness. A God-centered life implies that we love what God loves, including those on the margins of society—the poor, the needy, the downtrodden.

Of course, like the psalmist, we long for deliverance from whatever dilemma we're in. We can join in the hope that God will restore "the fortunes of his people." No matter how callous our sinfulness or how dire our circumstances, our faithful God will help us pick up the pieces of whatever is broken. Like the Israelites, we can rejoice!

How do you feel when you are out of touch with God's call to love and compassion? Know that God's faithfulness offers restoration.

The final words of Jeremiah's diatribe hold out a sliver of hope for the wayward Israelites. Verses 27 and 28 offer a surprising shift in tone as they speak of restoration in the face of desolation.

The same possibilities also exist in our lives. No matter how severe the despair in our personal and political realms, no matter how far we have strayed from divine purposes, God says, "And yet I will not make a full end." God implies that we are not ultimately finished or defeated. Our God of second chances never gives up on us! Nothing can separate us from this unmerited love.

My congregation's ministry to the addiction community, called The Way, emphasizes the spiritual aspects of AA's 12-step program. As those in recovery share their struggles with the demons of addiction, we hear amazing evidence of the second (and third and fourth) chances God offers. Folks who have experienced the depths of existence witness to divine deliverance through their allegiance to a "higher power." They find themselves strengthened and empowered by the God who compassionately utters, "And yet . . . . "

The leader of The Way reminds us that we are all in recovery; each of us receives the reclaiming grace of God. In such "and yet" moments, a soft note of grace comes regardless of how we've failed. Like the errant Israelites, we encounter hope as lament, hope as survival, and hope for restoration from a steadfast God, even in the face of judgment. Miraculously, God's hope for us feeds our hope for ourselves.

God may not always keep us safe, but God does indeed keep us. Thanks be to God!

Recall a time when you have experienced a second chance at a more abundant life, when you have heard God's "and yet." Express your gratitude for this steadfast love.

Paul joins a long list of biblical characters who engage in kingdom purposes despite their inadequacies. In this letter to Timothy, we read a portion of Paul's personal story. He tells of God's mercy flowing into his life, forgiving his wicked past and equipping him for holy service. It reminds us that every saint has a past and every sinner has a future!

And, yes, God calls even us, in spite of our weaknesses and flaws—often through them. Consider the credibility of a reformed addict who can lead another to recovery because "she has been there." When we find ourselves in difficult circumstances, we usually seek the counsel of someone who understands what we are going through. As human beings, we rarely share our troubles with those who don't seem to have any troubles!

Our human yearning for mercy takes a variety of forms. A young pastor serving a church that he described as a "wonderfully volatile congregation" recalls his frequent prayer, "Lord, you got me into this, now please get me through it!" He realized both his inadequacy and his dependence on divine mercy and grace. Many who may have a strong sense of "call" occasionally share the age-old query of Moses, who essentially protested, "Why me, Lord?"

God's mercy inspires and emboldens our own. The dictionary defines mercy as the compassionate treatment of those in distress. Like Paul, we are encouraged to show the same mercy to others that God showers on us. We set aside our feelings of unworthiness ("I'm not good enough or wise enough or talented enough") so God's grace can flow through us without restriction or excuses. The One who calls us to loving service will empower us to do it.

What specific act of mercy and compassion can you offer another today?

Paul celebrates what he experiences as Christ's remarkable patience. It isn't surprising that Paul's list of the fruit of the Spirit includes patience. (See Galatians 5:22.) As we attempt to embody the biblical call to patience, we run smack into a culture that values speed. Our microwave society is accustomed to power and productivity at our fingertips: strike a match and the fire erupts; turn a key and a two-ton automobile springs into motion; erase a thousand words by hitting "delete." We want to get the job done, respond with an instant solution, and find the answer right now. Our bodies often register impatience before we do. We tap our fingers on the table, swing a leg in rhythm, or pace the floor because quiet waiting is too uncomfortable.

Patience is often defined as "long-suffering" or "forbearance." All of us who have waited for a broken bone to heal or an illness to run its course know about forced lessons in patience. Our intellect tells us that impatience doesn't hurry the healing any more than it makes a long line at the supermarket move faster. So the ability to hang in there when the going gets tough is a virtue worth developing.

Nowhere is patience more necessary than in the arena of spiritual growth. After all, growing in grace sometimes feels like watching the grass grow. We all have experiences of falling off the spiritual rails only to be led back on track by the patience of others and of God. Surely we can be as patient with our plodding progress as God is! Then we can pass that serenity on to everyone we meet.

How does impatience show up in your life? Notice the physical and emotional clues—heavy sighs, fidgeting, harsh judgments. As you become aware of each sign, breathe in the patience of God, then breathe out your irritation.

Jesus comes under fire from the Pharisees for consorting with tax collectors and sinners and actually sharing meals with them! The dinner table, a place of acceptance and celebration, clearly brings to light Jesus' violation of society's standards, and the Pharisees feel understandably indignant.

Under the cloud of this criticism, Jesus challenges them with an example from their own culture. He asks them to imagine losing a sheep from their own flock. Wouldn't they search for the one they lost and celebrate when they found it? This image speaks to us of a God who never stops reaching out to us, who diligently looks for us until we allow ourselves to be found.

On the other side of this relationship, it's fair to say that we are born with an impulse to seek and yearn for meaning. As expressed by Saint Augustine, we remain restless until we find our rest in God. We are created to grope for the Light, to hunger for the One in whom "'we live and move and have our being'" (Acts 17:28).

The searching itself is key to spiritual growth. It upsets our inner life and casts light on what needs to change. One signpost of a faithful life is that we never stop hungering and thirsting for God. Rather than settling for a life of moral bookkeeping, we remain teachable, unfinished, and ever open to God's continuing refinement of our thoughts and actions.

Like the sinners and the tax collectors, we find ourselves welcomed and forgiven in Jesus' presence. We reach out our hand to discover a divine "hand" stretched out toward us in beckoning love.

Think of times when you have felt pursued by God. Imagine that pursuit as one of gracious invitation rather than condemnation.

All three parables in Luke 15 (the lost sheep, the lost coin, the lost son) end the same way: with a big, lavish, over-the-top party! In verses 1-10, the elation of the shepherd who finds the sheep and the woman who finds the coin is so great that they invite friends and neighbors over for a celebration! The joy of the occasion calls for lavishness and revelry. For those who seek the face of God primarily as stern judge or demanding taskmaster, this image of an exuberant host comes as a surprise.

The first two parables mention the joy of celebrating the return of the penitent sinner. Jesus' critics tied repentance to an adoption of their standards of purity and law observance. Jesus means something different. When people turn toward God and follow Jesus' way of compassion, they express true repentance.

Jesus' declaration that heaven is throwing a big, noisy party every time a single sinner sees the light challenges us to honor on earth the positive changes in our lives and the lives of others. On the smaller scale of daily existence, I believe that God (and the heavenly host) delights in every step of our growth in love and compassion. Celestial joy overflows each time we inch forward on the spiritual path, each time we reach a little deeper toward intimate relationship with the Divine, each time we include the outcast, each time we minister to the least of these, each time we become more deeply aware that God created us in love and for love, and each time we bear that love to others.

The next time we sing "Joyful, Joyful, We Adore Thee," let us remember the God who seeks us, finds us, and brings us home to celebrate.

Imagine God throwing a party out of love for you. Let your heart fill with gratitude for such lavish, holy joy.

Lessons in Respect

SEPTEMBER 12–18, 2016 • LEE ESCOBEDO

Scripture Overview: Three of the texts for this Sunday deal with intercession; although they certainly will not make praying any easier, they may make it more hopeful. The readings from both Jeremiah and the psalm depict the anguish of one who identifies with the pain of God's faithless people. Prophet and psalmist grieve with and for the people and join in the persistent and impatient plea for health and renewal. But God turns out not to be an impassive or distant deity but one bound up with the anguish of the prophet and the anguish of the people. Likewise, the psalmist discovers that the God who refuses to tolerate Israel's faithlessness nevertheless cannot finally abandon the chosen community. First Timothy also challenges readers to offer prayers of intercession and specifies that they be made for those in positions of political leadership.

Questions and Thoughts for Reflection

- Read Jeremiah 8:18–9:1. Jeremiah weeps for the self-will and disrespect of his people toward God. What do you see in the contemporary world that causes you to weep?
- Read Psalm 4. How do you, like David, acknowledge God's guidance in your life?
- Read 1 Timothy 2:1-7. Paul reminds us to pray for everyone, no matter their relation to us. How can you be more intentional in praying for others?
- Read Luke 16:1-13. In what ways can you take more personal responsibility in being a steward for the things God bestows to humanity?

Retired Christian radio announcer; member of Ascension Lutheran Church, Tucson, Arizona

Jeremiah mourns Israel's alienation from God. He proclaims, "Come back to God," but the people refuse. The drought in the land reflects the drought in their souls. The people wonder why God has abandoned them. Yet the people of Judah have taken God's mercy for granted.

Instead of relying on God, the people have relied on the Temple, false prophets, idols, and their own imagination. But God, through Jeremiah, cautions them about their folly. God warns that their disrespect will bring horrible consequences. The citizens of Judah believe their safety rests in being God's special people, but they forget that God disciplines the ones God loves. Long before Babylonia conquers the city and carries them away, they have many chances to repent; but they continue to disrespect the Lord. Such is the obstinacy of misconduct. They discover the pain of suffering as slavery, poverty, and hopelessness become their self-imposed penalty for disrespect.

Their mistake, like ours, comes in wrongly supposing that the relationship between God and humanity is just a game. It isn't. It's a responsibility and privilege. The people of Judah exemplify God's intentional love. God holds them up as a light to the world.

We can choose to respect or disrespect God. We cannot anticipate that our church, our education, or our reasoning will spare us from God's justice. Unlike the Israelites, we cannot ask, "Where is God?" when we turn our backs and ignore God's presence among us. Jeremiah warns, "Come back to God, for your own welfare."

Lord Jesus, may my life today show respect for you. Amen.

Jeremiah began prophesying to Jerusalem and Judah in 622 BCE, during the time of the reforms of King Josiah. Nebuchadnezzar, king of Babylonia, destroyed Jerusalem in 586 BCE, ending the southern kingdom of Judah—a tumultuous time. Today's verses express God's anger toward the Israelites for disrespecting the Lord, but they also illumine God's sadness and pain brought on by their disobedience. Judah's self-will and disrespect for God unraveled their protection and prosperity.

Obviously, when we know the right thing to do and refuse do it, we have only ourselves to blame for the ensuing difficulties. Consequently, we need to ask if we are conforming to God's life-giving principles or disrespecting God as the nation of Judah did. If we listen, read, or watch the news, we can quickly find evidence that we are not paying attention very well. We too stand guilty of ignoring sound advice. Yet, whether we cause our own affliction or it comes from an outside source, God shows constant concern for humanity.

Jeremiah could easily tread our streets and deliver this same message. Humanity does little to recognize God, and we also ignore God's concern for our pain and suffering. Shame on us. Yet, Jeremiah cries, "Come back to God!" And then weeps.

Why does Jeremiah weep? He weeps because he knows his fellow citizens possess a God-given choice between fullness and emptiness. While God is always present to comfort, we must desire the health and healing God offers.

God of healing, when we weep like Jeremiah, bring us your comfort as we live toward your final deliverance. Amen.

We want to find people we can look up to, don't we? Just look at the many TV shows and movies based on super-heroes and people who save the day. Our culture loves heroes.

TV or movie characters often capture our attention because of their ingenuity, goodness, and friendliness. In the Christian world, the mere mention of King David brings to mind the image of a hero of faith, both as a youngster who defeats a giant with a sling and as the great king of Israel who follows God throughout his life. While David wasn't perfect, God called him "a man after my own heart."

Psalm 4 offers another reason to emulate David: He respects God and speaks intimately with God. David doesn't consult the Lord as an afterthought. Rather, in bad times and good, David goes to God for a solution to his problem or to revel in God's faithfulness, and he affirms that "the Lord hears when I call."

David's prayer embodies boldness, confidence, humility— all traits similar to those of our top fiction heroes. David begins his prayer, "Answer me when I call, O God, . . . Be gracious to me, and hear my prayer."

David doesn't demand or worry. He closes with these words, "I will both lie down and sleep in peace; for you alone, O Lord, make me lie down in safety." He completely trusts in the Lord.

Today the Creator offers us an opportunity to imitate the best character. David has blazed a trail, showing us how to respect God and thrive in our temporary circumstances. Even when conflict and chaos seem to reign we can, as did David, sleep peacefully, knowing God as our defender, comforter, and protector.

Father, quiet our hearts and comfort us with your love. We look to you for peace and safety. Amen.

O ne of my Bible teachers noted that humanity's attitude is this: "Lord, tell me once, maybe twice, and I'll take it from there." It reminds me of a young child telling his or her parent, "I do it myself." Positive thinking and our self-help culture tempt us to believe we can do it ourselves—we don't need God. So while we're repeating, "I think I can, I think I can," we set God aside in disrepectful self-determination.

David demonstrates a positive attitude, yet not one based on smiley-faced bravado. A positive attitude results from respect for God. But positive thinking can enforce the idea that if we think the right thoughts or say the right words or visualize the right images, we will achieve our objective. We set goals, identify roadblocks, and work to eliminate these in order to get what we want. And, while we're choo-chooing along, we pray, "Lord, bless my plans."

David behaves quite differently. David's attitude indicates that he puts God before himself. He acknowledges that his success depends on God's guidance and intervention. When David keeps this focus, he avoids failure and experiences success. David not only proclaims God as his God but expresses his respect for God in his understanding of God as protector, deliverer, savior, and hope.

While positive thinking may carry us far, it is often insufficient and unreliable. Positive thinking that *excludes* God is not only disrespectful but idolatrous. Respect for God leads to contentment and security through trust in the Lord. Our day will look and feel different as we practice respect, which brings a bonus: the experience of God's peace.

Father, may I learn to keep my attitude focused on you, not me. Amen.

Some days at work I don't give my best. I just go through the motions. On those days my boss, the company, or the other employees barely cross my mind. On those days would I label my behavior as dishonorable? Would I admit to being irresponsible? Here Jesus addresses the issue of personal responsibility. Through the parable, Jesus indicates that personal responsibility entails respect for God, others, and ourselves.

The dishonest and irresponsible behavior of the manager in Jesus' story grabs our attention. Yes, he sort of does his job; but he also squanders his employer's assets. He disrespects his employer with incompetent management. However, when confronted, he accepts responsibility and attempts to make matters right. By acting with wit, the manager secures his future in case he loses his position. By doing so, he gains the admiration of his employer.

What does our workday look like when we take responsibility for our behavior? Would we even consider shirking our responsibility or stealing time or paper clips?

Personal responsibility reforms us. Those days when we act irresponsibly become red flag days that alert us to danger. They remind us to honor God's blessings in accountable ways and as opportunities to demonstrate trustworthy behavior.

Through our dependable actions, we show respect for God, respect for others, and respect for ourselves. Jesus asks that we demonstrate personal responsibility for the common good. Give your best.

Lord Jesus, thank you for today's opportunity to show respect to you for my many blessings. Amen.

The manager's job performance is only part of what Jesus addresses as irresponsible. In a broader context, Jesus teaches about service to God versus service to money.

The King James Version uses the word *mammon* for money. Mammon is more than pocket change or insatiable greed for material possessions. It refers to what a person trusts in. Jesus draws a distinction between trusting in material and earthly things rather than in what God gives. Jesus offers a lesson in selfishness versus selflessness, in living God's way instead of our way. Serving God requires an unselfish concern for the welfare of God's gifts. In our service to God we accept responsibility for what God has given us. And one gift we've received is the earth we inhabit.

It follows then that we treat the world like it's ours, because it is. But we have been guilty of disrespecting God's gift. We often hear stories of denial and self-justification: "That's not my fault. . . . It's your problem. . . . I'm not guilty of polluting . . . . It's my DNA. . . . I'm not responsible." Shunning responsibility and accountability for our planet has led and will continue to lead to dire consequences.

Jesus calls us to acknowledge where we place our trust. God notices our behavior; God knows what master we serve. God made us to be responsible and accountable. Accordingly, God lifts us to a standard God knows we are capable of maintaining. When we do, we choose to place our trust in God rather than the material. Service to God leads to respect for all creation. "Whoever is faithful in a very little is faithful also in much."

Thank you, Lord, for holding us accountable as we learn to care for the earth, the home you have given us. May we never take it for granted. Amen.

In our culture, we detest being conned. We're suspicious of everyone because anyone can mistreat us. Before we make commitments to another, we question why we should care about and respect the person. We even do this with God. "Why should I care? What's in it for me? Why should I respect God?"

Paul asserts God's desire for "everyone to be saved and to come to the knowledge of the truth." These verses support accurate knowledge of the gospel and makes note that Paul is a "teacher . . . in faith and truth." As we come to this knowledge, we experience benefits in committing to God. The first: A changed attitude toward others. Paul instructs, "Pray for everyone, including kings and all who are in high positions, so that we may lead a quiet and peaceable life." This is a Christ-alive-in-me prayer that hugs those we like as well as those we dislike. This prayer is the benefit of a changed attitude. It's Christlike.

Christ-thinking desires that everyone come back to God. The second benefit is a changed heart for the eternal well-being of others. Human nature has little interest in the everlasting welfare of anybody. But Paul calls us to demonstrate genuine concern for our neighbor's well-being. It's Christlike.

Christ-thinking cures our faultfinding. The third benefit is a changed message, one that dispenses empathy: "There is one God; there is also one mediator between God and humankind, Christ Jesus . . . who gave himself a ransom for all." The beneficial message offers a remedy of healing and hope. It's Christlike.

Why should we care? What's in it for us? Why should we respect God? By respecting God, we receive a changed attitude, a changed heart, and a changed message. Thus, our respect for God moves us to respect others and ourselves.

Father, may I desire truth. Help me develop a healthy respect for the benefits I have in Jesus. Amen.

It's time to order!

Upper Room Disciplines 2017

Regular print: 978-0-8358-1551-2

Enlarged Print: 978-0-8358-1552-9

Kindle Edition: 978-0-8358-1553-6

Epub Edition 978-0-8358-1554-3

Bookstore.UpperRoom.org

or

800-972-0433

Did you know that you can enjoy
The Upper Room Disciplines
in multiple ways?

Digital or print?

The Upper Room Disciplines is available in both regular and enlarged print, but are you aware that it is also available in digital format? Download a copy to your Kindle or choose an EPUB version for your e-reader. Whatever your preference, we have it for you today.

What is a standing order option?

This option allows you to automatically receive your copy of *The Upper Room Disciplines* each year as soon as it is available. Take the worry out of remembering to place your order.

Need to make changes to your account?

Call Customer Service at 800.972.0433 or e-mail us at CustomerAssistance@umcdiscipleship.org. Our staff is available to help you with any updates.

The Responsibility of Promise

SEPTEMBER 19–25, 2016 • JASMINE ROSE SMOTHERS

Scripture Overview: The Bible warns about the delusions that wealth brings, repeatedly directing readers' attention to the poor and the destitute. Luke's Gospel text culminates in Jesus' story of the rich man and Lazarus. Only in the next life, when the rich man is rid of his riches, can he see Lazarus, now secure at Abraham's side. First Timothy contains a series of warnings to prosperous readers that having the basic necessities of life should be enough. Greed diverts attention away from the God "who richly provides us with everything for our enjoyment." And against the best wisdom of all the financial planners of Judah, Jeremiah purchases the field at Anathoth. The prophet invests his money in the divine promise, in the outlandish conviction that God is faithful.

Questions and Thoughts for Reflection

- Read Jeremiah 32:1-3a, 6-15. Where do you see God's promises in your life? How do you act on them? What keeps you from acting on them?
- Read Psalm 91:1-6, 14-16. In what setting do you experience a sense of God's shelter?
- Read 1 Timothy 6:6-19. With what do you find yourself content?
- Read Luke 16:19-31. How do you maintain an ability to see those in need? How do you address those needs?

Ordained elder, North Georgia Conference, The United Methodist Church; coauthor, *Not Safe for Church: Ten Commandments for Reaching New Generations*

The prophet Jeremiah receives a promise—a word from the Lord—which seems poorly timed. A war rages, and Jeremiah is in jail. Those looking at the situation from the outside would find God's promised future for Jeremiah and the Israelites hard to believe. God's promise of a new covenant with the people (31:31) and of redemption and deliverance (32:15) appear far from current reality. Yet, God tells Jeremiah to act on the promise.

The Israelites have put their trust in the power of Egypt to save them from the Babylonians. Jeremiah's warnings to King Zedekiah have gone unheeded, and Jeremiah finds himself under "house arrest" for his prophesying. If you were in Jeremiah's situation, what would be at the forefront of your mind? I cannot imagine that buying property in a city under siege would be a priority for many of us when battles rage around us and we are held captive in the walls of our lives. Worry about survival would probably occupy all our time. But the prophet Jeremiah acts (with God's prompting) on God's promise of redemption and restoration.

In believing a promise from God, we accept responsibility to act. Acting on promise, when we cannot see promise's fulfillment, is the responsibility that comes with the privilege of being an heir to promise. When life is hard, and we cannot see our way forward, we continue to remember and act on God's promised redemption and deliverance in our lives. Jeremiah bought land in his doomed hometown because he listened and acted on the word of the Lord. What has God promised you? What keeps you from acting on the promise?

> *Lord, when it is hard to see that you will keep your promises to us, give us "strength for today and bright hope for tomorrow" so that we may act on what you've said and see your promises fulfilled. Amen.*

M y real estate agent asked as we stood outside the office for my house closing, "Are you ready for this?" I wanted to shout, "No way! What crazy person decided it was a good idea to allow *me*—a soon-to-be seminary graduate about to start my first full-time clergy appointment—to buy a house?" Instead, I said, "Of course!"

Half an hour later, after signing what seemed like endless documents, I received the keys to my first house. Just like that, I was a homeowner. How odd that signing a stack of papers, handing over a big check, and receiving keys created such a shift in my life. Suddenly I felt grounded and rooted in a place that I would call my own.

People tried to warn me that a home comes with a great deal of responsibility. Having a mortgage really did turn me into a grownup. When the dishwasher gave out, I had to figure out the repairs. When the toilet backed up, there was no one to unclog it but me. Even still, it was mine. The house became my home. And my home became the place where so many of God's promises were realized. The promise of home comes with responsibility; yet, never a day goes by when responsibility outweighs the benefits of home.

While Jeremiah is in jail, God makes an odd request. God tells him to purchase and redeem the land of his kinsman in his hometown. For Jeremiah, the option to buy confirmed the truth of God's request and signaled God's follow-through on the promises made to the Israelite people. "Houses and fields and vineyards shall again be bought in this land."

Faithful God, thank you for keeping your promises. May we accept responsibility to act. Amen.

Twenty-four-hour news broadcasts leave us longing for peace, mercy, justice, hope, and love. Children lose their lives, leave families; and friends wonder why. Young adults feel a sense of insecurity in life, love, and livelihood that demands justice. Older adults feel cast away by society—by employers to whom they have been loyal and by a church consumed with preservation instead of transformation. The church is under fire for not acting like Jesus and remaining silent when it should act. Yet, the psalmist proclaims, "[The LORD] will cover you with his feathers, and under his wings you will find refuge; his faithfulness will be your shield and rampart" (NIV).

While the days seem dark and the times make it difficult to find anything or anyone to trust, God promises us a refuge and fortress worthy of trust. Yet, the psalmist calls us to the responsibility of dwelling: "Whoever dwells in the shelter of the Most High will rest in the shadow of the Almighty" (NIV). The promise of resting, refuge, and faithfulness comes through our choosing to dwell in the presence and shelter of the Most High God.

Psalm 91 extends an invitation to peace, protection, and promise fulfilled. Yes, life is crazy! Yes, cancer, car accidents, and careless violence cause us to question our safety and make us wonder about God's faithfulness.

Even so, God remains faithful. God is our refuge, our fortress. God covers us, saves us, and keeps us from living in fear. Divine nature and action do not depend on our feelings about God. Rather, we realize and acknowledge promises kept when we dwell in God's presence.

Most High God, draw us near to you so that we may dwell in your shelter. When life feels unwieldy, steady us in the safety of your wings. Grant us your peace. Amen.

Songwriter Diane Warren penned a Grammy award-winning tribute to her father, "Because You Loved Me." The lyrics of the song proclaim a love that profoundly influences the life of another. In verses 14-16, the Lord turns the tables on us. "Those who love me, I will deliver; I will protect those who know my name." The Hebrew word for love used in this verse implies an attachment to, a connection with. God responds to the reciprocal love and faithfulness of the relationship. We do not earn or merit God's protection; we ground ourselves in God, receiving nurture and safety that satisfies. While Warren is "forever thankful" for the one who "saw [her] through, through it all," the psalmist takes comfort in God's promise-keeping because of the investment on both sides of the relationship.

Honestly, some days I do not prioritize conversations with God or acknowledge God's faithfulness in my life. Many of us have days when we slip off our Christian pedestal, and we take actions that could make God question our love and commitment. However, I expect God to protect me and to be with me in times of trouble. I recall an old adage that states, "With great privilege comes great responsibility." Or even more, Luke 12:48, which notes the following: "To whom much has been given, much will be required."

Yes, God is faithful and will answer when we call. But the psalmist points to the importance of mutuality in our relationship with God. How many of us expect God to hold up God's end of the deal when we do not? What can God expect from you? How do we live into God's promises?

Gracious and loving God, thank you for first loving me. Remind me of my responsibility in our relationship. Show me the way forward so that your faithfulness is not met with my faithlessness. Amen.

The Responsibility of Promise   319

Newsflash: Christmas is three months away! Do not panic! Rather, consider this an invitation to ponder what it means to be content. Very soon, the "best sales events of the year" will commence. People of all ages will become kind and cooperative as they drop not-so-subtle hints regarding what should be under the Christmas tree. In no time at all, we will ignore the cries of Advent to wait, slow down, and draw near to God in expectation of the gifts of hope, peace, joy, and love that the Christ child will bring. Our more, more, more meters will turn on, and we will trade family time for frenzied lines and clicks of the mouse. In today's passage, Paul invites us to take stock of what is most important in our spiritual lives so that we will not wander from the faith and cause ourselves much grief.

The promise of "great gain in godliness combined with contentment" is clear. This reading offers a gut check for the people of God. From dust we came and to dust we shall return. After all, we seldom hitch a trailer of possessions to a hearse. Food and clothing—learn to be content with these, Paul instructs. Money is not evil; however, the pursuit of and the love of money distract from our responsibility to God. In our eagerness to obtain and protect our riches, we stray from our faith and from living out of contentment. When we stray from our faith and do not hold ourselves accountable for Christlike living, we cause pain in our own lives and in the lives of others.

Christmas is coming, but Advent comes first. Take care to make contentment and godliness a top priority in your life.

Dear Lord, save us from becoming "trapped by many senseless and harmful desires that plunge people into ruin and destruction." May we attend to contentment and godliness in this life. Amen.

Wake up. Go to work. Sit in traffic. Engage with members of your family. Eat. Go to bed. Rinse. Repeat. For many people, this pattern represents a good life (well, minus the traffic). Having a routine, a job, a family, and a steadiness about life is more than many can hope for. However, God imagines more for us and promises more to us. More than going through the motions, God promises a life, richly provided for by God, that takes "hold of the eternal life, to which [we are] called."

Paul turns his attention from the folly of those who desire wealth to address Timothy himself: "But as for you, man of God, shun all this; pursue righteousness, godliness, faith, love, endurance, gentleness. Fight the good fight of the faith." Paul invites Timothy and us into a pursuit of "the life that is really life," the life that exemplifies faithful living. "Real" life can take on many meanings. Caught up in a "seize the day" mentality that lacks grounding in community and compassion, some approach life with destructive and reckless fervor. Others "seize the day" with a passion for a deeper engagement with God and community. Faithful life is not about steadiness and routine. Faithful living involves our willingness to "do good, to be rich in good works, generous, and ready to share." Faithful living lays a good foundation through reliance on God.

Faithful living is not easy. It does not manifest itself simply because we breathe. A faithful life challenges and compels us to "fight the good fight of the faith" and "keep the commandment." Our responsibility to faithful living allows us to "take hold of the life that really is life."

Merciful God, give us a zeal for faithfulness in living so that we may experience all that you have promised. Amen.

A few years ago, I helped celebrate Holy Communion at an affluent church. We used the liturgy of The Great Thanksgiving for Advent. In the middle of the liturgy, the celebrant speaks these words: "You fill the hungry with good things, and the rich you send empty away." I heard an audible gasp mixed with an uncomfortable silence in the majestic sanctuary. The liturgy continued, "Your own Son came among us as a servant, to be Emmanuel, your presence with us" (*The United Methodist Book of Worship*, 54). I saw the people relax. The gasp, the silence, and the settling back in stayed with me for weeks. Why are we okay with Jesus as servant but uncomfortable with a faith that challenges us?

The Gospel text once again contrasts the rich and the poor, pulling off a reversal of circumstances after death. The rich man finds himself in the tormented place of Hades and the poor man rests on the bosom of Abraham. We do not know that the rich man did nothing in life to change Lazarus's circumstances, but now in Hades the rich man actually *sees* Lazarus for the first time. His wealth has limited his perspective on people and the world. Money and sumptuous living are not the evils in the text; the lack of acknowledgment and action on behalf of others less fortunate is the sin. The Gospel calls us to do good in the world, to see the other and offer care. Riches are not worth our souls.

The Great Thanksgiving instructs, "You have mercy on those who fear you from generation to generation. You put down the mighty from their thrones and exalt those of low degree." We have been convinced of God's promise of abundant and eternal life by someone who rose from death. We *see* the other and conduct ourselves in such a way as to reveal God's promise to others through our living.

Dear Lord, free us for joyful obedience through Jesus Christ our Lord. May it be so. Amen.

The Tracks of Our Tears

SEPTEMBER 26–OCTOBER 2, 2016 • STEVEN R. GUTHRIE

Scripture Overview: Moving from the sadness of Lamentations 1 to the thanksgiving prayer of 2 Timothy 1 is to move from total darkness to "the appearing of our Savior Christ Jesus, who abolished death and brought life and immortality to light through the gospel." Lamentations 1 and Psalm 137 are both painful laments from the vantage point of the exile. Both laments dramatize the expression of honest pain, which offers to God anger as well as grief. In contrast, the New Testament texts speak of faith. The writer of the epistle delights in Timothy's heritage of faith, nurtured by mother and grandmother and empowered by divine gifts of love and self-discipline. But it is a heritage that must put itself at risk for the sake of the gospel and not flinch in the face of inevitable suffering. The disciples ask Jesus for "more" faith, only to be told that faith cannot be quantified.

Questions and Thoughts for Reflection

- Read Lamentations 1:1-6. When have your tears of regret washed away illusion? How do you begin again after repentance?
- Read Psalm 137. Recall a time when someone angered you. How did you deal with your anger?
- Read 2 Timothy 1:1-14. The author states that when we shed tears for another person we "testify to our profound connectedness to others." When in your life have you shed tears for the suffering of another?
- Read Luke 17:5-10. How do you experience gratitude even as you live with the demands of the Christian life?

Associate Professor, Theology/Religion and the Arts, Belmont University, Nashville, Tennessee

One of the great Motown hits of the 1960s is the Smokey Robinson song, "The Tracks of My Tears." Three of the four passages we'll encounter this week mention weeping in one way or another, and the fourth alludes to suffering. As we'll see, however, the reasons for these tears are varied. It may help us to follow "the tracks of our tears," to consider the different sources of our sorrows. Even more important than understanding the source of our tears, however, is discerning their destination. Where might God lead us through the different kinds of sorrow we encounter?

In Lamentations 1, we meet tears of loss. The writer poignantly describes a ruined Jerusalem; once the prosperous center of Israel's life but now a ghost town "after . . . Judah has gone into exile" (NIV). It seems likely that this poem describes Jerusalem after it has fallen to Babylonia in 586 BCE, carrying its leading citizens into exile. What intensifies Israel's mourning is that this exile comes as the consequence of her sin. These are not only tears of loss, then, but tears of regret.

These kinds of tears represent both a danger and an opportunity. Tears of regret may simply cause us to long for the good times long gone, but that would be a mistake. Tears of regret are meant to wash away illusion. The poet now recognizes that the false friends who filled Israel's streets back when times were good have abandoned her. These tears of loss and regret are, above all, tears of repentance, a gift that clears away the false promises of our self-centered loves and misplaced hopes and invites us to start again.

Lord, we give you our regrets. Do not let our tears lead us back into nostalgia or second-guessing but forward, with our eyes fixed on Jesus Christ and his kingdom. Amen.

Like Lamentations 1, Psalm 137 is a poem of lament arising from Israel's captivity in Babylon. Lamentations 1 is written from the perspective of those left behind in Jerusalem. Psalm 137 is written from the perspective of those carried off into exile.

One reason for the tears of Psalm 137 are the taunts of Israel's "captors" and "tormentors." But even more than this goading, the exiles weep because they are far from home; strangers "in a strange land" (KJV).

Few of us have faced captors or tormentors, so we may not feel much of a firsthand connection to this lament. But then we remember that the apostle Paul declares that our "citizenship is in heaven" (Phil. 3:20) and that Jesus tells Pilate that his "kingdom is not from this world" (John 18:36).

Those who follow Jesus are indeed like these exiles, strangers in a strange land. So we weep when we watch the news, when we encounter cynicism and cruelty, when we hear of a friend's cancer diagnosis, or when we stand by the grave of a child. In each case something in us says, "This is not how it should be." Or at least, we hope this is our response. These tears are the appropriate response of those whose citizenship is in heaven. They are the tears of alienation and exile. They remind us that we are out of step with the ways and powers of this world and that for a time we are separated from the Garden for which we were created and the New Jerusalem for which we are destined.

Lord, we weep over the brokenness and brutality of our world. May our tears spur us to pray all the more passionately: "Thy kingdom come. Thy will be done in earth, as it is in heaven" (Matt. 6:10, KJV). Amen.

The Tracks of Our Tears

Psalm 137 is, as previously noted, written from the perspective of those carried off into captivity in Babylon. Verses 1-6 give voice to moving and heartrending lament. Weeping grows into rage, however, and in verses 8 and 9 we encounter some of the most troubling lines in the Bible. These verses shock and terrify. What shall we do with them?

Israel has suffered severe violence and injustice. Jerusalem was reduced to rubble as Israel's enemies looked on and mocked. The exiles weep because of the wrongs committed against them. But verses 8 and 9 show us another feeling. Here we encounter tears that flow not only from the violence others committed against Israel. These tears flow from the exiles' own festering hurt and rage, from their own desire for retribution and vengeance.

If this desire is the source of these tears, then where should they flow? Psalm 137 tells us they flow into the very presence of God—the right place to bring our hurt and anger. What would we say if we were sitting with the writer of this psalm—the one who has seen his city demolished and has been carried off into exile? Indeed, what would we say to others who have suffered great violence? Do we say, "Get over your anger"? "Forgive and forget"? "Two wrongs don't make a right"? No. Those who have been wronged want to cry out—and they should. But Psalm 137 tells us the appropriate place for these cries is the sanctuary of God. These tears lead us not to vengeance or denial but to the compassionate embrace of the One who judges justly.

Lord, we give you the hurt and anger we feel toward those who have wronged us. Thank you for allowing us to bring our wounded hearts into your presence. Hold us there until you have healed us. Amen.

For eight years my wife and I lived in Scotland. Our three oldest children were born there. I remember how my parents would cry when, after a short visit with them in the United States, it was time for our return to Scotland. They knew it would probably be a year before they would see their grandchildren again, and the prospect of separation broke their hearts.

In this letter Paul remembers Timothy's tears when they were separated from each other. Paul, likewise longs to see Timothy. This letter reminds us that one source of our tears is the deep connection we have to others in Jesus Christ. As Christians, we find ourselves bound not only to biological relations but to a much larger family. Indeed, Timothy is Paul's "beloved child"; Paul is Timothy's spiritual father. (See Philippians 2:22.)

Nor do tears flow only because Paul and Timothy miss each other. Paul writes Timothy at a time when Paul is suffering, and, what is more, everyone has deserted him. In this context he urges Timothy not to be "ashamed of the testimony about our Lord or of me his prisoner" but rather to "join with me in suffering for the gospel." Love involves us in both the joys and the sufferings of others. We do not simply become fond of others; we find ourselves bound together with them in their triumphs and tears. When we shed these sorts of tears, it signals spiritual health. They testify to our profound connectedness to others. And they indicate that God has so broadened our hearts that we feel concern not only for our own well-being but for the needs of others.

We thank you, God, for the life we share with our sisters and brothers in Christ. Give us courage to share not only in others' joys but in their sufferings as well. Amen.

The Tracks of Our Tears

Join with me" Paul urges Timothy, "in suffering for the gospel." "For this gospel I was appointed a herald and an apostle and a teacher" he writes. "For this reason I suffer as I do." In these verses, Paul relays the word that we will shed some of our tears for the sake of the gospel. Jesus tells his disciples the same message on more than one occasion: "'Servants are not greater than their master.' If they persecuted me, they will persecute you" (John 15:20).

We may not understand how these words apply to us. Many of Jesus' followers in the early centuries were imprisoned or martyred for their faith. In what meaningful sense can contemporary American Christians suffer for the gospel? Yet, even apart from persecution, the ordinary Christian life includes an element of suffering for the gospel.

We suffer for the gospel when we prefer others' needs to our own, when we obey Jesus by serving "the least of these"—the naked, the hungry, the imprisoned. We suffer for the gospel when we refuse to sacrifice time with family, church, and community in exchange for success and advancement; when we go out of our way to befriend those who are difficult and unpopular; when we refuse convenient but dishonest shortcuts in our work.

But these tears of suffering are also tears of joy because they involve us in walking alongside Jesus, sharing in his work. Moreover, they are shed in hope and confidence because we know that "our Savior Jesus Christ . . . abolished death and brought life and immortality to light through the gospel."

Lord, we "want to know Christ—yes, to know the power of his resurrection and participation in his sufferings, becoming like him in his death, and so, somehow, attaining to the resurrection from the dead" (Phil. 3:10-11). Amen.

The wide-ranging sources of sorrow and human suffering can overwhelm us. We may feel tempted to add tears of self-pity to our long list of tears. Why is life so hard? Why does God call us to travel such a difficult road? It doesn't seem fair.

We hear a similar complaint in verse 5 of today's reading. The disciples aren't simply making a generic request for more faith. Instead they are responding to a difficult teaching. In Luke 17:3-4, Jesus tells them that they must forgive those who sin against them. In fact, he says, if someone sins against them seven times—in a single day!—they still must forgive. In response to this call to extraordinary forgiveness, the disciples exclaim, "Increase our faith!" In other words: Jesus, you're asking us to go pretty far above and beyond the call of duty here! If you're going to ask us to do something that demanding, then you'd better give us an extra dose of faith to carry it off!

Jesus responds with a parable. When a servant has worked hard at his job all day, is it above and beyond the call of duty to expect that he would also prepare the master's evening meal? Would that task call for special provisions or special commendation? Of course not. This is what servants do. They are called to put another's needs before their own. And this, Jesus says, is the way of the gospel as well. Forgiving, serving, laying down rights, preferring others' interests to your own: these aren't above and beyond the demands reserved for "super disciples"! Rather, these are the basics of life in God's kingdom, where the one who would be first must become the servant of all. (See Mark 9:35.)

Lord, keep us from self-pity. Teach us to love, serve, and forgive joyfully and without resentment. Amen.

The disciples, amazed by Jesus' demands, plead, "Increase our faith!" Jesus then responds with a parable that, at first glance, seems rather harsh. A servant doesn't receive special praise for obedience. What kind of response is this? Is Jesus telling the disciples: "Shut up and do what you're told"?

No. First of all, we notice that Jesus begins by saying, "Suppose one of you has a servant." Jesus begins, in other words, not by describing how God relates to us but by describing how human masters and human servants normally relate to one another. We wouldn't imagine a master feeling indebted to a servant simply because the servant did his job. An employee who does the job she was hired to do wouldn't ordinarily think, *OK, I did it—but my boss really owes me one now!*

We don't relate this way to those who have authority over us on a human level. How much less would we relate to God in this way? Serving and forgiving others is hard (as the disciples recognize). But the demands of the Christian way do not justify going through life feeling exasperated, as if we have been enormously inconvenienced by God. No service we render, no obedience we offer ever puts God in our debt. That is not the character of our relationship to God.

We can state the same point positively: Even when faced with the demands of the Christian life, our attitude toward God is one of gratitude. Among the various tears we shed, we mingle them all with our tears of gratitude.

We thank you, Lord, for your goodness to us. We thank you that we always have cause for gratitude and that you call us not only to the way of the cross but to the joy of the resurrection. Amen.

Joy and Obedience

OCTOBER 3–9, 2016 • KATE OBERMUELLER UNRUH

Scripture Overview: One might have expected Jeremiah to advise the exiles to maintain their independence and be ready to return to Judah. Instead, he tells them to settle in, to build and plant, to seek the welfare of Babylon, even to pray for its prosperity. The judging purposes of God call for extended exile and not impatient rebellion. In the story of the ten lepers in Luke, one returns to praise and thank Jesus for giving him health. Only then do we learn that he is a Samaritan. The ultimate outsider becomes the model of faith. Second Timothy bears witness to the awesome character of God that always honors divine commitments, thereby appearing to humans full of surprises. For the psalmist, God merits the worship of all the earth.

Questions and Thoughts for Reflection

- Read Jeremiah 29:1, 4-7. When have you found yourself in exile? How did you cope with the situation? What reminded you that God had not abandoned you?
- Read Psalm 66:1-12. When has the testing of God brought you out to "a spacious place"?
- Read 2 Timothy 2:8-15. How do you ready yourself to present yourself as one approved by God?
- Read Luke 17:11-19. The writer states that Jesus' question, "Where are the other nine?," invites us to receive God's healing of illness and inner wounds. What in your life needs God's healing touch?

Doctoral student in education and formation, Princeton Theological Seminary; more than a decade of ministry experience in various roles; coauthor, *Words That Give Life*

*B*loom where you are planted. Handstitched and framed in blue, these words adorned the wall of my grandmother's kitchen. My mother repeated them to me during my first semester away at college, when I got my first job a thousand miles from home, and many times since. That old blue frame now graces the wall of my own home. It has accompanied me from city to city, state to state, and across the Atlantic when I lived and worked overseas.

The Israelites, however, did not choose to leave home for a new adventure. Instead, the Babylonians destroyed their homeland and carried the leading citizens to Babylon to serve as slaves. And God engineered this exile. They find themselves in foreign territory, and now God tells them to settle in. This will not be a temporary situation; they are in Babylon for the long haul. Amidst the chaos and homesickness, God desires a good life for the chosen people. God wants them to flourish. So God speaks the same words to the Israelites that God spoke to me through needlepoint: *Bloom where you are planted.*

For the Israelites, blooming means making themselves at home in a foreign and uncomfortable place. It means putting down roots, building houses, establishing families, and helping to build their community. God intends that Israel not only survive exile but thrive in the midst of it.

The fulfillment of God's promise sometimes requires discomfort on our part. Whether it involves geography or not, God often plants us in foreign circumstances that leave us longing for the security of the way things used to be. When life is not ideal, when we feel exiled, when we are away from home or in a metaphorical new place, God still wants a good life for us. God wants us to flourish and bloom.

In what places of discomfort and unfamiliarity has God placed you? How could you follow God's call to make yourself at home under these conditions?

Shortly after beginning work for Chevrolet, I received an e-mail from one of my college professors who reminded me of the old adage that "what's good for General Motors is good for the country." GM's prosperity indicated a thriving national economy; it was also his way of encouraging my work.

The prophet Jeremiah has a similar message for the people of God in exile: What's good for Babylon is good for Israel. Their welfare is bound up in the welfare of the place of their exile. Thus, God calls them to make Babylon a good place to live.

We still discover that our well-being is tied up in the well-being of others. God created us to need, give, serve, and desire—together, in community. Instinctively, we know that our steady connection to family, friends, and neighbors affects our well-being. And we affect the well-being of others when we are present in their moments of joy and need.

What often remains hidden to us, however, is our tie to the well-being of the invisible in our community. We are no less connected to the homeless person on the corner we drive past every day than we are to the person sitting in the pew next to us. Our link to the abandoned, the poor, the marginalized, and the forgotten exists, but we have forgotten it. Seeking the welfare of the seen and the unseen in our communities offers unique challenges because we must reach outside the boundaries of our daily lives. Yet as the story of God's people tells us, in seeking good for others we can live the good life ourselves.

How is God calling you to make your community a better place? Who or what could benefit from your attention?

Lord, show us the people who need to be seen. Empower us to serve in your name that we may brighten the world with your light. Amen.

When I became a mother, people naturally wanted to know about the baby. How much did she weigh? Who did she look like? How did we choose her name? After several months, I began to emerge from my sleep-deprived stupor and reenter the world, happy to get out of the house and interact with grown-ups about life outside the home.

Despite my desire for adult interaction, in the middle of a conversation my mind would wander back to my daughter. If she was with me, I wondered what her facial expressions meant. If she was with someone else, I would worry that she needed me to feed her or rock her to sleep. Sometimes I literally forgot what I was talking about midsentence or interrupted myself with a sidebar on spit-up or feeding schedules. My singular focus on the baby made me seem a bit crazy.

Paul also maintained a singular focus that changed his life and made him seem a little crazy to others. In fact, he wound up in jail for it on a number of occasions. Yet, his focus on the gospel of Jesus Christ motivated his endurance. Paul is so fixed on Jesus that there is no room in the spotlight for his chains. Paul does not dwell on what he must endure; rather, he endures persecution because he tightly grasps the promise of the resurrected Lord.

Paul's concentration does not waver. He attends to the gospel with proclamation, with attempts to help others grasp it and to keep it constantly in their sight. Doing so doesn't mean talking about it but actually going before God. If you set your sights on Jesus, Paul says, then you set your sights on ultimate faithfulness.

What is fighting for your attention right now?

Faithful God, I want to put you first. Help me to see you before all and in all, until you are all I see. Amen.

Paul clearly evidences God's power. Sometimes when I read his letters, I picture myself next to him, chained to the stone wall of a small, dark cell. I can feel despair closing in through the moist walls, the frightening silence interrupted only by the distant din of life on the outside. Then I read Paul's words, and that image transforms into a vision of strength in which the power of God enables me to stand up and walk, unfettered, into the sunlit streets.

As I boldly step into the world with a newfound courage, I feel in my soul the truth I have just read: "The word of God is not chained." I can breathe deeply, knowing that through Christ, I am not chained. I am wonderfully free and whole.

Yet with each step, I exert a little energy. I exhale some of that deep breath. I engage in the tasks of everyday life, and I begin to run out of steam. Before I realize it—and sooner than I like to admit—I find myself back in those chains. The house needs attention; the children need attention; my tasks require attention. Suddenly I look at my to-do list, which I never seem to complete, and I feel burdened by my inability to keep up. I am out of breath and out of energy. I am empty.

The good news is that I am never out of God's love. I wear myself out doing "my best to present [myself] to God as one approved by him, a worker who has no need to be ashamed," but in that very effort I forget that it is not my effort that warrants God's approval. The unbounded word of God has already granted me that. God's grace is sufficient.

When do you feel the most free? When do you feel empty?

God, thank you for being faithful when I am faithless. Forgive my tendency to attempt to earn your approval, and help me to surrender to you so that I can live in your freedom. Amen.

Sunny blue skies, hot chocolate on a cold day, fresh flowers, fireworks, babies—all these things bring me joy. It comes to me in a burst of energy, gratitude, and happiness that makes my heart smile, and for a moment I experience the sheer goodness of creation. These moments often last only a short time, so I do my best to recognize and savor them for the fleeting gifts they are.

I often feel jealous of the psalmists who seem ready to break into joyous songs of praise at any given moment—deep, genuine praise at the drop of a hat—a trait I both admire and envy. In today's passage, the psalmist calls "all the earth" to "make a joyful noise to God." I acknowledge that I don't always feel the sense of amazement that characterizes the writer of our psalm.

As I contemplate this psalm, I realize that the psalmist is disciplined at remembering. It may not be inherent perfection that causes the psalmist to overflow with God's praises but rather the intentional remembering of God's mighty acts and sustaining presence that naturally calls forth praise from all creatures of the earth. Verses 5-7 evoke images of the miracles in Exodus and other deeds God accomplishes toward humanity. Just as a clear blue sky stirs praise within my own heart, so here the parting of the Red Sea summons the praise of God's people, for God "has kept us among the living" and continues to preserve those lives. The miracles of God in the service of God's people, both then and now, provide cause to remember and to engage in repeated and endless praise of the One who brought Israel "into a spacious place."

This week, make it your practice to remember and share those stories.

God of glory, help me remember and proclaim your work in my life that I may experience your joy and share it with others. Amen.

Each week, my church engages in the practice of sharing joys and concerns. Sharing details of our lives before the community of faith allows church members to get to know one another, making us truly invested in those around us. That shared investment means that people not only participate in appealing to God on behalf of others but also that they eagerly wait to participate in recognizing God's answer.

If we share burdens and hardships, then we also share joys. If we cry out to God and beg for mercy, for healing, or for help, then we certainly must return to God with thanksgiving for those very things. The discipline of asking for help requires the discipline of recognizing God's response and appropriately responding ourselves. Jesus seems disappointed that nine of the ten lepers he healed failed to grasp this concept.

The sick in this story appear to know the rules of engagement: They keep their distance because they are considered "unclean" and address Jesus as "Master." These lepers exhibit signs of faith but fall short when they fail to acknowledge God's role in their restoration. They ask, receive, and go without so much as a thank-you.

Like the lepers in this story, we often exhibit the same kind of behavior. We ask for mercy, for healing, for a divine hand to improve our circumstances. God responds, and we often receive what we ask for. Yet when our circumstances improve, we tend to forget that it was and is God at work, listening to us, talking to us, and responding to us. We go on our way without returning thanks and without adding our testimony to God's story.

In what ways has God worked in your life recently? What answered prayers have you unwittingly overlooked?

I am grateful, Lord, for all that you are and all that you do. Thank you for always hearing and responding. Stir within me a proper response to your handiwork, O God. Amen.

Joy and Obedience

As an adult I found myself intrigued by the Harry Potter series. In it, witches or wizards whose parents are Muggles (ordinary people) are a genetic phenomenon. The series carries a strong theme of prejudice against those who are not full-blooded wizards.

A similar prejudice existed in Jesus' day. The exact reasons behind the animosity between Jews and Samaritans have been lost to history, but the New Testament gives ample evidence of ethnic tension (see, for example, John 4:9; 8:48). Whether motivated by questions over ancestry or religious practice, a number of Jews treated Samaritans as outsiders. Some would even say they resented them.

In today's scripture, we follow Jesus "going through the region between Samaria and Galilee," which tells us that the Samaritan leper is not far from home. Jesus does not brush off these men as unclean lepers or treat them as second-class human beings. He heals them. Jesus does not reserve his healings for a special group; he responds to those who approach him in faith. While Jesus heals all the lepers, the Gospel of Luke emphasizes the faith of the one who returns. His faith makes him well.

Wherever we find ourselves in our faith journey, Jesus will respond if we reach out in faith. His actions challenge us to inspect our attitudes toward others. And in practicing the humility that allows us to consider others better than ourselves, we may be surprised at where and in whom we find great faith. Those outside our Christian circles might seem unlikely witnesses but often exhibit God's redemptive work in bold ways.

When have you considered yourself better than others? When has your faith made you well?

Jesus, have mercy on me. Forgive my haughtiness. Remind me, daily, that you died not just for me but for the sins of the whole world. Amen.

Teach Me Your Way, O Lord

OCTOBER 10–16, 2016 • JAN SPRAGUE

Scripture Overview: Christians want help in understanding the significance of the Bible. Psalm 119 delights in the instruction of Yahweh. The text of the Torah is valued, not as a legal document but as an occasion for meditation and for the shaping of values, intuitions, and sensitivities. Scripture in Second Timothy is the gift of God and a guide for the practical life of God's people. Its instructive role equips believers for every good work. Jeremiah 31 anticipates the time when God will write the law on the hearts of the people and reminds readers that at the core of "the law" is the covenant relation God establishes: "I will be their God, and they shall be my people." The parable of the persistent widow directs us to the companion of Bible study: prayer.

Questions and Thoughts for Reflection

- Read Jeremiah 31:27-34. In what sense do you perceive God's guidance coming from within you?
- Read Psalm 119:97-104. How immersed are you in God's word? How does scripture guide your decisions?
- Read 2 Timothy 3:14–4:5. Who in your life has been a courageous teacher leading you toward God? How has he or she helped sustain your faith?
- Read Luke 18:1-8. How have your attitudes toward prayer changed? How does this passage help you to view prayer in a new light?

Pastor, Marengo United Methodist Church, Marengo, Ohio

As a child, Timothy learned more than rote words of scripture. The words came to life as he heard the stories of how those words sustained his grandmother, Lois, during the stormy moments in her life. The prayers of his mother, Eunice, covered him. He heard those words sung with praise for God's blessings and prayed with human tears. Timothy personally experiences what Hebrews 12:1 calls a "cloud of witnesses," as persons of influence in his life spoke into his heart the words of God that nurture believers in all circumstances of life.

Paul joins Timothy's "cloud of witnesses." He becomes yet another of Timothy's teachers and continues to nurture those seeds and words of faith sown early in Timothy's life. He reminds Timothy that the witnesses and teachers in our lives are God-given blessings and resources; they serve as mentors and spiritual trail guides. The retelling of the biblical narrative and the vulnerable sharing of personal faith journeys provide sacred teaching moments and expressions of love and faith. These are not simply shared and passed on like dusty keepsakes kept on a shelf. Retelling and sharing faith stories plant seeds that can teach and grow into something personal and soul-sustaining.

Ever the teaching preacher, Paul entreats Timothy to honor the courageous faith of his teachers, to let the words he knows in his head become the words of his heart that buoy up faith. Paul reminds Timothy that God inspires each word of scripture. These words aren't dry words on a page; these words speak into our lives. They become our mirrors, our words of challenge and comfort. They become our goal and our inspiration. The words teach and sustain us wherever our journeys take us.

Thank you, God, for our faith mentors, teachers, and cloud of witnesses. Lead us to be the same for those whose faith journey follows ours. Amen.

Walking the cookbook or diet book aisles of a bookstore overwhelms me with the myriad choices, all claiming to be the best. Each author makes his or her case for eating certain foods and not others. The books offer different approaches: you may count calories, carbs, or points. Some writers champion specific proteins or vegetables as the key to eating right. We have to sort out what makes sense in terms of what we choose to feed our bodies.

The psalmist makes a case for the same process of discernment as we choose what we feed our souls. Our access to seemingly endless information, wisdom, and opinion can often overwhelm and confuse us. We accept the validity of the adage that proclaims that not everything presented on the Internet—or anywhere else—is necessarily true or good.

The psalmist realizes how easily we can wander away from God's laws and intentions, no matter who we are. His resolution focuses on total immersion in God's word. He feeds his soul with God's laws; he knows them inside out. He commits them to heart, and they never leave him. God's word becomes his soul's food, his strength and his comfort.

The psalmist loves God's instruction and finds himself connected to the true source of life. Armed in this way, the psalmist knows God's expectations and can stand down his enemies and temptations. His God-directed life allows for a new perspective. With God as his teacher, he experiences healing and learns God's ways. His life changes as he listens to the only voice that matters, and he aligns his life choices with those of God.

God, so many voices claim to have the answers. Teach us to listen and tune our hearts to yours. Amen.

Our society trains us to expect immediate gratification. Crisp photos and videos appear immediately on multitasking phones we carry faithfully. We have thousands of songs or dozens of movies and television shows at our fingertips for instant entertainment. We can collaborate with or instantly connect to coworkers and friends.

This immediacy makes the mode of perseverance a rare commodity. How do we practice and take action that requires commitment over the long haul? Jesus tells this parable of a widow who takes her situation that calls for justice before a judge who really doesn't care. She pesters him to the point that her persistence and perseverance finally wear him down. The judge pragmatically decides to care for her situation, reasoning it is his only chance for peace.

Jesus tells the disciples to pray with the same constant fervor and persistence that this widow employs. He assures them that God—the polar opposite of the uncaring judge—will respond and help them.

Though we struggle with perseverance and prefer immediate gratification of our wants, we seek to find fulfillment in God's timing. We can easily link God to that disconnected judge, but God is anything but disconnected or disinterested. Our faith and prayers need to be consistent, constant, and committed, just like God. Our constancy comes in our confidence in the character of God who is responsive to our prayers, especially when we lift up issues of justice. It may be that as we spend more time in persistent and consistent prayer, we will discover that prayer relies less on our swaying God's opinion and more on allowing God to teach us divine ways and timing.

Teach us how to pray, Jesus, even as we aspire to your unwavering faith. Teach us tenacity in praying for justice. Amen.

The Lord makes the Israelites the offer of a lifetime—even better than a clean chalkboard or dry-erase board! No matter how hard you work to clean those surfaces, you can still see the faint images of what has just been written and now erased.

The new covenant God espouses is like installing brand-new dry-erase boards! Everybody gets a new, never-before-written-on surface. God will lay the past behind and start over, fresh and clean! The destruction, brokenness, and heartbreak of the past will give way to a time of new birth and hope. For generations, the faithful have worn millstones of guilt and sin around their necks, knowing that the sins of previous generations have been bequeathed to the heirs apparent. God now declares that policy null and void! No longer will the sins of family members outlive them by generations. This is good news!

Although God has taken the Israelites by the hand, provided for them and loved them, the people have broken the previous understanding, even as they broke God's heart. Here God makes a new covenant with the faithful.

This new day begins with a new covenant that God engraves upon the hearts of the faithful. There will be no losing of documents, no erasing of promises, no telltale residue or shadows from the past! Writing the covenant upon the hearts of the people internalizes and centralizes it. No one depends on another person to learn about God. God will live within their hearts. This is good news!

Engrave your word, your presence, your grace upon our hearts, O God. You have given us hope, freedom, and forgiveness in this new covenant, and we are grateful. Amen.

Timothy is blessed by the many people and avenues that have nurtured his faith: the teachings of his mother and grandmother and his own reading and study of scripture. His soul is convicted of the truth and power of "the sacred writings." Leaning in, looking him straight in the eye, Paul tells Timothy that once his spirit has heard beyond the words, once God has convicted him, once his heart has engaged and yielded, Timothy now shoulders a sacred responsibility to live and share God's message of salvation hope.

People in our lives have shared the power and strength, the call and conviction, the grace and hope found in scripture. They have shared those places where God has met them. We have been blessed and spiritually uplifted by those who have taught and reminded us what it means to live a faithful life. Their witness enables our witness; we accept the task of persistence in "favorable or unfavorable" times. And we acknowledge that we will endure suffering for the sake of our conviction.

In the midst of a difficult season, I found myself surrounded in a church Bible study by new friends who ignited questions and wonder in my soul. My spiritual hunger bewildered me. My pastor played "Paul" to my awakening "Timothy." My companions fed my soul, answered my questions, and became the nurturing faith family that propelled my faith to turn a corner and come home, forever changing my life.

I soon became convicted and called; nothing less would satisfy my soul. Convicted to stand strong with eyes focused on God while ridiculed. Called to preach in the face of manipulation of the sacred word. Commissioned to share hope in the midst of darkness and to speak truth that eternally changes lives.

For the blessings of those who have loved us into the arms of Jesus, thank you, Lord. Amen.

I sometimes forget stuff: names I know as well as my own, things I remembered an hour ago, where I put my keys or what I set on top of them! But some people and situations I never forget: broken covenants and pain. I may forgive and choose not to allow brokenness to imprison me, but I don't forget.

In these verses God recalls a broken covenant, a time of judgment. But now "the days are surely coming" when God will initiate restoration: "I will forgive their iniquity, and remember their sin no more." God makes a deliberate choice to forgive sin and not remember it—an intentional decision not to allow the power or influence of sin to stand in the way of our relationship. God's conscious choosing to cast aside our mountain of iniquities speaks volumes about the grace of our God who so desires a relationship with us that nothing will stand in the way.

God ups the ante and goes straight to the heart. In the past, God took Israel and Judah by the hand and tried to lead them home into the land of milk and honey, into relationship. Anyone who has ever dealt with a two-year-old or a mule or a headstrong person knows how that goes. God did not break that covenant; the faithful did.

God will write the new covenant on our hearts. It resides and operates from within. We don't have to learn it; we simply have to receive it. God offers the gift of life, hope, and grace to each of us, despite our obstinacy and waywardness. God renews the possibility of relationship by restoring our hope and watching over us as we "build and . . . plant."

Remember me, Lord. Amen.

She doesn't have a prayer. Some dismiss her as "simply" a widow. Without family to care for her in customary ways, she doesn't seem to matter or to fit anywhere. She finds herself involved being denied justice. Having no one to go for her, she takes up her own case. The judge perceives her as nothing more than an embarrassing nuisance because she keeps coming back, demanding justice. His decision to grant justice does not come from righteousness of heart; he simply wants to get rid of her incessant clamoring.

We might conclude from this story that persistent prayer wears God down until God grants our wishes. But that would be an inaccurate interpretation. Jesus actually juxtaposes God to the unjust judge. If the "unjust judge" offers justice, how much more will a caring God offer to those God loves? God does not demean and label us as "simply" this or that, nor is God a genie in a bottle who grants wishes.

Jesus calls us to perseverance in prayer not to wear God down but to build us up. We pray in order to strengthen our faith and our relationship with God. We pray for God's intercession in situations of injustice, even as God moves us to speak up and take action for justice and for those without advocates.

Prayer changes us just as it changes situations. So we pray like this widow approached her unjust situation: without discouragement, without losing heart. We, like the disciples, must answer Jesus' question: "When the Son of Man comes, will he find faith on earth?" Through our perseverance in prayer, God moves in us and for us. And while it may seem delayed, in God's time our help will come and God's justice will prevail!

Teach us your ways, loving God. Help us persevere in prayer so that our faith can grow even stronger. Make us faithful. Amen.

Gratitude: Foundation of Faith

OCTOBER 17–23, 2016 • JAY M. HANKE

Scripture Overview: The Hebrew scripture readings declare the salvation of humankind and insist that the initiative for that salvation comes from God alone. The prophet Joel looks forward to the day when all Israel's sons and daughters will become as prophets in the land. Psalm 65 is a psalm of thanksgiving for the "God of our salvation." The writer of Second Timothy elevates his own achievements by means of athletic imagery, but the reading concludes with an acknowledgment that strength and deliverance have come and will come from God. The story of the prayers of the Pharisee and the tax collector in Luke suggests the perils of ignoring the fundamental truth of Joel 2 and Psalm 65. The Pharisee presumes that his achievements are his alone; the tax collector knows that prayer begins and ends with a cry to God for mercy.

Questions and Thoughts for Reflection

- Read Joel 2:23-32. In the face of tragedy, how can we encourage one another to see with Joel's eyes?
- Read Psalm 65. What in the created world brings words of praise of the Creator to your lips? What ridges and furrows in your life need God's softening?
- Read 2 Timothy 4:6-8, 16-18. What would it look like in your life to run the race God has set before you without striving to outrun others?
- Read Luke 18:9-14. Where might God be inviting your gratitude? How can your gratitude to God lead to tangible love of a neighbor you might have otherwise disregarded?

Retired United Methodist pastor, member of Burnt Factory United Methodist Church, Winchester, Virginia

On sunny days when the air is crisp and the colors spectacular, gratitude flows so easily. Awe, wonder, and thanksgiving easily slip out of our mouths. Even our posture signals our sense of well-being and praise as we experience God's blessings and grace full strength. The psalmist seems to be enjoying this full-strength kind of day. Superlatives describing the character of God jump off the page to remind us, fill us, and encourage us in our own experience of the Almighty One. Our God answers prayer, forgives our brokenness, and even satisfies our longing for intimacy. And there is yet even more: The God we worship provides deliverance and salvation, hope and strength. When we allow this psalm to wash over us, we feel humbled before the expansive nature of our God.

Recently I drove through the "big sky" region of the western United States. The ever-changing vista of thousands of acres of lush, green, ripening grain, from horizon to horizon, set against a backdrop of majestic mountain peaks capped with snow amazed me. What an egregious sin it would be were I to express no gratitude to God in response, to turn away from verse 8 of this psalm as it calls me to stand in awe as I witness God's signs. Or, perhaps, to feel some sense of awe but not remember the One who gives this wonder.

Not all our days lend themselves easily to gratitude. But today may this psalm serve as a call to worship for a week of spiritual work: remembering awe for our God, establishing anew the gratitude that forms the foundation of our faith in Jesus.

Read aloud these verses, holding them in prayer, in silence, in awe.

Among Jesus' teachings on prayer we find this parable of the Pharisee and the tax collector—perhaps a favorite because we all know that we are not Pharisees! Clearly, this Pharisee has several spiritual "growth areas." And yet, it's all too possible that we recognize these growth areas in his prayer because they appear in our own.

At the outset, Jesus identifies in the Pharisee spiritual issues of self-righteousness and contempt for "others." The Pharisee happily steps on the head of the tax collector, so that in contrast, he will appear taller, more praiseworthy, more justified before God. His recital of his own goodness stands out as a poor attempt to hide his fear of personal unworthiness, his death grip on a worldview that has no grace.

This parable gets sticky for us when we recall our tendency to put "others" in groups that are "less than" in our eyes. When we reflect honestly, we thank God that we are *not* members of certain groups (immigrants, specific political adherents, competing companies or fellow-employees, family members, welfare recipients, annoying neighbors, certain nationalities, ethnicities, even whole occupational sets). Much of our culture lauds our contempt, our standing on the heads of "others."

Could this "less-than" posture be a gratitude issue? The Pharisee addresses God and yet sings a hymn of praise not to God but to himself. He asks God for nothing, offers no praise, and defends himself against God's desire for intimacy. His gratitude is blasphemous, suggesting that God has elevated him above all the undesirables around him. How different and humble his prayer and life would be if he were to rediscover the depth of gratitude we were created to give to God alone.

Begin your prayer time by making five statements of gratitude about who God is.

In this parable of contrast, the Pharisee actually asks God to compare and contrast his life with that of the tax collector, hoping for a favorable result. But the resulting contrast reveals both his shallow spirituality and his self-righteousness. Conversely, the tax collector offers a profound seven-word mantra that embraces two significant realities: He is a sinner, broken before God; and the God of mercy is his only hope. Clearly the qualities that drive this second prayer are humility, transparency, and vulnerability, none of which appears in the Pharisee's prayer. This second prayer is not overtly thankful, but gratitude forms the foundation of the tax collector's confessional stance before God.

We have choices to make about the ever-present interplay between light and dark in our lives. We tend to polish brightly the light side of ourselves, while hiding the shadowy dark side from everyone else, even ourselves. In vain we hope that others —especially God!—will not notice the shadow. This dishonesty about ourselves makes gratitude especially difficult to embrace.

In his confessional prayer, the tax collector achieves an honesty and humility about himself that allows the juxtaposition of his confessed sin and God's mercy to be life-giving! His prayer anchors his real life of quiet desperation, which he is powerless to change, in the real mercy of God's almighty power and love.

The tax collector may not name his experience either as grace or gratitude. But as he leaves the Temple, God declares him justified. Perhaps he realizes he has been made "right" before God. His steps are lighter, his breathing more relaxed, for at some level he knows God has heard him yet again, and he is thankful.

Ask God to help you know the depth of God's mercy for you. Feel the darkness recede, and be thankful.

The sports-mania of Western culture quickly brings to mind the image of the raised index finger. We want to be first, not second; winners, not losers; victors now, not next year. Preoccupation with winning dominates more areas than our sports venues. We want to be first in everything: our relationships, our projects at work, our house on the block, and even our church among other churches.

As Paul contemplates his death, he recognizes a change in his life flow: Now his life is a poured-out offering (libation) to God. His amazing journey with God will now end as a blessing *to* God and a blessing *from* God. He couches his enormous gratitude in deeply felt humility and an unspeakable joy.

But talk of being first . . . not Paul. Notice that he fought the good fight but no talk of winning the fight; that he finished the race but no talk of coming in first; he kept the faith but no talk of having the best, most superior faith of all. Well-known for his fits of arrogance and self-focus, this season in Paul's life is differently powered; a spirit of humility brings his gratitude to the forefront. The crown of righteousness that awaits him is not earned but received as a gift.

When grasping for first place gets in the way of serving our Savior, then humility, gratitude, and peace will shun our lives; joy will seem elusive. Our culture despises the concept of "enough." May we witness to our faith by pointing to Jesus, who makes every day more than enough. Thanks be to God!

Talk with God about the contests you are running today. In silence, ponder what it means to be faithful.

Locusts, grasshoppers, fire, invaders, destruction, desolation, dust, death—these do not foretell the future but rather Judah's current-day reality. Devastation and defeat overwhelm, and deportation to Babylon looms. Yet, following his descriptions of ruin in chapter 2, Joel moves toward words of hope. Joel does not shrink from the apparent disconnect between this good God and the devastating plight of God's chosen ones. Joel sees a day when abundance and blessing will return to God's people and their shame cast aside. Indeed, twice Joel speaks for God saying, "My people shall never again be put to shame."

We too experience the challenges of shame: the eroding of our self-worth when the course of our lives has taken a devastating turn. Do bad things happen because we are bad people? Perhaps our shameful embarrassment hides an awareness of our ever-present brokenness and unfaithfulness.

Joel's prophecy pushes beyond the shame issue and seeks to rebuild hope. Joel speaks boldly for God: God's Spirit will return, and many will be touched by that Spirit. The people will gain confidence to dream dreams and see visions. God will again do that which is powerful, unexplainable, magnificent, and bring persons to salvation and wholeness.

Is this not the message we need to know in our own lives today? Joel's words assure us of God's relentless outpouring of the Spirit. Not surprisingly we hear them again on the day of Pentecost; they echo throughout scripture to give us the hope of healing someday soon. The goodness of God will surely be our reality in this life and the next. Thanks be to God!

Ask God to show you how you can bring hope to others today.

The psalmist expresses his deep gratitude to God using the metaphor of water. His imagery reminds me of a dear friend who loved to quip: "A day without rain is like a day without sunshine." From beginning to end, the topic of water flows through scripture. Although water can be out of control with devastating results, water is life-giving, and its absence is cause for alarm.

The psalmist writes that God visits the earth and waters it: two life-giving truths, both literal and metaphoric. God's visitation, God's presence of blessing impacts our lives in so many ways—just like water. God waters us, provides, enriches, blesses. The psalmist gives us the visual image of the earth being enriched by its watering Creator, that we may also see the image of our lives being enriched by our ever-visiting God!

Verse 10 is especially powerful: God waters abundantly—settling, softening, and blessing. I have plenty of furrows and ridges in me, places that are hard and impenetrable. Even in the midst of God's abundant blessings, I can refuse to acknowledge God's power to gently pull down my rigidity, to soften my intractable hardness. What a refreshing, transforming image: God's love pours down on me like rain, and I become pliable and permeable yet again. What a blessing God has for me if I will just let it rain!

If I pause to consider all that lies behind me, I would see what the psalmist sees: deep wagon tracks from the heavy load of God's bounty and richness in my life. How appropriate that this half of the psalm begins with God visiting and ends with shouting and singing for joy. Bring on the rain!

Confess to God your ridges and furrows. Find a place where water flows, sit awhile, and listen for God's life-giving grace.

On this sabbath day in thousands of settings, faithful Christ-followers take their places of leadership to teach, praise, preach, and pray. They have studied, prepared, and centered themselves in the presence of God's Spirit in hopes that the people of God on this day might be led to worship with transforming sincerity. Hopefully, most who gather will participate with enthusiasm and abandon. But some will be distracted and some will only look on or sit with arms folded across their chests, judging all that happens before them.

As Paul concludes this letter to Timothy, his words come from the depths of his spiritual journey with the Lord. He is well-acquainted with onlookers, doubters, detractors, and self-appointed judges. Living boldly as a disciple of Jesus is daunting in our secular and humanistic culture. Many around us look with a wary eye on our devotion to Jesus, our radical commitment to the way of the cross. But Paul cheers us forward: be persistent, proclaim the message. In these closing words, Paul reminds us that God's loyalty to us and our loyalty as messengers are intertwined. Our task as leaders comes in our faithfulness to the God who stands beside us, in our willingness to be servant voices to the truth of God's message.

As we hold God's word in our hands this day, may we be filled with gratitude for this gift and both humble and patient as we teach it and preach it. It will take our whole lifetime to receive the blessing God intends for us. How audacious that God would entrust this powerful message to us! With grateful hearts we embrace it and with glory to God forever and ever we tirelessly proclaim it.

Pray your favorite scripture, acknowledging it as God's gift to you.

Our Joy in God's Righteousness

OCTOBER 24–30, 2016 • ROSEMARY D. GOODEN

Scripture Overview: Habakkuk stands aghast at the "destruction and violence" all around and wonders how justice never seems to conquer. At the end of the reading, God contrasts the proud, whose spirit "is not right in them," with the righteous who live by faith. The psalmist delights in God's righteousness and in the commandments of God; however, he admits that "I am small and despised." The psalmist's "trouble and anguish" appear in Second Thessalonians also, but here the "persecutions and the afflictions" endured by the faithful serve a particular end: They stand as signs of the imminent return of Jesus Christ. In the Gospel reading Jesus tells Zacchaeus, "Today salvation has come to this house," which reminds us that the righteous who live by faith are not necessarily the socially or religiously acceptable.

Questions and Thoughts for Reflection

- Read Habakkuk 1:1-4; 2:1-4. What situations in your life and world cause you to cry out to God, "How long?"?
- Read Psalm 119:137-144. Who have you known who trusts God implicitly? How has that person's example helped you in the past? How might you let it help you in the future?
- Read 2 Thessalonians 1:1-4, 11-12. How will you offer Christ's peace to someone you meet today?
- Read Luke 19:1-10. Jesus' interaction caused Zacchaeus to trust God and straighten out his life. Where and with whom might God be leading you to share with others the heart of Christ?

Episcopal layperson; former lecturer in Modern Church History and Mission, Seabury-Western Theological Seminary, Evanston, Illinois

In today's passage, the beginning of a dialogue between the prophet Habakkuk and God, Habakkuk complains vehemently to God and questions God, who seems to be silent and inattentive in the face of the tyrannical rule of the Chaldeans: "O LORD, how long shall I cry for help, and you will not listen?"

I have questioned God, even railed against God, not only about my own suffering but also about injustice in the world. Perhaps you have done the same. Like the psalmist who desperately cries for deliverance from personal enemies in the fourfold "How long?" of Psalm 13, we question God and wonder where are God's justice and deliverance in an increasingly scary world.

On March 7, 1965, commonly known as "Bloody Sunday," several hundred people were tear-gassed and beaten with billy clubs as they began a nonviolent march for freedom and justice across the Edmund Pettus Bridge to the Alabama state capitol. The march resumed on March 21 and ended March 25, 1965, before the state capitol, where Martin Luther King Jr. delivered a speech that also included a fourfold "How long?":

> How long? Not long, because no lie can live forever.
> How long? Not long, because you still reap what you sow.
> How long? Not long. Because the arm of the moral
> universe is long but it bends toward justice.
> How long? Not long. . . . Our God is marching on.

When we experience injustice, unfairness, and intense personal suffering, let us freely cry out to God in our prayers. Let us also live in hope and wait for God.

O Lord, hear my prayer. When I call, answer me. O Lord, hear my prayer. Come and listen to me. Amen.

Habakkuk positions himself to hear God's response to the dominant question posed in yesterday's reading, "How long?" In his declaration that he will be at his "watchpost" waiting for God, Habakkuk acts as one who lives by faith, demonstrating hope and expectation despite the despair he voices in the first chapter. God's answer reminds Habakkuk and modern readers that God is sovereign and will deal with injustice, suffering, and evil according to God's timetable and as God deems fit.

As we await God's appointed time, we live by faith. And living faithfully is more than mere survival, getting by, or muddling through. We live fully in the face of suffering, persecution, and violence. We live expectantly, knowing that God will answer personally our cry for help and deliverance: "For there is still a vision for the appointed time. . . . It will surely come."

Martin Luther King Jr. and countless women, men, and children endured suffering, persecution, and violence in the struggle for freedom. Many sacrificed their lives for the cause of freedom and justice. Along with King's, the names of forty individuals who were killed between 1954 and 1968 are inscribed on a circular black granite table, which is part of the Civil Rights Memorial in Montgomery, Alabama. Designed by Maya Lin, who also designed the Vietnam Memorial in Washington, D.C., it was dedicated in 1989. Another part of the memorial, a curved water wall, includes an excerpt from King's "I Have a Dream" speech, a paraphrase of the prophet Amos (5:24, KJV): "Let justice roll down like waters, and righteousness like a mighty stream." May we be willing to live by faith in the stream of righteousness.

Gracious and loving God, help me to live by faith. Help me to remember that you are sovereign and will act in your own time and way to bring about justice. Amen.

Our Joy in God's Righteousness   357

In this prayer of lament, the longest psalm in the Psalter, *righteous* is a key word and is repeated five times. The psalmist points us not only to God who is righteous but also to God's justice. Like the prophet Habakkuk, the psalmist complains to God but in a different tone. Rather than cry out "why" and "how long" this lament is contemplative.

The psalmist delights in God's instruction even while facing "trouble and anguish." God responded to Habakkuk's complaint with the words: "The righteous live by their faith" (Hab. 2:4). Similarly, in today's passage the psalmist prays, "Give me understanding that I may live." In *The Message*, Eugene Peterson translates verses 143 and 144 this way:

Even though troubles came down on me hard,
your commands always gave me delight.
The way you tell me to live is always right;
help me understand it so I can live to the fullest.

Psalm 119 is a hymn of praise for the law. The psalmist's delight is in God's law, the source of understanding. In Psalm 1 the psalmist describes the happiness of the righteous: "Their delight is in the law of the LORD, and on his law they meditate day and night" (v. 2). In the same manner, the psalmist in today's passage speaks of delight in God's law and of the joy in keeping God's law, even during suffering.

To delight in God's commandments when trouble and anguish come over us is a gift from God, not something we conjure up on our own. This disposition goes beyond optimism and mere positive thinking. The word of God and Christ the living Word give us hope and encouragement to be faithful and to live in hope, especially during times of trouble and anguish.

Lord, you are my song and my praise: All my hope comes from God. Lord, you are my song and my praise: You are the wellspring of life. Amen.

Grace to you and peace from God our Father and the Lord Jesus Christ." What a way to begin a letter! Perhaps, like me, you receive voluminous e-mails daily, many unwanted and unsolicited. Yet I also receive personal notes that, despite the intervention of a machine, provide a sense of connection to distant friends and colleagues. Some of these letters close with "Grace and peace."

Today a common practice in many Christian churches is "the exchange of peace," or "passing the peace." In my Episcopal church, we exchange peace with the words: "Peace be with you" or "The peace of the Lord be with you" as we clasp hands, hug, or even plant a "holy kiss" on the cheek of the other person. At the end of the service, a deacon sends us into the world with the words: "Go in peace to love and serve the Lord." In offering peace to others, we also point them to the incarnate Christ, who is our peace.

The church in Thessalonica grows and flourishes, despite problems and hostility from non-Christian Thessalonians. What an inspiring portrait of a Christian church! Paul is moved to offer prayers of thanksgiving to God for this vital community. Like the Thessalonian Christians, we too can flourish through grace freely given to us by God through Jesus Christ. We are enabled to live a life of faith, love, and steadfastness, especially during times of suffering, hostility, and persecution. Grace renews, transforms, and leads us to wholeness.

Just think of what could happen not only in our congregations but in our world if we demonstrated abundant faith in God and love for one another.

In what ways do you extend grace and peace to all, not just to members of your church but especially to those who suffer and the strangers you encounter daily? Before attending your next worship service, reflect on the practice of exchanging the peace.

The first chapter of Paul's second letter to the Thessalonians begins and ends with grace: "grace and peace to you" in a salutation and the "grace of our God" in a closing prayer. Paul often included prayers in his letters to the churches he established. In yesterday's reading Paul indicated that he continues to offer prayers of thanksgiving to God for the exemplary faith, love, and steadfastness of the Thessalonians.

Recently I complimented an elderly woman in my neighborhood on her dark brown shearling coat with matching hat. She responded, "Thanks for the encouragement." Her comment prompted me to think about compliments in a new way. Indeed, sincere compliments are a form of encouragement, as is intercessory prayer.

In today's reading, Paul includes a prayer of encouragement to the Christians in Thessalonica, "asking that our God will make you worthy of his call and will fulfill by his power every good resolve and work of faith." Their steadfastness, love, and faith continue to grow, even in the face of persecution, because of Paul's pastoral ministry, which includes intercessory prayer. We too are called to intercessory prayer.

Like the Thessalonians, we need encouragement and prayer as we seek to live out our call to discipleship, especially in our vocation and daily life ministries. Through God's grace we can reflect the same type of commitment and thus honor God, even as we suffer and face difficulty.

Thank God for family, friends, and others who have encouraged you in your journey of faith. Think about and pray for those who need your prayers of intercession.

On his way to Jerusalem, Jesus encounters in Jericho a throng eager to see him, a familiar scene in Luke. Jesus also encounters a rich tax collector, also familiar. In the preceding chapter in Luke, Jesus has told two parables: the parable of the Pharisee and the tax collector and the parable of the rich ruler.

Today's reading carries a tone of immediacy, even urgency, in the narrative as well as in the action itself. Aware that Jesus is "passing through" Jericho, the rich tax collector Zacchaeus runs ahead and stakes out a strategic position in a sycamore tree. Its wide, low branches and short trunk make it easy for a short man like Zacchaeus to climb. As Habakkuk positioned himself at his watchpost to receive God's word, so Zacchaeus positions himself above the crowd to see Jesus as he passes by. Miraculously, Jesus notices him poised above the crowd. When Jesus reaches him, he looks up and tells him to "hurry and come down; for I must stay at your house today."

Of all the people in the crowd, Jesus fixes his eyes on Zacchaeus! And despite Zacchaeus's occupation, not to mention his reputation and position in the community, Jesus invites himself to his house for a meal.

Jesus' willingness to dine with Zacchaeus extends his concern to everyone in the crowd, especially outcasts, the marginalized, and those on the fringes of society, including the rich. Jesus looks directly into our eyes, seeks us out of the crowd, and invites himself into our lives. By welcoming Jesus and responding affirmatively to his invitation, we can know the salvation, grace, and wholeness that Christ has generously given to everyone, even those who have caused our suffering.

Gracious and loving God, as you have welcomed me, help me to invite and welcome others, especially the marginalized and dispossessed, to your gospel feast. Amen.

Our Joy in God's Righteousness   361

As Zacchaeus hurries down from his perch in the sycamore tree and welcomes Jesus to his house, everyone witnessing this scene starts murmuring. We can hear them now: "What kind of man would go to the house of a chief tax collector for dinner? Is he out of his mind? Who does Zacchaeus think he is?" Just imagine the scene.

During the time of the Roman Empire, a tax collector, or publican, was an outcast for several reasons. A type of entrepreneur, the chief tax collector contracted to collect taxes and tolls and hired local residents to assist him. He was responsible for paying the government but was also free to collect extra taxes. Such a system invited abuse and resulted not only in the tax collector's making a profit but also in corruption, theft, and fraud becoming part of the system. Jews rejected tax collectors because in the course of their work, they came in contact with ritually unclean people.

Despite Zacchaeus's ill-gotten wealth, tainted occupation, and undignified sitting in a tree, Jesus seeks him out of the crowd, showering him with loving attention. Jesus recognizes an outcast, whose entire family probably suffered shame, embarrassment, and rejection because of his occupation. His acknowledgment of Zacchaeus and his family's human worth and dignity fills their need for Jesus' redeeming grace.

Zacchaeus repents, promising to give to the poor and to make restitution to those whom he has cheated. Jesus then tells Zacchaeus, "Today salvation has come to this house." For Zacchaeus and for all of us, the day of salvation brings transformation, deliverance, and new life in Christ.

Holy and life-giving God, thank you for seeing us in the crowd and offering us the gift of salvation through Jesus Christ. Help us humbly to repent and follow you daily. Amen.

A Place in the Choir

OCTOBER 31–NOVEMBER 6, 2016 • JONATHAN C. WALLACE

Scripture Overview: The rebuilding of the Jerusalem temple became a test of God's promise. The prophetic word of Haggai insists on courage and labor, reminding the people that God's Spirit is already present among them and points toward the future. In Second Thessalonians, some Christians have grown extremely agitated by claims that the "day of the Lord" has already come. The passage recalls what Jesus and God have already accomplished and insists that God's future may also be trusted. Jesus' response to the Sadducees confutes them, not merely by its cleverness (their question also is clever) but by its truth. The eschatological future cannot be understood simply as an extension of the present, except in one profound sense: God is Lord both of the present and of the future. This profound truth demands the praise to which Psalm 145 calls all creatures.

Questions and Thoughts for Reflection

- Read Haggai 1:15b–2:9. The people return home from exile—but home has changed. When have you returned "home" to a different setting than the one you left? How did you feel the changes?
- Read Psalm 145:1-5, 17-21. How fully do you participate in worship? In what areas are you more reserved?
- Read 2 Thessalonians 2:1-5, 13-17. The phrase "shaken in mind" may be better translated as "shaken out of mind," implying great distress. What basics and foundation do you return to when you are "shaken out of mind"?
- Read Luke 20:27-38. The Sadducees miss the core of who Jesus is. When has an "old" religious mind-set blocked your ability to see and hear a "new thing"?

Pastor, First Presbyterian Church, Foley, Alabama

Ah, the "good old days"! How we miss them! In a rapidly changing world, nothing is more appealing than memories, real or imagined, of greater glory than what lies before us at the moment. How can our present attempts or future dreams possibly measure up to the "good old days"?

We are not the first faith leaders to deal with the impossible expectations of an idealized past. Consider the rather put-upon prophet Haggai. Haggai lived in the first few decades of the Israelite return from exile. Visions of a glorious return to their land have sustained the people whose hopes are dashed by scarred fields, ruined homes, and the Temple in rubble. No attempt at rebuilding, especially the Temple, measures up to the splendor of days gone by.

Haggai gives his people a word that's worth hearing today as we face similar reviews of our efforts. He reminds them that God's interest focuses less on good beginnings than on good endings. Though the ancient promises may not be fulfilled in their entirety at the moment, God remains steadfast and continues to uphold those promises.

We do not fear. The future is still unfolding, and it rests in God's hands. Though things may not be as they once were, we acknowledge that with God (as the great baseball philosopher Yogi Berra noted): "The game ain't over till it's over!"

Despite it all, God stays with us. God brought the people out of exile and continues to work to bring us out of our exiles. The good news: Even when we return and find a world we no longer recognize, God is not through with us yet. With God, the "good old days" are yet to come!

Gracious God, may I bask in the glow of your work in the present, knowing that the best is yet to come. Amen.

ALL SAINTS DAY

I am uncomfortable with the idea of saints. Hearing the word *saint* conjures up images of serious-looking people dressed in robes with huge golden halos encircling their heads. Saints stand taller than us; they're different from us, possessing gifts we cannot hope to call our own and achieving things we cannot ever hope to attain. Strange as it may seem, however, Jesus' most famous sermon may help us appreciate the saint that is in us all.

The sermon resembles Matthew's Sermon on the Mount. In Luke, however, Jesus does not preach from on "high." He does not preach in the third person: "Blessed are the poor, . . . the mourning," and so on. In Luke, Jesus speaks from a level place. He sits among the suffering as a healer and a herald of good news. He speaks in the second person, as we do when we look someone right in the eye: "Blessed are you who are poor." In Matthew, Jesus seems to speak abstractly. In Luke, Jesus speaks as someone who takes the people's pain upon himself. He moves among them, talks with them, touches them. He stands on level ground with them.

That is what saints are: People who stand on level ground with those who are hurting, look them in the eye, and have the audacity to tell them they are blessed. Saints bring blessing to people by taking them seriously and tending to their needs. Saints are those who by word and deed dare to take sides because they believe that God sides with love and mercy. May we do to others as we would have them do to us. Saints alive!

Holy God, may we have the audacity to stand with the poor, the hungry, and those who weep. Amen.

The priestly Sadducees are rich, educated, and serious. They reject the notion of the resurrection of the dead and view Jesus' teachings on that subject as dangerous. In an attempt to discredit him, they pose a question designed to humiliate him publicly: What if a woman marries a man with six brothers, and her husband dies with no heir? According to the law of Moses she marries the eldest brother. Then he dies, and so on until she marries all seven brothers at one time or another. In the resurrection, whose wife will she be?

Their question is so absurd that it would be hard to stifle a snicker! Were these brothers accident-prone or suicidal? Who was this woman? Lizzie Borden? Typhoid Mary?

The fact that the Sadducees have no sense of humor about this matter makes it even funnier. Jesus plays along by saying that all our social arrangements pale in comparison to what God has in store for us. God's relationship with us will still exist when everything has turned to dust. Nothing, not even death, will separate us from God. That is all we need to know.

Encountering the gospel of Jesus Christ requires a sense of humor. The more serious we become about limiting the bounds of God's working, the sillier we look. The farther we extend the "rules" to exclude others, the farther we move from the kingdom. How can we not laugh? What could be funnier than an uneducated carpenter from Nazareth promising the things he does? What could be funnier than seeing serious people pelt Jesus with questions and then look embarrassed when Jesus answers them? All shall be well if we laugh at ourselves, quit trying to embarrass and humiliate our neighbors, let God be God, and see how it all turns out!

O God, may your upside-down kingdom bring me joy and laughter. Amen.

The fact that we have a hymnbook in the center of our scriptures has always impressed me. That placement makes sense to me as a pastor. Poll any random sample of people leaving the sanctuary on Sunday morning. Most won't remember the Bible verses that were read or have the first idea of what the sermon topic was. But they will tell you every hymn that was sung—and offer a strong opinion about them!

We seem wired for music, and the Christian faith places it at the center of its worship life. The Psalms capture the various moods, convictions, hopes, and dreams (both realized and dashed) of the people of Israel in the form of song. Put into writing for the first time in the Babylonian exile, these songs helped preserve the faith of the Israelite people and gave them strength in the midst of the most trying of circumstances. Like any hymnbook, some songs are not well known, but others have been written into our very souls.

Psalm 145 may not be one that we know by heart, but it begins an important section of this hymnbook that is dedicated to the praise and adoration of God. The psalmists acknowledge that we may have our laments and complaints. But in the end, God is our creator. Therefore, the worship and praise of God must be at the center of our lives.

How do we do that? Perhaps the last verse of Psalm 145 gives us a good place to start. We don't have to have all the answers. We don't have to be particularly talented. However, our mouths can speak the praise of the Lord. We can sing God's praises. It may not seem like much, but those kinds of songs have a way of catching on. It's the kind of song that can change the world!

Lord of life, may I sing your praises and encourage others to take up the song. Amen.

The first chapel service I attended while in seminary is a favorite memory of mine. My classmates and I filed into the sanctuary after our first morning of tackling New Testament Greek. The organist launched into one of the great hymns of the church, and the gathered body stood to sing. However, I hesitated. After that first class, I did not feel at all sure that I belonged there. My academic talents and spiritual gifts did not measure up to those of my peers. I thought I was kidding myself by even participating in that worship service. I took the posture of a bystander, content to let the "real" students and future ministers perform the tasks of worship.

As the voices of the congregation rose to the familiar tune, I became aware of the two people seated next to me. One had a pure, beautiful, and trained voice. The other person was . . . well, not nearly as talented. His gift lay in areas other than singing! However, that did not stop him from offering his best. He lifted his song every bit as loudly and confidently as our more polished colleague. After listening to a few verses of his singing, I shrugged my shoulders and joined in with everything I had.

The singer of Psalm 145 would have approved. He suggests that worship and praise of God is not limited to the professionals. God reigns over all people and all things. Therefore, every person and every thing finds its destiny in praising God. Oh, we need leaders, those who possess talents and gifts to help us. But in the end, praise and worship involves us all. In worship, God is the only audience—and God expects our participation, not perfection. Worship is not for bystanders. This God is not a God of the few. God is Lord of all. That means we all have places in the choir.

Loving God, accept my offering of thanks and praise as I lift my voice in song. I give you all that I am. Amen.

When Franklin D. Roosevelt looked over the crowd gathered to hear his first inaugural address in 1933, one emotion dominated the nation: fear. An unprecedented economic collapse, an agricultural disaster, and the rise of totalitarian regimes overseas combined to produce suffering on a scale beyond anything our nation had ever experienced. It seemed like the end of the world. Roosevelt stared out at the crowd and said, "The only thing we have to fear is fear itself."

Paul addresses the Thessalonian Christians fervently. The Greek words used in this passage evoke the image of the community being "shaken out of their minds." They are quite distraught, perhaps even bordering on institutional paralysis. They too look at the signs of their times and feel deeply confused about what they see. They think the end of the world is upon them. They are deeply afraid.

Though Paul never uses the familiar refrain found in other places in scripture, his response reflects the same comforting exhortation that comes to us again and again: "Fear not." That is not a statement of denial. Some situations that we find troubling lie before us, making us understandably anxious. Our misunderstandings and fears, however, create more danger than the challenges we face. Mortals can do great damage in the name of fear. Paul seems to sense this as he admonishes his congregation to remember what they have been taught: The future lies in God's hands.

Our circumstances may feel like the end of the world. Truthfully, worlds end all the time. What remains is God's love and the hope that we have a place in God's future. After all, hope is stronger than fear! So let us comfort our hearts and "strengthen them in every good work and word."

O God, may I believe in your truth, standing firm and holding fast to the proclamation of the good news. Amen.

A professor of mine once said that there are no bad questions, only bad answers. I used to believe that. However, as I write this meditation, election season has rolled round again. I deeply respect the democratic process that resides at the heart of our form of government. However, I have a hard time keeping my cynicism in check with all the negative ads. In the process, we do not learn from the questions why someone favors a particular candidate, party, or policy. The questions posed simply humiliate those with whom we disagree. We ask bad questions—questions to discover how well opponents fall into rhetorical traps.

This episode from Luke's Gospel shows one way that Jesus handled that kind of situation. A group of Sadducees approach him with a question they hope will belittle him in the eyes of his adoring fans. Jesus responds by calmly reminding them of what their own law says about the subject of resurrection. We gain some satisfaction from Jesus turning the tables on his opponents and giving them a taste of their own medicine. As the Gospel notes, "They no longer dared to ask him another question" (20:40).

I believe this text also teaches a lesson about the kinds of questions we ask. Jesus calls us into relationship with one another. He does not seem to care about winning arguments. The questions we choose to ask each other and God may reflect more clearly the character of our heart and our commitment to following Jesus' teaching—even more than the answers we desperately want to advance in the public square.

Knowledge and passion are wonderful virtues. Humility and respect for others are even more precious in God's eyes.

God, may I ask the questions that lead me to faithfulness and community. Amen.

Telling a New Story

NOVEMBER 7–13, 2016 • ASHLEE ALLEY

Scripture Overview: Isaiah 65:17-25 looks toward God's creation of "new heavens and a new earth." Jerusalem itself is not to be restored but created anew, a place in which life will be revered and protected and in which God will permit no harm to any of creation. The New Testament lessons remind us of the reality—the sometimes painful reality—of the present. Second Thessalonians 3:6-13 warns against the disorderly conduct of those who believe that the newness of the eschatological future permits them license in the present. Luke 21:5-19 adds an element of sobriety to the singing of new songs and the expectation of a new future. The faithful are called to bear witness to God's future in the present, precisely when the new future cannot be seen and even when it seems most improbable.

Questions and Thoughts for Reflection

* Read Isaiah 65:17-25. How does the promise of the new heavens and new earth encourage to tell a new story?
* Read Psalm 118. Which story will you tell? The one of your captivity . . . or the one of your salvation?
* Read 2 Thessalonians 3:6-13. Where in your life do you need to be more disciplined so that you do not deceive yourself?
* Read Luke 21:5-19. What signs from God are you seeking instead of trusting in what you know about God's character?

Clergy Recruitment and Development Coordinator, Great Plains Annual Conference of The United Methodist Church, Lincoln, Nebraska

It's easy in our darkest hour to despair. We rehearse the tribulations, trials, and troubles that bring us to the height of our pain. I suppose something helpful comes from telling these stories in that we confess our sin, which may have conspired in drawing us to the depths. The prophet Isaiah has plenty of words that express the pain of the depths. Yet, these words from Isaiah don't rehearse the past; they claim the future.

The drama of salvation for God's people takes shape through this vision of new heavens and a new earth! The pain of the past, of death, hunger and strife, are passing away. Isaiah's words inspire and redeem! They remove the sting of the past—the weeping, the babies gone too soon, the sacrifice without benefit—and tell a compelling new story that becomes the vision of the people of Israel when thinking about the future. The vision of the new heavens and new earth culminates in Revelation 21:1-2—a life that awaits us when we endure through our present suffering.

Isaiah's vision reminds us that God hears our call, and we have a new story to tell. Though our familiar story of trouble often springs to our lips, the story of new heavens and new earth bring purpose to our pain. Our passage today reminds us that what we see is not the end of the story. May this compelling vision give us courage and strength to face more days, each one bringing us closer to the new heavens and new earth.

God, I rejoice that you redeem and reform all my pain. May I glimpse your restored creation today and tell that story. Amen.

As we would expect from a prophet, much of the book of Isaiah contains warnings and pronouncements about the sins of the people. The prophet has warned them of the coming destruction that results from their sin. Yet the words in Isaiah 65 offer a new vision for the kingdom to come, one that can stir the heart of even those most desperate in their circumstances. Existence as previously known will be turned on its ear. The images of the wolf and the lamb lying together and the lion eating straw like the ox reveal that in the new creation, the people can expect a rebirth of their human nature. No longer will the inclination of their evil and destructive hearts possess them, but, rather, the prince of peace will reign. The image exists not just for the hearers of Isaiah, but for anyone who hears the words. Our natures are reborn; our hearts will host the Prince of Peace.

Beyond wolves and lambs, lions and oxen, one other creature in Isaiah's list doesn't benefit from the new creation. Isaiah proclaims that the serpent will eat dust. Genesis 3:14 sealed the snake's future: "Upon your belly you shall go, and dust you shall eat all the days of your life."

That proclamation by God came as the consequence for the serpent's deception of humanity. God still hates deceit. When we think that sin must rule in our hearts, we've not told the story of God's promise for the new heavens and new earth. God's promise holds power. May the story we tell be the promise of new heavens. That story has the power to defeat the deception of our hearts until promise becomes reality.

Powerful God, grant me peace as I await the new creation. Strengthen my heart as you hear my prayer. Amen.

The single most important event of the Old Testament, the story that the Hebrew people told about themselves, was that of the Exodus, their release from captivity in Egypt. They go to Egypt willingly because of famine in their country; God uses Joseph to prepare for the famine (Gen. 37–41). They become captives as their numbers threaten Pharaoh. Perhaps because humanity seems destined to repeat history if we don't retell it, the Israelites choose to retell their release story in their worship. Psalm 118 closes what is identified traditionally as the *Hallel* collection. *Hallel*, as in *hallelujah*, "Praise the Lord."

Verses 1-4 praise God for the foreverness of God's love, "God's steadfast love endures forever!" And the opening verses give way to a recounting of deliverance by God. God answers the psalmist's cry of distress by setting him in a broad place. Surrounded on all sides and pushed hard to the point of falling, the psalmist triumphs with the Lord on his side.

It is important to repeat this truth because God's people will face captivity again in Babylon. Through the recitation of Psalm 118, they choose their story. Rather than focusing on captivity, they focus on praising God forever and remembering God's faithfulness.

We all have stories of captivity in our lives. We are captive to our pain, our families, our choices. And sometimes, things that we had no control over tie us to a life in captivity. But the people of God choose to remember and recite the story of God's faithfulness, not the years of captivity. Perhaps we can join in their refrain and "Praise the Lord" as well.

O God, I praise you because you deliver us from our captivity, both individual and corporate. I remember that you release me from that which binds me and for that I say, "Praise the Lord! [Your] steadfast love endures forever!" Amen.

The psalmist praises God for being his salvation. The verses prior recount the many ways divine salvation has come. God has been the psalmist's refuge, his strength and protection, and now his saving help. What astonishes is not that God has helped but that God has helped when situations looked impossible.

I suppose we look for help to come in certain ways. We want to be plucked out of our difficult circumstances, but often we receive strength in the midst of them. The psalmist calls to mind that the Lord's salvation didn't come as he would have thought. He uses the illustration of a stone that is rejected by builders. Perhaps it was too large. Or too small. Or not square enough. Thus, it sits on a pile, waiting for someone else to pick it up or toss aside. But in God's perspective, that rejected stone becomes the cornerstone, thus anchoring the rest of the building. Jesus mentions this verse and refers to himself as that cornerstone.

These words from Psalm 118 remind us that the story we read isn't the full story. What may look like captivity becomes an occasion for rescue. What looks like imperfection can become the foundation for the way forward. Verse 25 even recalls that while God has already rescued, our need for salvation is ongoing.

We are brought through our difficulty with words of praise on our lips. Perhaps that ability to praise God in the midst of our trials is the source of our salvation. We've got a story to tell. May it be the story of our salvation.

God, so often I feel the need of a savior. In the midst of my trouble, I recognize that you have already rescued me and you will do it again. Praise the Lord! Amen.

The author of Second Thessalonians surely takes the church to task for its laziness. He tells the faithful to "keep away from believers who are living in idleness." Ostracism: that seems a pretty harsh admonition for laziness.

As always, there is more to the story. While First Thessalonians is in response to the church's looking for signs of the Lord's return, Second Thessalonians is written in response to the church's living as if he had already come again. The epistle writer cautions the church against an untrue story that some seem to be living out of, a story that implies that because Jesus will come again soon, they don't need to plan for the future. They take advantage of others' generosity, living undisciplined lives and knowing that someone else will meet their needs.

How tempting it is to tell the version of the story that benefits us the most! Christ has commanded us to deal generously with others. But at what point does our self-talk become deception? When does our deception—even of ourselves—begin to separate us from God and from others?

In Second Thessalonians, the people have crossed that line. Their undisciplined lives have become a stumbling block for the community, and they are in danger of being given the cold shoulder. The writer advises that those who can take care of themselves, do so. Discipline teaches us what it means to be a disciple. May we be honest in our work as we face the true story about ourselves.

God, I confess that sometimes I tell my story in the way that benefits me the most, even if it is deceptive. I pray that I would see the truth about myself and others more clearly and, in doing so, would honor you with my discipline. Amen.

Wow! What beautiful work! It's amazing that someone possessed the skill to make this!" I overheard this comment when visiting the grand cathedral of Notre Dame in Paris. Yes, it is indeed admirable, but I could not shake the feeling that we tourists had missed the point. While it represents the artistry of a skilled worker, anyone willing to look beneath the surface at the art itself can see the narrative of scripture and find the story of the world's redemption. The tourist saw the signs and missed the point.

Perhaps that explains Jesus' animation in this passage when people focus on beautiful stones rather than on his transformative story and work. They see the stones of the Temple and admire their beauty. Jesus' words of caution surely catch them off guard: "The days will come when not one stone will be left upon another." He may have intended this statement to serve as a warning so that they would not abandon their faith in him as the Messiah when the day of the Temple's destruction arrived.

Jesus meets their natural questions of when and how with words to this effect: "Trust me. Listen to me. Persevere." Jesus knows that other stories will creep in and try to supersede the story of his return. He warns them about following after false messiahs who claim to usher in a new age.

How easily we explain away difficulties! How tempting it is to look for signs as a means to control our fears! But the story we must heed is the one that reminds us that troubles befalling us are not without the promise of Jesus' presence. May we have the eyes to see more deeply the transformative story of Jesus.

God, I am often tempted to look for signs of what is to come in order to control that which I cannot know. Give me the faith to trust you when difficulties arise. May I see beyond my present circumstances. Amen.

It seems that every year as Hollywood looks for another story to tell, they find a summer blockbuster that narrates the cataclysmic destruction of the world. Perhaps the writers take their plotlines from these words of scripture: natural disasters, political persecutions, famine, and epidemics are voiced by Jesus himself as threats to the lives of his listeners. But Jesus speaks to their fears through a bigger and more powerful story than the most vicious peril.

Jesus doesn't speak magic words that remove the people from their circumstances. In fact, he tells them not to prepare words in advance if they get taken before a court and put on trial for their faith. Jesus' words of encouragement help them realize that the absence of difficulty is not the mark of faithfulness. Difficulties are guaranteed. And the difficulties don't mean that they are experiencing punishment. As they await deliverance from their present (and future) problems, Jesus admonishes them to receive what they encounter with a posture of openness to being rescued by God's hand. He even goes so far as to say that not a hair on their head will be lost.

What a bold statement! We know that people have and will lose their lives due to persecution, disease, and other disasters. His words suggest that we hold fast to gain our lives, which reorients our perspective so that we can remember the deeper reality of life spent with God both now and in eternity. May we hold fast, living our earthly lives shaped by that hope; for it is in doing so that we truly learn to live. That story carries a better plotline than any Hollywood blockbuster!

God, I trust that you will give me words to speak in times of difficulty, and wisdom and strength to endure whatever comes my way. May I hold fast and gain true life. Amen.

A Different Kind of King

NOVEMBER 14–20, 2016 • SARAH PURYEAR

Scripture Overview: Each of the passages for this week addresses the ends served by divine power. Jeremiah characterizes kingship by wisdom, justice, and safety. The exercise of kingly power is on behalf of God's people rather than against them. The reading from Colossians praises the cosmic dimensions of Christ whose exaltation is not an end in itself, for the task of Christ is one of reconciliation. The goal of Christ's kingship moves to center stage in the passage from Luke. The bystanders and one of the criminals executed with Jesus know what it means to be a king, so they taunt Jesus with the demand that he use his power to save himself. For Jesus, however, a king is not one who saves himself but one who saves others.

Questions and Thoughts for Reflection

- Read Jeremiah 23:1-6. What experiences do you recall of leaders in various arenas not being wise shepherds of the people and the people's resources?
- Read Luke 1:68-79. The song of Zechariah is this-worldly *and* political. In what ways does the song encourage you to view the baby in the manger in a different light?
- Read Colossians 1:11-20. How has Jesus revealed himself as your king this past year?
- Read Luke 23:33-43. Jesus came as a different king, a different kind of messiah than people expected. Recall a time when God's response in a situation differed from your expectation.

Associate priest, St. George's Episcopal Church, Nashville, Tennessee

This coming Sunday we mark the close of the church calendar. Once again we have walked through the events of Christ's life, death, and resurrection, and the life of the church. This cycle concludes with the Sunday known as "Christ the King" or "Reign of Christ." Over the course of this week, our readings will re-present the story of how God in Jesus fulfilled his promise to send the true king, not only for the people of Israel but for the whole world.

We close the church year with a reminder of the very beginning of the biblical story. The prophet Jeremiah tells us that God will gather the "remnant of my flock" and return them to their land where they shall "be fruitful and multiply." This promise echoes God's original intention for humanity from Genesis 1:28. God created us in love and placed us in a world where we could flourish and live into our identity as divine image-bearers.

When God called the people of Israel to be the chosen, God intended that they would live into this full-bodied vision. By the time of Jeremiah, however, the people of Israel and Judah have strayed from God's desires for them. In these verses, God's wrath extends particularly to those who shepherd the people, the leadership who has scattered the flock. But God reaffirms a steadfast love for the "scattered sheep," promising them a way of return to the fold.

God wants us to grow into the fullness of who God created us to be. In what areas of our lives do we see ourselves coming alive, aware of God's presence and of the divine gifts given? In what areas of our lives do we feel diminished by fear, distraction, or selfishness? May we find greater freedom to embrace the abundant life God intends for us.

Lord, help me to live into your vision for my life that I may bear fruit that reveals your glory. Amen.

By the time of Jeremiah, the people of Israel and Judah have seen more than their fair share of bad kings, who have ranged from the merely lousy to the downright diabolical. With a few notable exceptions such as David, Hezekiah, and Josiah, their leaders excel in their unfaithfulness to God and their shocking treatment of the people. These developments don't surprise God. Back in 1 Samuel 6 when the people had clamored for a king like the nations around them, God had warned them of a king's likelihood of exploiting them. God mentions that by asking for a king, they are rejecting God as their true king. At the people's insistence, God grants the demand.

In today's verses God expresses anger and dismay with the kings who have so thoroughly failed their people. Rather than saying, "I told you so" and leaving them to their own devices, God promises to intervene, removing these bad leaders and appointing good ones in their place. God will send kings who, like David, will rule like shepherds rather than tyrants. The "righteous Branch" of David will tend the people with compassion and justice. He will not seek his own comfort at the people's expense; instead, he will "execute justice and righteousness in the land." This king will create a safe haven for the people. Most importantly, he will faithfully serve the God who has appointed him king.

Of all the images that God chooses as a descriptor in the Bible, that of shepherd speaks the most comfort. How does the image of God as shepherd speak to you today? How are you in need of God's tending, care, and compassion? Invite God to shepherd you today.

Lord, remind me of your shepherd's heart toward me; help me recognize the good pastures into which you lead me; and give me wisdom to tend with compassion and justice those you've entrusted to me. Amen.

Centuries after the time of Jeremiah, the people still await the shepherd king God had promised. They have returned from exile to their homeland but still feel displaced, for God has not spoken to them through the prophets for many years, and the promised Messiah has not arrived. The people still remember the ancient prophecy, but its memory raises poignant and painful questions: Will the Messiah, the one who will save us, ever show up, or has God forgotten God's promises to us?

At the opening of Luke, Zechariah bursts into song, answering those long-held questions with a resounding word of hope: God has remembered, and the Messiah is on his way! The "mighty savior" is about to arrive, and Zechariah's newborn son will prepare the way for him. God remains faithful to God's promises after all and will deliver the people. Zechariah likens this deliverance to the sun's rising after a night so long and dark that he has wondered if it would ever rise again.

Perhaps an area in our lives feels like a place where we "sit in darkness . . . in the shadow of death"—an unanswered prayer, an estranged relationship, or a persistent feeling of restlessness. We long to leave this sense of exile behind and see God's promises come true. Yet, as time goes by and nothing changes, we wonder if God has forgotten us. In times like these, Zechariah's song invites us to recall the times when we too have burst into a song of thankfulness because of God's saving help. May we trust that the same God who inspired Zechariah's song will give us reason to sing once again.

Lord, when I feel like I'm in exile, help me to believe in your tender mercies toward me. When I feel like I am sitting in darkness, guide me into the way of peace. Amen.

The Messiah did indeed come, fulfilling God's promises; but he proved to be different from what people had expected. As in the time of Samuel, they think that having a king made to their liking will solve all problems, but God intends to send a king who will transcend all expectations. This king will do something greater than overthrowing the Romans; he would deal fully and finally with more ancient enemies, the ones that have lurked and prowled and devoured since the garden of Eden—the enemies of sin and death.

To accomplish this, God's appointed king will submit himself to humanity's sinfulness; he will let them do their worst to him, and then, rather than taking revenge for their cruelty, he will forgive them. He will offer himself up to the punishment they deserve and open a way of freedom from sin and death.

In Luke 23, we see Jesus living out this call to be the suffering king as he hangs upon the cross. Bystanders mock him with ironic taunts: "He saved others; let him save himself if he is the Messiah of God, his chosen one!" They cannot comprehend that precisely because Jesus *is* the Messiah, he refrains from using his power in such a limited and self-serving way. Most who witness his crucifixion consider it the definitive sign that he isn't their king; but it is there upon the cross that Jesus delivers his people and restores the rightful rule of God.

When we are tempted to think that a king made to our liking will solve our problems, may we embrace our suffering king— God's perfect plan of salvation for us.

Lord, forgive me for trying to remake you in my image; help me to see you in your true glory—as the king who gave his life for me. Amen.

Few who witness Jesus' crucifixion understand that despite his ignoble death Jesus is in fact the true king. The disciples themselves, though they have heard Jesus say multiple times that he will suffer, die, and rise again, do not hold on to hope during his crucifixion. Instead, most of them flee in fear, afraid that their association with Jesus will lead them to a similar fate.

As often happens in the Gospels, the person whom we least expect to "get it" has eyes of faith to see who Jesus really is. One of the criminals crucified beside Jesus recognizes that he is the "King of the Jews," as the sign above his head proclaims. This nameless criminal believes that contrary to all appearances, Jesus will usher in a new kingdom, and he asks to be part of it in some small way: "Jesus, remember me when you come into your kingdom."

Surely this criminal, sentenced to death for his crime, wouldn't be at the top of most kings' list of recruits. But Jesus does not scoff at his request; Jesus speaks a word of promise and of hope: "Truly I tell you, today you will be with me in Paradise."

Once again our king operates by a different standard when it comes to welcoming people into the kingdom. To enter Jesus' kingdom, we don't need wealth or social standing or power or even righteousness; all we need is faith in who he is and what he has done for us. May we have faith like this criminal, who was the first to be welcomed into Jesus' kingdom.

King Jesus, remember me, even when I forget you; remember me when I lose faith in you; remember me when I run away like the disciples. In your mercy, welcome me into your kingdom—not because of my merit but because of your passion. Amen.

Colossians 1 provides a magnificent conclusion to the church calendar and to our reflections on Christ's reign. Now that we have walked through the story in detail, Paul takes a step back and offers a glimpse of the bigger picture. In all the twists and turns of the biblical story, God's intention to rescue us from sin and death never wavers. Through this king named Jesus, God has woven together a master plan to save all creation.

As in all his letters, Paul tries to help his readers better understand what God has done for them in Christ. In Christ, Paul says, God has "rescued us from the power of darkness and transferred us into the kingdom of his beloved Son, in whom we have redemption, the forgiveness of sins." Here Paul focuses on forgiveness of sins as the inheritance of those who have entered Jesus' kingdom. Forgiveness is the trademark of this king who brings his people back from exile, who tends them with compassion like a shepherd, who prays that they receive forgiveness for their very worst cruelty toward him. His kingdom is not a place of darkness, guilt, and punishment but of light, freedom, and forgiveness.

Paul may paint a grand picture for us, but he also describes a practical reality for us as Christians. We can turn to our king to receive his gift of forgiveness whenever we go astray. We can release any burdens of guilt and live in the freedom he won for us. We can represent his kingdom to the world by offering forgiveness to those who have hurt us. Thanks be to God for the inheritance King Jesus has won for us.

Jesus, thank you for the forgiveness of sins you have lavished on me. Help me live as a representative of your kingdom to the world around me, forgiving others as I want to be forgiven. Amen.

REIGN OF CHRIST SUNDAY

Jesus ushers in a different kind of reign than the world has seen before. He doesn't rely on flashy entourages but leads a band of fishermen. He doesn't use powerful weapons but multiplies loaves of bread. He doesn't operate through threats of punishment but forgives those who persecute him. All these differences prompt some to ask the question, Who is this man? Who is this king who acts so counter to what we know of this world?

Paul tells us in soaring and exalted language about the true nature of this unusual king. Jesus has no need for big weapons or threats or stashes of money, for as the "image of the invisible God, the firstborn of all creation," he has a deeper, truer source of power than any worldly ruler. Paul says that everything, whether "thrones or dominions or rulers or powers," has been created through him and for him, and therefore they are subject to him. Jesus has been the world's true king from the very beginning of creation, and now through his resurrection he has become the "firstborn from the dead," taking the lead in God's new creation as well. In doing so he has made a way for us to find reconciliation and peace with God.

As we close out this cycle of the church calendar, I invite us to reflect on how Jesus has revealed himself as our king this past year. When have we especially felt the compassion of our shepherd? Where have we experienced God's faithfulness in fulfilling divine promises? In what circumstances have we received Jesus' forgiveness on a new level? May we learn to trust him as our true king in new ways during the year ahead.

Lord Jesus, thank you for being a different kind of king. May I open my life to your gracious rule so that I may know more of your compassion, your faithfulness, and your forgiveness. Amen.

Walking Joyfully with the Lord

NOVEMBER 21–27, 2016 • JOHN FRYE

Scripture Overview: Advent is a new year, new time, new life: a genuine newness wrought by God in the world. As both the prophetic oracle and the psalm attest, Israel hopes for justice, peace, and well-being. The biblical community knows God's intention for these matters and trusts God's faithful promise. Thus Advent begins in a vision of a healed alternative for the world. The New Testament readings intensify the long-standing hopes and make the promises of God immediate prospects. The intensity and present tense of New Testament faith revolve around the presence of Jesus, whose very person initiates a new beginning in the world. The church at Advent watches in order to notice where God is bringing justice, peace, and well-being.

Questions and Thoughts for Reflection

- Read Isaiah 2:1-5. What are your experiences of freedom and un-freedom? Consider how your demands for freedom in certain areas cause others to experience un-freedom.

- Read Psalm 122. When have you gathered for worship with a diverse community? What do you perceive as the benefits of such a gathering?

- Read Romans 13:11-14. The writer suggests that we consider our salvation as a journey. Where are you along the way?

- Read Matthew 24:36-44. We are to KEEP CALM AND CARRY ON. How do you manifest your "readiness" for the coming of the kingdom?

Priest and pastor under Desmond Tutu; now retired and working at St. Margaret's Anglican Church, Fish Hoek, Cape Peninsula; living in Cape Town, South Africa

Many of us demand to live in a "perfect" environment: free from fear of harm, and nice and quiet. Some people who spend time in Africa working on contract are glad to go "home" to the United States or Europe where "everything works," as one of our friends said. This demand for security and peace on the part of some represents a kind of un-freedom for others.

Another un-freedom comes in the demand to live among people of our own faith and practice—or race and culture. Untold misery has been unleashed on the world because of this demand; for example, the racism of South African apartheid. Freedom for Afrikaners brought bondage to others.

How we yearn for the realization of God's dream and will among us here on earth. The prophet Isaiah shows how God's plan benefits all: God will be present as teacher, arbitrating peace among nations; conflict will recede. Thy kingdom come, O God. . . . please, and soon.

Can we possibly move in this direction? Our South African experience says *yes*! Archbishop Desmond Tutu consistently spoke nonviolence to his people in the midst of their suffering. He noted that the unrighteous and illogical nature of the apartheid state would bring about its failure. The process did not require martyrs and killing but faith in God and love and prayer for all. Tutu based his theology on the Exodus tradition: It is God who frees people from oppression. Believe in God's plan, and work without violence to achieve it. This principle holds true for oppression related to gender, ethnicity, my demands over against yours.

May we subject ourselves to this principle now in the name of Jesus Christ and evaluate all our relationships honestly.

Lord, free me from the things that cause me to oppress others; forgive me and help me serve them with respect and love. Amen.

Good faithfully and consistently desires that the chosen people join him in bringing peace and good government to the world. The whole of history seems to show God's plan being frustrated, and any object lesson that Israel and Jerusalem might provide falls to the ground.

Among a sea of destruction and devastation Isaiah 2:1-5 offers a tiny alighting place. In Isaiah 1 "the faithful city has become a whore" (v. 21) and from 2:6 onward shock and doom increase. Thank God for the prophet's vision of God's gracious will and proclamation.

God's plan involves Israel's educating the nations of the world and drawing them close to God. God-in-the-Temple will "teach us his ways" and open divine paths to us. Instruction, which will include God's wisdom as Israel knew it, and the "word of the Lord" will woo all nations to God. The people of the world will freely choose the options that make for peace. We hear the prophet wail words to this effect, "O Jacob, when will you come into your heritage?" It calls to our minds Jesus' lament over Jerusalem.

As with Isaiah, some of us are called to speak truth to power and to break down strongholds of lies. Tyrannies based on lies crumble, as in East Germany and South Africa, and when they are gone people wonder where their power originated. Today in South Africa the Christian church speaks truth to white racism and to black racism. Based on the truth and faithfulness of God, a Tutu or Mandela and Christians in gang-ridden areas—and in your area—bring truth to bear and tear down strongholds.

Dear Lord, show me whom I should approach prophetically about wrongs, and give me the power through your Spirit to speak without fear or favor. Amen.

In reading this psalm, we may feel angry or overcome that the reality of Jerusalem's history is so very far from peaceful. We may pray, "When, O Lord, will you do these things for this poor, besieged city?"

This may be our reaction, but we can and do feel the pilgrim joy of the writer and his friends who gather to worship and celebrate Israel and Israel's God in one of the great annual festivals in Jerusalem. Psalm 122 is one of fifteen Songs of Ascents (Psalms 120–134). Psalm 122 specifically falls within the category of a pilgrimage psalm, one that pilgrims sang on the way. The Songs of Ascents prepare the worshipers to come to the Temple in the right spirit. The festivities unite the whole nation. The king and secular authorities attend; representatives of all the tribes come to worship. Conditions like war must often have interfered.

Even after the destruction of Jerusalem and the sojourn in exile, the hope remained that one day every Jew would participate in worship like this. Israel then looked to the messianic era for its fulfillment.

The importance for us today lies in what the psalm says about the quality of relationship among the pilgrims and worshipers. The New International Version Study Bible (1985) notes as follows: "These constitute a loving brotherhood, who worship together, [and] pray together." In South Africa we experienced such quality of relationships in the 1980s when large, united worship services became the spiritual powerhouse leading to the overthrow of the racist regime in South Africa. There was joy, and glory was given to God.

The whole community experiences the beneficial effects of such inclusive worship; when that fails, the community suffers.

When have you entered into joyful worship with many different kinds of people? Do you desire such inclusiveness?

Thanksgiving Day, USA

Thanksgiving Day as embraced in the United States wonderfully asserts the place and power of love and gratitude within families—a wholesome national celebration that other nations may regard as exceptional. Ties of blood and friendship, openness to strangers and the poor, truly reflect the Bible passages for this day. You "shall celebrate with all the bounty" (Deut. 26:11), and Psalm 100 offers these comforting words: "We are [God's]; we are his people, and the sheep of his pasture" (v. 3).

In the Gospel reading for today, the crowd comes seeking the miracle-maker who has just fed five thousand people; they want more of the same. "I want it all, and I want it now" is a common twenty-first century cry. But Jesus says that we've got to move on from the food and drink celebration to receiving the bread of God that comes down from heaven. "Whoa! What's this then? We like big parties and being well fed, but you're talking about something much different. We don't understand."

Can our Thanksgiving Day take us into eating the bread of heaven? "Oh, Dad, don't be so religious" is a common response from younger family members to suggestions for praying on the day. It requires great creativity and sensitivity to eat both bread and the bread of heaven. Paul, in Philippians, moves us through celebration, supplication, and thanksgiving to a continual mindfulness of the kind of thoughts that God deems "worthy": truthful, honorable, just, pure, pleasing, and commendable. The daily actions that flow from these will bring us the peace we need for life. In response to God's great gifts to us, we give God ourselves. *We* are the gift, the thanksgiving present that God desires.

Here we are, Lord God, to be yours—body, mind, and spirit. Amen.

Chapters 24 and 25 of Matthew emphasize persons' taking responsibility for their own salvation. We "must be ready." But in the meantime, what about the world and those who don't seem to respond to God? We have a mission to them and, for many of us, this includes interceding with God for their salvation.

While all prayer is good, I have experienced some helpful and unhelpful ways to pray for the "lost." I have found it unhelpful to give God orders as to how to bless the people we pray for. I have been in the position, as a pastor and as a parent, of praying wrong things for my charges: out-of-date information, an undue slant toward my own benefit, worldly outcome oriented, and not lovingly concerned with their salvation. It's sometimes a shock when I'm confronted with the actual person to see how far wide of the mark my prayers were!

So how can we most usefully employ our intercession in this Advent season? We can always pray for love, forgiveness, and peace in their lives and share these things with them. We may want to pray that no one be left behind at Christ's return.

Paul's intercessory prayers for believers provide good examples for us. In praying for the church at Colossae, where he has never been personally, Paul says, "We have not ceased praying for you and asking that you may be filled with the knowledge of God's will" (1:9).

Jesus himself is the great Intercessor who prays for all. Because only the Father knows "about that day and hour," we gratefully accept Jesus' intercession for us as we intercede on behalf of others.

Lord God, I entrust you with the destinies of all those for whom I pray. Amen.

Paul writes this letter several decades after the death and resurrection of Jesus Christ. Christian believers in Rome need encouragement. Paul knows many of them himself, as Romans 16 indicates. He desires to visit this group of Christians who reside at the center of the Empire to see that they are in the center of God's will and purposes.

"The present time" (NIV) refers to "the last days," the time between Christ's resurrection and his coming again, or *parousia*. Some Christians expected his immediate return; but as year follows year and he hasn't returned, they have to think and pray differently. Paul uses the phrase "our salvation is nearer to us now" to indicate that the whole process of salvation will be consummated on Christ's return and not before, and there is no way of knowing when that will be. But we must be ready.

The old, unbaptized life he describes as "night" and with it go the "works of darkness," which the believer lays aside in the sacrament of baptism when first coming to Christ. We enter into Christ, the body of Christians, and Paul says we must renew the life we receive at our baptism by daily entering into the mind of Christ and growing to be like him. We "put on the armor of light," just as we "put on the Lord Jesus Christ."

Paul tries to convey the urgency of his request; Jesus' return is closer today than it was yesterday. He exhorts the Romans to heed the nearness of the day and take appropriate action. For some of us the image of taking off and putting on is very strong; it's something we can do and note our progress. Being ready, being awake: We as a church can become more Christlike daily, and we hold this opportunity in the forefront of our minds and our attempts at loving.

Lord, what habits and attitudes do I need to lay aside? Help me put on the Lord Jesus Christ this day. Amen.

FIRST SUNDAY OF ADVENT

England feared invasion by Hitler's armies. Through the summer months of 1940, fear, uncertainty, and a kind of paralysis grew among the population. Government used all means available to bolster morale, including billboard-sized posters like this one: KEEP CALM AND CARRY ON.

Jesus of Nazareth taught about the "end of the age" and about the "day of judgment." After his Ascension, the young church felt uncertain about the timing of such events. Details in the various New Testament books do not allow us to construct a detailed chronology of future events: Only God the Father knows. We, like the early church, must wisely entrust ourselves to God's care and our personal readiness. This is true whatever our circumstances: in prison, out of work, jet-setting, wealthy, or in the caring services—even traveling and on holiday! Yet that trust becomes more difficult when we find ourselves in crisis. We "keep awake therefore." We keep calm and carry on with our daily dedicated, purposeful activities and relationships. We don't allow our sacred space, our safe place of companionship with God, to be broken into and destroyed.

Jesus emphasizes watching and staying awake. We remember that in the garden of Gethsemane before Jesus' arrest, he asked his disciples to "keep watch with me" (Matt. 26:38, NIV). In times of heightened drama, opportunities for both good and evil abound. Jesus desires that we join him in his watching, identify with him and participate fully in that final act of redemption. Paul says that we know "what time it is" (Rom. 13:11), and we will be of better service to our God as we stay mindful of that.

What spiritual discipline will best promote my watchfulness—for now and for always?

The Wilderness of the Heart

NOVEMBER 28–DECEMBER 4, 2016 • AMY L. MEARS

Scripture Overview: The Old Testament roots of Advent hope are cast in royal imagery. The psalm marks the king as one whose work is to bring justice to the weak. The new king makes a new world possible. The Gospel reading is both invitation and warning that we must make concrete decisions to reorder our life in ways appropriate to God's new intention. Characteristically Paul makes the grand, sweeping claim: The new behavior appropriate to God's new governance is that the strong and the weak, the haves and have-nots, relate to each other in new faithfulness. Advent is spent pondering specific decisions about bringing our daily life into sync with God's rule.

Questions and Thoughts for Reflection

* Read Isaiah 11:1-10. When do you allow yourself "fallow" time? How does that time of "resting" nurture your fruitfulness?

* Read Psalm 72:1-7, 18-19. This prayer for the king expresses the qualities that the people desire in a leader. What would you add to the list?

* Read Romans 15:4-13. Paul notes that Christ welcomed you for the glory of God. Consider the last several months: Whom have you welcomed for the glory of God?

* Read Matthew 3:1-12. What is growing in your heart's wilderness this Advent season?

Pastor, Glendale Baptist Church: A Caring Community of Equality and Grace, Nashville, Tennessee

Frustrated gardeners and farmers of the world, unite! By late November, even the fall greens are looking pretty brown, but we can't risk our emotional health by pulling out the seed catalogs just yet. It is fallow time. We cover the soil with compost and mulch and leave it there, bereft, with only our hopes for next month's solstice to reverse the length of day and light and warmth. In the meantime, only twinkle lights hanging everywhere sustain our spirits.

Isaiah comforts the frustrated gardeners of his exiled community with words of fruitfulness, hope, encouragement. "The stump appears to be dead, I know. Our family tree is cut down. It looks like we are finished as a people, as a nation."

But wait. Something is afoot. Deep in the dark recesses of the earth, life stirs even yet. "This is not over," Isaiah tells the bereft people. "Life is here. This stump of our family is not done. Our roots are sound and grounded." A shoot, a sprout, a branch, a canopy is in our future. Then grows a tree of righteousness, shelter for the people, protection and provision.

Isaiah promises that the Spirit of the Holy will guide their new leader. The selection of the nation's new hope won't rest on looks or brute strength. God's people will be led with wise words and impulses toward justice and respect. Love for the Holy will produce a crop of fruitful people of peace, reprieve for the suffering, and comfort for the grieving.

God of hope, when we are in darkness, remind us that you and life exist here too. Amen.

The nature channels on television offer great episodes on strange animal buddies: a deer that comes to the fence every morning and runs up and down playing with a dachshund; a box turtle playmate for a fox kit; a yellow Labrador's daily swim with a dolphin in an Irish bay. Isaiah's peaceable realm has little in-breaking hints—but they're certainly not the norm.

What would our world be like if there were no predator and no prey? If all animals ate grass and hay and grain, the carnivores would surely have less energy. Their lives might be less productive, more lethargic; fewer offspring, less energy for doing carnivorous things. Perhaps the scavengers would become a bit more competitive. Would the prey animals develop some new purpose for life instead of survival?

And what of people? What of us? Our paintings show the peaceable realm with the toddlers playing with a bowl of colorful snakes like it's a bowl of sour candies, a tiny lamb curled in the forepaws of a hugely maned lion. (Despite Isaiah's noting that the *wolf* shall live with the lamb.) "And a little child shall lead them," Isaiah depicts it for us.

When the earth is filled with the knowledge of God, peace reigns. But will we appreciate that peace? Will the little child be petulant, prone to tantrums? Will the lambs demand their turn to dominate the lion pride? Will the scavenger animals require mediation?

Our seasonal contemplation about the advent of peace is not a simple proposition. If we hope for peace, we would do well to work for it.

Spirit of peace, we would not be naïve. We would be thoughtful and careful as we pursue peace and justice. Challenge our oversimplification; make us brave. Amen.

This psalm, in its references to both king and king's son, brings immediately to mind David and Solomon. In this psalm attributed to King Solomon, the psalmist asks the Holy One for help. Let's see what he seeks in his prayer-song. He seeks God's faultless judgment. He asks that the king be a good person of sound judgment, particularly with regard to the impoverished citizens of the realm. He requests peace and righteousness. He desires his own ability to bring justice for the poor ones and for children who are in need. He asks to defeat those who oppress the poor ones.

The psalmist solicits a long life for himself and his administration—and a reign that will bring good things, like rain upon the earth. He asks that those who pursue goodness will have success and that peace prevail on earth "until the moon is no more."

The psalmist notes the qualities desired in the new leader in a repetitive phrasing: righteousness, justice, peace. These are the qualities that support the king in his duty, the qualities valued by the people. And so the Son of David comes, bringing righteousness, justice, peace.

The community likely used this psalm when the nation crowned a new ruler, perhaps also on special anniversaries of the reign. What a great idea! Do you have a psalm that lists the intentions of your reign over your personal realm? For what characteristics would you pray? For the increase of what abilities and awarenesses would you ask? What will you plead for your children? Would you have the courage to return to the psalm each year on your anniversary to assess your progress and restate your interest in righteousness and goodness, kindness and peace, justice and good judgment?

Spirit of peace and beauty, help me to focus my life on peace and beauty. Remind me of my purposes and my intentions. May I align my words and actions with my psalm. Amen.

God, the Eternal Giver; humankind, the eternal receiver. This Advent we receive once again the amazing gift of God's love. A gift we could not give ourselves: the gift of God incarnate. And God's glory fills the whole earth.

It was a stunning moment. Seven children, ages four through twelve, sat around the low table in little chairs drawing expressions on empty paper faces with crayons and talking about God. Little B said, "When I close my eyes, I can see God!"

"Really?!" I responded to him with big, surprised eyes. And then, just to throw a twist into the conversation, I asked him with a sly smile, "What does *she* look like?"

"No!" he exclaimed to me, indignant.

"No? What, then?" I asked.

At that, he closed his eyes, lowered his face into his hands, looked at God for a moment, and murmured, "All the beautiful colors. God looks like all the beautiful colors."

Young M, sitting next to B, said to herself mostly, "God is a shining ball of light."

Psalmists and theologians surround us. Given a chance to write a song or draw a picture or dance a step or tap a rhythm about our God "who does wondrous things," the less inhibited among us have an easier time of it. For this, the hymnist writes, "Little children praise you perfectly, and so would we." Blessed be the God of Israel.

Glorious God, we would bless your name forever. May your glory fill all the earth, and may it fill my life this day. Amen.

Chirst is drawing, drawing near, Christ is coming, coming here!" So ends a stanza of Tom H. Troeger's Advent hymn, "Wild the Man and Wild the Place." The Romans writer, Paul, hearkens back to the prophets—Isaiah in particular—in proclaiming that the one who saves is coming from the root of Jesse. The one who saves is coming to bring hope and the realm of the holy to all the world—not just to the people of God from among the Hebrew people—but to everyone. Christ is drawing near; Christ is coming here!

Paul stresses unity of all who profess Christ and "glorify the God and Father of our Lord Jesus Christ." He notes God's steadfastness that encourages believers to live in harmony. The stump of Jesse came for the salvation of Israel and, through Israel, the world: Jews and Gentiles.

So what do we do? How do we prepare for the coming of the one who saves into the world and into our lives? And how will we know when the stump of our old way of being has produced new shoots and vines and leaves and blossoms and fruit?

Paul boils it down to this: "Welcome one other, therefore, just as Christ has welcomed you, for the glory of God." Advent is a time of preparing our interior house in order to welcome Christ. Further, it is a time of preparing to become like Christ as we welcome other people into all the abundance that love brings to life.

Hospitable God, we want to share in your hospitality by welcoming others in love as you welcome us. May we be awake, aware, and ready to welcome. Amen.

The desert. What grows in the desert? John the Baptist "appeared" in the desert, the scripture story tells us, and begins wreaking havoc, the likes of which have not been seen for generations. He dresses funny; he eats peculiar things; he bellows like a crazy man about getting ready for the coming One.

All that time in the wilderness has caused some seeds to germinate in a people hungry for evidence of the presence and activity of God in the world. They swarm out of the cities and villages to gather around John and hear the call. "Get ready! Get your hearts and your actions lined up together! Heaven is drawing very near!"

John calls for a change of heart. He speaks of a God who cares and holds people accountable for their thoughts and actions. This God holds out the offer of ultimate justice in a world that seems haphazard at best in its morals. So change your ways! Change your hearts!

What is growing in your heart's wilderness this Advent season? Where is an unexpected shoot sprouting from a region of your heart that you had thought defunct? To what is the voice of the prophet calling you? To more consistent quietness, meditation, and prayer? Are you preparing for the presence of the Holy by speaking more pointedly about truth when you encounter it? Are you singing or painting or opening your life and your home to the hospitality of the Holy?

The desert is wild and sometimes desolate, but it is certainly not empty. Life thrives there—it's just not always obvious. Maybe this is your day to hear John's call, "Wake up!"

We know that you wait for us in the desert, Jesus of Nazareth.
Awaken us and teach us to follow. Amen.

THE SECOND SUNDAY OF ADVENT

My college botany professor was a bit of a strange fellow. He had a good sense of decorum as far as plants might be concerned. With people, though, he lived just outside the realm of expectation.

One day my professor explained the idea of "dormancy" in plants. If someone prunes a tree too dramatically, the tree could respond by going into a deep tree-sleep, not putting out leaves or fruit or new growth—perhaps for years. However, a person could shock a tree out of dormancy. "Once," he told us, "a tree had split, so I cut it off straight across the trunk, six feet from the ground. Nothing but a trunk. It went into dormancy and just sat there for three years. I was sure that it still lived, so I stood there in the yard one day, took off my belt, and whipped that tree to wake it up." We students pictured the bizarre image of our professor, safari hat on head, belt in hand, whipping his maple tree in the suburbs.

John the Baptist tells the gathered folks that trees need to demonstrate their worth by doing what trees do—producing good fruit. Rather than being allowed to stand dormant, John notes that "the ax is lying at the root of the trees." They will be cut down and thrown into the fire.

Preparing ourselves to follow Jesus, John says, is our purpose in life, and we must be about that work. What "fruit worthy of repentance" will you bear? How will you prepare for the One who is coming?

Bless me this day, O God, as I search my life for evidence of good fruit. Make me able and willing to produce the goodness and kindness, peace and mercy, to which you call your people. Amen.

Living Water in the Wilderness

DECEMBER 5–11, 2016 • HEATHER MURRAY ELKINS

Scripture Overview: These readings convey that God's coming, or the coming of the Messiah, will be profoundly transformative. The promises of messianic possibility work against our exhaustion, our despair, and our sense of being subject to fate. The psalm provides a comprehensive summary of the miracles wrought by God in the past to make new life possible. Jesus' life and ministry embodied these large expectations of Israel. The prophetic oracle, psalm, and Gospel reading all move toward the practicality of the epistle reading, which demands that we allow this claim of new human possibility to permeate all of life. Our life is directed to the reality of God, the very God whom we discern in our present and to whom we entrust our future.

Questions and Thoughts for Reflection

- Read Isaiah 35:1-10. Where in your life do you feel that you have gone astray? After you realize you are lost, how do you return to the way that is God?
- Read Luke 1:47-55. When have you spoken fearlessly about a situation in your life?
- Read James 5:7-10. For what do you thirst?
- Read Matthew 11:2-11. What characteristics draw you to a spiritual leader?

Professor of Worship, Preaching, and the Arts, Drew Theological School, New Jersey

I was born with a genetic disadvantage; I lack what is called "sense of direction." It's not that I cannot find my way around a map; I can't seem to map my mind to remember the four directions. To cope in the years before GPS, I asked for directions frequently. I made friends with people who could find true north. I also married well; my husband can find his way to new spaces with ease. I think he has a map chip in his DNA.

Imagine the consolation this Advent text of Isaiah brings to those of us who are perpetually lost: "No traveler, not even fools, shall go astray." Not even fools will get lost. This highway is not an aging interstate suffering from cloverleaf confusion. This is the Holy Way. Whimsy aside, this promise has the power to calm our fear of being lost. It offers the best medicine for Israel's fear of being left behind.

And who walks on this Holy Way? God's people. *Only* God's people. Isaiah insists no one "unclean" will be allowed. Is God saying, "My way or no highway?" Yes. But this is not a pilgrimage of people who are perfectly spotless; this is a very human company of the forgiven. These are the ones who determine that God will be both their beginning and their end. If you, be you wise or foolish, choose this Way, you will not travel alone. You will not be lost or left behind. If God is your destination, if the One who is the Way has called you, this journey is home.

Holy One, help me find my way to your highway. Amen.

Augustus 8, 2014. The bad news comes by e-mail, phone, and Facebook. John, the beloved, born of water and the Spirit was gone. John Mogabgab, who wove a witness of justice, mercy, and spirituality together in words and images, has entered the communion of saints. Sadness deepens with each message given and received, and under all is the sound of hearts breaking.

The text for this day lies open on my writing table as I process the news. John, founding editor of *Weavings: A Journal of the Christian Spiritual Life*, a designer of the core curriculum for the Academy of Spiritual Formation, a senior editor of Upper Room Books—now gone. How will this work go on without John?

In today's passage, Jesus questions those who express concern and anxiety about the loss of their beloved leader John who has been imprisoned. His voice sounds clear and close as I study the text. It is as if Jesus is examining those who grieve now just as he did those who struggled in his day. Jesus interrupts their anxiety with a question, "What then did you go out to see?"

What had John's followers seen? What had drawn them to John's ministry? What served as the source of his spiritual and social power? Jesus wants the community to remember what they know: "What then did you go out to see?"

What did they go to see? What do we look for in prophetic leaders? Not a reed but an oak. Not a mouthpiece but a witness. Not someone who does it his or her way but someone who prepares *the* Way.

Jesus' question is unexpected, as is the teaching that follows. One of the greatest prophets on earth is not greater than whoever's least in the "kin-dom" of heaven. John would have agreed.

Spend a few moments in prayer for those who are or who have been your teachers of the Way.

The third week of Advent is a time when patience wears thin. When will it rain? When will this child be born? When will Christ come again? James addresses his words to a people whose teeth are set on edge as are their lives. His community lives in a drought of truth; their riverbeds of justice are bone dry; they suffer a fierce thirst. Patience is in short supply when you thirst. But for what did they thirst and what does their thirst share with our common experience?

Contrary voices about minimum wage fill the morning news, forming a soundtrack to this text and other verses that lie just outside this day's passage. "Listen! The wages of the laborers who mowed your fields, which you kept back by fraud, cry out, and the cries of the harvesters have reached the ears of the Lord of hosts" (James 5:4).

James urges patience to those who cry out for justice. He promises his beloved community that the Holy One not only knows their suffering but will act on that knowledge. The Holy One will come.

James doesn't counsel his community to be silent; his letter conveys the scorching heat of a prophet's public protest preserved in the verse that introduces this Advent instruction: "Strengthen your hearts!"

What keeps a heart strong? Hope, certainly. Christ will come again. That is the gospel promise, then as now, but the promise isn't easy. How does the first coming of Christ that we celebrate this season make a difference to that beloved community and to ours? This is the tough edge of Advent. James invites us to the hard work of waiting and praying for the life-giving rain.

"Come, Lord Jesus!" Bring the living water that will quench our thirst for justice and mercy. Amen.

The Magnificat is aptly named. Mary's words offer a magnificent declaration of the nature of the Holy One who is intimately involved with our humanity. It's a song in honor of the Unmoved Mover who shatters the illusions of the self-sufficient and flips the pyramids of power and the pharaohs who build them upside down. Mary gives voice to the freedom song of Christians throughout the centuries.

This scriptural song and proclamation also represents performative speech. It helps accomplish what it describes—language that does what it says. And we could apply the term that Michel Foucault uses to Mary's song: *parrhesia*. The term comes from the Greek and means "fearless speech."

Four conditions identify this scripture-song as fearless speech. First, it tells the truth. Second, the speaker risks real danger in speaking the truth. Third, the declaration contains criticism of the unjust situation and those who profit from an oppressive status quo. Last, the speaker/singer understands that she speaks from a calling, a sense of duty. So truth, danger, criticism, and duty are all conditions of this fearless speech.

In addition, this young, soon-to-be mother isn't trying to convince her community to believe what she's saying by using powerful images or persuasive arguments. Mary means what she says and is saying what she means. She believes that the Holy One is with her, and the world will never be the same.

When did the Holy Spirit empower you to stand by the word of God within you?

"Could you repeat that?" If you've ever had the experience of going for snacks just as a game-winning basket occurs, you know the importance of repetition. When we miss out, we want to hit the replay button. A really significant experience fosters our desire to hear or see it again even if we didn't miss it the first time. "Read it again, Daddy."

Neurobiology is demonstrating the great influence of repetition in the molecular conversation between nerve cells in the brain. Learning takes place when the nerve cells make new connections; repetition enhances the special communication channels. Initial learning will last if the connections are repeated in significant encounters throughout our lives. Even one new connection can create a network of "knowing."

Psalm 146 is a song that Mary and her community would have known and sung by heart. The ancient songs from the psalms repeated the creation stories of Genesis and the salvation history of the people of the God of Jacob (and Rachel and Leah), and they show up again in the Gospels.

Advent presents a good time to repeat in song, prayer, and preaching what we believe to be true about the One we worship. Each time we repeat these ancient songs of faith and freedom, we make new connections. It's how we learn to think and feel, part of how we live and move and have our being.

So who is our God? Repeat after me: Creator of heaven and earth, the sea, and all that is in them. Feeder of the hungry. Helper of the helpless. Judge and Restorer of justice. The One who keeps faith forever.

Let a song come to mind that reminds you of God's faithfulness.

Nancy Mairs, poet, essayist, teacher of embodied spirituality, came to lecture at Drew University several years ago. Much of her writing and teaching was engaged in the struggle for justice, artistic expression, and recognition of the humanity of those with handicapping conditions. She was in a wheelchair and had limited use of her hands at that point of her life, but she made a lasting impression on individuals as well as the institution.

Handicapping conditions? Disabled? Or should I use the term *differently abled*? What language could I borrow or invent or honestly use to name without blame? Since I had the honor of introducing Mairs, I decided my best course of action was to ask, despite her reputation for not tolerating fools. What did she want me to say? Was there a right way?

"Be specific," Mairs replied. "I have MS. Say so. I'm not blind or deaf. Tell them I'm a cripple." I know my face registered shock at the word I'd been taught never to say. I was, for a moment, speechless. Later I would read her essay on why stating it that way was speaking the truth, but at the moment I felt at a loss. She took pity on me and offered a piece of wisdom I've learned to treasure. "You know, it may help if you remember that you're only temporarily able."

Matthew and Isaiah (35:5) are also specific. Eyes. Ears. Legs. Skin. They name physical conditions that have represented loss and limitation to human communities for centuries. They employ these physical descriptions to demonstrate the depth of healing that God will give. The Holy One's coming will free us. We will be *imago Dei* ("image of God") without limitation. Does that mean only temporarily able-bodied? No. It means freedom in the mystery of the One who was both wounded and whole.

Dear Healer of the wounded, keep me alive to your love. Make me able through your baptism to be a disciple. Amen.

THIRD SUNDAY OF ADVENT

Every year or so I take a group of students on a pilgrimage to Almost Heaven. Its institutional label is Appalachia: Arts, Energy, and Education. Most of these pilgrimages are to West Virginia, my place of birth and ordination. Some students come willingly, some from obligation; but all are pilgrims in the end.

We see rough areas where mountains used to be and meet people who know how to do good in hard times. If the class has become a community through our travel, the last stop is Palestine, West Virginia. (I sometimes wonder what wandering Aramean was father to these names.) We turn left at the Blue Goose, round the curves on Sonoma Road, and park on the edge of the steep hillside that has a sign MARKS' MANOR.

Burt watches for us from the top of the hill, and his hound wags welcome. Burt was a famous raccoon hunter in this corner of the world. At ninety-four, he's given away his guns, and the young dog at his feet doesn't know what an easy life he's got.

Burt bewitches my students with stories of moonlit nights and the music of baying hounds. It's as though "we're not in this century," one whispers. The magic deepens when he cuts a branch from the peach tree and shows them how to search for water. It's a gift he says; he's the only one in his family that got it. I tell my students that Burt's known for finding water on hillsides of stones and in bad seasons of drought. Some of them try out the peach branch; others watch, skeptical and silent. What does it take to find water in the wilderness?

The prophet reminds us that it takes a gift—a gift of the Giver. "Here is your God." When the Holy One comes, there is water, living water everywhere, and not a single life will die of thirst.

Holy One, form pools of living water in these burning sands of time. Amen.

The Shape of Waiting

DECEMBER 12–18, 2016 • MARK W. STAMM

Scripture Overview: We are close to the reality of Jesus, in whom we have invested so much of our life and faith. Jesus is larger than life, shattering all the categories of conventional religious recognition. On the one hand, it is asserted that this is the "Son of David," in continuity with the old dynasty and the old promises. On the other hand, this is one "from the Holy Spirit," not at all derived from the human dynasty. This twofold way of speaking about Jesus does not reflect vacillation or confusion in the community. Rather, it is an awareness that many things must be said about Jesus, because no single claim says enough.

Questions and Thoughts for Reflection

- Read Isaiah 7:10-16. How and when has God saved you in unexpected ways?
- Read Psalm 80:1-7, 17-19. What grace-filled steps have you taken to bring salvation and restoration to the world?
- Read Romans 1:1-7. The author suggests adding a chair to your feasting table. Whom will you invite to fill it?
- Read Matthew 1:18-25. When has God meddled in your life? What was the outcome?

Professor of Christian Worship, Perkins School of Theology, Southern Methodist University, Dallas, Texas

Advent calls us to the discipline of waiting. But, for what are we waiting, and how do we wait? Preachers and worship leaders will respond to that question in differing ways, including those who respond something like this: "We don't sing Christmas carols or talk about the birth of Christ until Christmas Eve." But today's Gospel lesson makes that negative commitment somewhat harder to sustain, with its "Now the birth of Jesus the Messiah took place in this way" (Matthew 1:18).

This birth narrative is not the greeting card story that we sometimes like to construct, is it? Suffice it to say that we have a complicated story here, and it's complicated because God started meddling in the lives of perfectly innocent and upstanding folks like Joseph and Mary. Watch out when the Holy Spirit starts to work in your midst. But, please, we're talking about a baby here, so let's not make this story too abstract. Anyone who has welcomed a new child into the family knows that it's a wonderful experience, but it's also more than a little disorienting. Nothing will ever be the same. Welcoming another human being will change you, as every married person learns, as the church experiences when it receives new and different people.

You can see, then, that this text is not just about what happened to Mary and Joseph two thousand years ago. It's also about our discipleship and the way the Holy Spirit is moving to bring Jesus into our midst today. We wait for him and he comes to us in the face of our neighbors, even in the face of neglected and abused children. Ready or not, Christ is coming, and we won't have to wait long. So, be ready for God's meddlesome and disruptive work; but be prepared for an adventure as well.

With the church in all times and places, we pray, **Maranatha,** *"Come, Lord Jesus." And we wonder how God will show up today.*

Many of us are used to reading this text as directly related to Jesus' birth and specifically to the virgin birth of Jesus. That's one perspective, but let's do our best to hear it as the ancient prophet might have intended. Notice the reference to Ahaz. Who was he? The writer of Second Kings summarized the reign of Israel's ruler in the eighth century BCE as follows: "He did not do what was right in the sight of the LORD his God, as his ancestor David had done" (16:2). The writer lists child sacrifice as among Ahaz's sins (2 Kings 16:3). His kingdom is crumbling, and judgment comes upon the land in the form of two kings, Rezin and Pekah, who lay siege to Jerusalem.

It doesn't look good for the country, but perhaps Ahaz is receiving what he deserves—only that doesn't happen. Instead, we hear this unusual promise of an unlikely birth and recall similar Bible stories of unlikely births: from Isaac to Samuel (Genesis 18:1-15; 1 Samuel 1:1-20), to this Immanuel, to John the Baptist (Luke 1:5-25), to Jesus—all unlikely births, not to mention the oddity of children as a sign of God's salvation. But that's the God of Israel. We don't always get what we deserve, and when God saves, it's not always through the means we had anticipated. God tells Ahaz that by the time the child is weaned, the threat of the besieging kings will be past. And it was so.

Sometimes we wait in fear, expecting the worst, but instead God raises us up, offering a new possibility. If you're anything like me, you may struggle with what some call "blue" Christmas. It's like a low-grade depression that creeps in this time of year, making it difficult to enter fully into the holiday spirit, whatever that may be. It lays siege to your heart. If that's where you are living, Immanuel is with you in the midst of it; but perhaps this year the siege itself will withdraw.

"Stir up your power, O Lord; . . . and let your bountiful grace and mercy speedily help and deliver us." Amen. (BCP)

The Shape of Waiting 413

We wait in prayer, praying with the psalmist: "O Shepherd of Israel, . . . stir up your might, and come to save us." We hear the word *save* quite often around church. What do we mean by it?

Some hear it as a question of who gets to go to heaven and, perhaps more darkly, as a question of who *doesn't* get to go. I'm convinced that God cares about what happens to us after we die and that God offers far more mercy than we allow ourselves to expect. Nevertheless, if we understand the focus of God's saving work to be primarily this set of questions, then our faith is rather lackluster and not very biblical. Such a narrow focus would leave us with little to do after our justification by grace. But God's saving work addresses so much more. The Shepherd of Israel loves the world—not the thought of its coming to an end and our escaping from it. So salvation and restoration of creation go together and, indeed, are one and the same. We pray, "Restore us, O God." God is accomplishing that work right now in our midst, and we get to be part of it.

We confess our sins, and God begins saving us from our self-centered preoccupations. Then we begin looking at our neighborhood in a more discerning way. We pray for the hungry and the homeless; God nudges us as we pray, encouraging us to become part of the solution. We end our silence against domestic abuse, first having the courage to name the problem in our public prayers and then through support of the local battered women's shelter. Our prayer doesn't bring the reign of God in its fullness, but it contributes to giving the world a little foretaste of it. We wait for God's final salvation by inching forward, one small grace-filled step after another.

Come, Lord Jesus. Show us little glimpses of your grace and mercy and perhaps some big ones every now and then. Amen.

THURSDAY, DECEMBER 15 ～ *Psalm 80:4-7,17-19*

Those of us who live in the northern hemisphere have come to the shortest days of the year. With the psalmist, we continue to pray for restoration—for ourselves, for those who suffer, for all creation, even for the church. This prayer calls for light in the midst of darkness and shadows: "Restore us, O LORD God of hosts, let your face shine, that we may be saved." God is the eternal source of light, and so God's face shines, bringing light to all who need it.

Perhaps we don't see light as a gift in the way that ancient peoples experienced it. Nevertheless, a necessary household chore in the days before electricity included the lighting of the evening lamp and quite early in Christian history, our sisters and brothers began using it to remind themselves of Jesus, the one whose light shines in darkness, whose light darkness does not overcome. (See John 1:5.) Sometimes we find it easier to believe in this light than others. Look into the night sky and think of the stars that we sing about this time of year. While some stars shine brightly, others present but a tiny point of light, barely visible in the night sky. Each star sheds some light. When we gaze at the stars, we look toward the very beginning, in some cases almost to the dawn of creation. The light that began its way toward us millions of years ago . . . waiting to be seen . . . now . . . by us . . . God affirms as "very good" (Gen. 1:31). Whether the light burns brightly or dimly, its source is God. Our confidence resides in that affirmation. Even as we wait in darkness, we catch a glimpse of the eternal future, the "city [that] has no need of sun or moon to shine on it, for the glory of God is its light" (Rev. 21:23). So again, we wait with the psalmist and we pray, "Let your face shine, O God, on and through us."

"O gracious Light, pure brightness of the everliving Father in heaven, O Jesus Christ, holy and blessed! . . .Thou art worthy at all times to be praised by happy voices, . . . and to be glorified through all the worlds." Amen. (BCP)

The Shape of Waiting

For Paul and for us, the shape of waiting is discipleship in Jesus Christ. Christ is our brother, "descended from David according to the flesh" and also raised from the dead, the "Son of God with power." It may seem odd to ponder the Resurrection during Advent, but remember that the Christian Year doesn't call us to act as if Christ were not yet born, much less not yet crucified and risen. Christians live in the midst of these spiritual dynamics, regardless of the season. Advent forms us to look for the places where the life of Christ is coming to birth, to look for places where it emerges from death. We wait, but with open and expectant eyes.

But how do we approach that waiting? I'm reminded of John Wesley's General Rules, that address all those who "desire to flee from the wrath to come." If you're willing to hear it, that's an Advent image for you. Notice that the Rules don't call us to do anything spectacular about that word of judgment but rather encourage the normal round of discipleship: "[Do] no harm" and "[avoid] evil"; do as much good as possible and use the means of grace, such as praying, studying the Bible, receiving Holy Communion, even fasting and abstinence. When those "who are called to belong to Jesus Christ" do these things, they will likely encounter the One who brings life from dead places.

Often we find Jesus Christ in the midst of our lives in the flesh. I remember an elderly woman in church who told me as a five-year-old that I was special. I remember a grandfather, himself a pastor, who told me as a twenty-year-old preacher that I had gifts for the work. Those words encourage me, even today, and I know you recall similar experiences.

"I am no longer my own, but thine. Put me to what thou wilt, rank me with whom thou wilt. . . . " Amen. (UMH, 607)

Many times, our waiting will take a countercultural shape. Christ entered creation fully in the flesh, becoming part of human experience. Thus we believe that the gospel can take root in every culture, and we believe that this rootedness expresses God's deep desire that the good news be sung in every language and played by every instrument. But today's reading insists that the gospel is at one and the same time countercultural. When Paul greets Christians at the heart of the Roman Empire in the name of "the Lord Jesus Christ" and when he refers to "Jesus Christ our Lord" (Romans 1:5) he isn't simply dressing up his letter with high-sounding religious language. Rather, he makes a sharply political statement by saying that Caesar is *not* Lord. That dynamic can change everything, and it can even get you into trouble, as we see with Jesus and Paul and with many Christians of conscience throughout the ages.

But you don't have to commit treason in order to be countercultural. Consider baptism, which redefines what we thought we knew about family, making it far wider than we had thought. In the baptismal rite of The United Methodist Church, we're reminded that baptism places us in a fellowship with "people of all ages, nations, and races" (UMH, 34), and we're asked to commit to that fellowship. Consider the Eucharist, which redefines what we thought we deserved, what we thought belonged to us, and what we thought about who gets to eat. The gospel uses these common elements as the first step in redefining almost everything. What will you do about these things? For this year's holidays, consider placing a chair for Christ at your feast day table, and then invite someone to fill it.

"Purify our conscience, Almighty God, by your daily visitation, that your Son Jesus Christ, at his coming may find in us a mansion prepared for himself; who lives and reigns with you, in the unity of the Holy Spirit, one God, now and for ever." Amen. (BCP)

And so we wait, now one week from Christmas; even more, we wait for Christ to appear in our midst today. The angel quotes the Isaiah 7:14 text to Joseph: "Look, the virgin shall conceive and bear a son, and they shall name him Emmanuel, which means, 'God is with us.'" Why this statement? We know that Matthew opted to translate the Isaiah text as "virgin" (*parthenos*), a reading that stands at the heart of our creedal life: "Jesus Christ . . . born of the Virgin Mary." Whether Isaiah's "young woman" or Matthew's "the virgin," this birth bears witness to God's unique activity and relates to the refrain, "All this took place to fulfill what had been spoken by the Lord," that we hear at many points throughout Matthew's Gospel. What is going on here? Matthew believes that the gospel stands in continuity with all of God's covenant work: The God who spoke the first words at Creation is the God who delivered the children of Israel from Egypt, who gave the Law, who raised Jesus from the dead, and the one who continues to send us into the mission of making disciples. He comes even today as Jesus the Messiah, the one born in our hearts.

This title *Messiah* speaks to God's intentions. The Messiah ushers in a new era of shalom, where the wolf will lie down with the lamb and all of God's people will join in a great feast marking the end of death (see Isaiah 11:6-9; 25:6-9). Those who first heard this gospel would've heard those intentions in the word *messiah*, and we can learn to do so. Realists may ask, "So where is this messianic age?"—a good question. It hasn't appeared in a flash, but the narrative remains incomplete. The Spirit brings it to birth in us in every act of compassion and justice.

We continue to pray, "Come, Lord Jesus," even in us, even today. Amen.

Sing the New Song: Our God Reigns!

DECEMBER 19–25, 2016 • JOHN H. COLLETT JR.

Scripture Overview: Ecstasy over the Christmas miracle is the theme that binds this week's passages together—unrestrained joy over what God has done and over who God is. These texts celebrate a God who reigns in strength. Yet this God is near and immediate, a participant in the human struggle for light and salvation. As worshipers, we join in rejoicing over the coming of the messenger "who says to Zion, 'Your God reigns'"(Isa. 52:7). We also celebrate "the Lord, for he is coming to judge the earth . . . with righteousness, and . . . equity" (Ps. 98:9). Then the note of immediacy is struck by the focus on what God has done just now, in these "last days," in which "he has spoken to us by a Son" (Heb. 1:2). The One who was present at creation, the eternal Word, "became flesh and lived among us" (John 1:14).

Questions and Thoughts for Reflection

- Read Isaiah 9:2-7. What or who in your life helps you to continue to walk in the world's darkness?
- Read Psalm 98. How do you discover hope even in the midst of difficult times for the earth? How does this hope allow you to shout for joy and sing the Lord's song?
- Hebrews 1:1-12. Advent reminds us of Jesus bridging the gap between God and humanity. How does this reality change the way you experience the world?
- John 1:1-14. Reflect on the incarnation of God in the form of a baby. In what ways does this influence the way you see and understand God's nature?

Executive Assistant to the Bishop, Nashville Episcopal Area; pastor in The United Methodist Church for forty-four years; previously superintendent of the Nashville district

Get ready to sing and shout for joy! Let's clear our throats, stretch our vocal cords, and expand our lungs. We've been rehearsing and preparing for a month. Now get ready to sing the Lord's new song. Advent days allow us to rehearse the joyful music of God's gracious rule in and through Jesus Christ. We reclaim the lyrics of promise from the Hebrew prophets, and we refresh the melodies embedded within our spiritual consciousness. We practice the songs of redemption individually and in congregations. We warm up for the big day.

In these remaining Advent days, we still watch and wait, ever ready to burst into song at the climactic moment. We are like the sentinels in Isaiah 52:8 who peer toward the mountain horizon, awaiting the runner from the battlefield. The runner, by his very body language, will herald whether the news is good or bad. When the good news comes, the sentinels burst into song!

Advent and Christmas prepare us to bear witness: "Our God reigns." Jesus Christ bears the good news that God's battle with sin and death has been won. It's all over but the shouting. The cleanup is ongoing and will continue until the last days, but as every commemoration of Jesus' birth dawns, we sing and shout for joy. You might say we are "staying in voice" for God's salvation crescendo when all the ends of the earth will see the salvation of our God.

Help us see, O God, your coming peace, good news, and salvation. Make us alert and ready to sing the song of your reign through love and justice. Amen.

How will creation sing to the Lord a new song in the age of climate change? With our belief that the earth demonstrates God's glory and serves as God's living creation and our abundant home, will not God heal and save the earth? But how will God's justice come to our greenhouse, gas-emitting way of life and fossil fuel-driven economies? Is there time, and will it hurt?

Naomi Klein, an award-winning journalist, writes that the *really* inconvenient truth is that climate change is not about carbon but about capitalism (*This Changes Everything,* Simon and Schuster, 2014). She argues that our economic system is waging war against life on earth. Our chances for survival hinge on our reducing carbon emissions by 8% each year through 2020! Ouch, that hurts! Yet, Klein believes that we have the capacity to impact climate change and that signs of transformation are everywhere. If climate change presents potentially catastrophic consequences for life on earth and if God loves the world, then when and how will God's justice come? And will it hurt?

The psalmist believes "the LORD rules!" "[God] set the world firmly in place; it won't be shaken. . . . Let the earth rejoice!" (CEB). Sounds like we need to support God's justice for the earth with our best science, technology, wisdom, courage, and willingness to sacrifice. If God wills to heal the earth, then we had best get busy joining in God's wondrous works. Bring gifts. Enter God's courtyards! Bow down to the Lord. Tremble before God, all the earth! And sing to the Lord, all the earth, the sea, countryside, trees, forests, fields, rocks, hills, and plains. Joy to the world, the Savior reigns!

May we take hope and courage, O God of creation, in your steadfast love for the world. May we all produce and consume in ways that also love your world. Amen.

The Creator and Ruler of all creation comes in this psalm as Judge. God "will judge the world with righteousness, and the peoples with equity." God comes to judge creation and its inhabitants. Can we have hope?

It is well documented that the gulf is widening between the haves and the have-nots, between developed and developing nations, between northern and southern hemispheres. Yet we increasingly share one world, one environment, one economy, one biological ecosystem. If God's righteousness and equity are coming, what changes might we get ready for?

Dr. Pardis Sabeti is an Iranian-American computational biologist and geneticist with Harvard University who participated in the fight against the Ebola epidemic in West Africa. Sabeti is also a musician and songwriter. While working in Africa, she often gathered coworkers to sing. She reflected on that experience, "after an hour of trying to sing through despair, my band mate played the beat of an old forgotten song and I began to hum. . . . We sat there together—women of different countries, ethnicities, and religions—in our seemingly forsaken temporary state on this earth with one truth, that 'I'm alive and so are you, we are here, we are the proof.'" The song "One Truth" became an anthem for people who struggle to stay alive in the world.

What is that beat of an old forgotten song—the Lord's song of life, healing, and hope? Our God is good, compassionate, and abounding in steadfast love. There is always hope, and we can sing the Lord's song. "Shout for joy to the LORD, all the earth, burst into jubilant song with music; make music to the LORD."

Let us hear afresh, O Lord, your song of life, healing, and hope.
And may we sing even in the face of dire conditions. Amen.

Advent soberly acknowledges the darkness in the world. We are reminded of wars and rumors of wars, disease, death, and despair. How are we to walk forward?

A mother asked her young son to go into the dark of night and shut the barn doors. The son protested that it was too dark and scary and that his flashlight didn't shine all the way to the barn. His mom then said, "Just walk to the end of the light." If he kept walking to the end of the light, he would safely arrive at the barn.

During the Advent days of life, if we keep walking to the end of the light we have, we can see shades of life, hope, resolve, grace, and peace. Isaiah kept walking to the end of the light and envisioned a world of joy—as an abundant harvest or the close of successful battle. God is coming with justice and righteousness to shatter the yokes and burn the boots of warriors. Isaiah kept walking to the end of the light, and there he perceived that God would save the world in the most surprising and disarming way. A new heir is coming: "A child is born to us, a son is given to us, and authority will be on his shoulders" (CEB).

My friend Bill Dockery wrote the following: "God rights our wrongs, not with the power of the rushing wind nor with the fury of the pelting rain nor with the fire of lightning. . . . God simply births a child and waits. . . . for each child brings the message that God is not discouraged with us but is still expecting to become incarnate in each human life."

Not a king, not a warrior—but a child is coming to bring light to our darkness. May we walk in that light.

"O come, O come, Emmanuel, and ransom captive Israel, that mourns in lonely exile here until the Son of God appear." Amen.

The opening words of Hebrews soar with Christological passion: "In the past God spoke through the prophets. . . . In these final days, though, he spoke to us through a Son" (CEB). And who could not hear these overtones in the Nicene Creed: "We believe in the one Lord, Jesus Christ, the only Son of God, eternally begotten of the Father, . . . begotten, not made, of one Being with the Father."

God gave God's self, in the form of the Son, as a sacrifice to cleanse people of sin. God thereby set about saving and redeeming the world in the same way God created the world—through goodness, blessing, and love.

Jesus, unlike any angel, human, or other entity of God's creating, is exactly like God from the beginning and is God's fullness in human form. Jesus gave himself to God's saving work so completely that he lived and loved fully, and he gave his life as the redeeming power of God's love and grace. In the Son, God fully closed the gap between God and humanity.

In two days we will try to take into ourselves the reality of what God did through that one birth. A son is given. "In these final days" . . . would that we could place ourselves in the bliss and urgency of "the final days" when in Christ, God perfects the world and we become all that God ever dreamed we could be. Jesus' birth affirms again that God believes in us and is never finished with us. In Jesus, God gave God's whole being and took up residence with us. And God will reside with us as long as it takes for God's sovereignty of love and grace to redeem all of creation.

"Love divine, all loves excelling, joy of heaven, to earth come down; fix in us thy humble dwelling; all thy faithful mercies crown!" Amen.

CHRISTMAS EVE

Christmas Eve services across the land now host the largest number of worshipers of any throughout the year. Like those in the time of Caesar Augustus who traveled to their birthplaces to be enrolled in the census, we make our way to candlelight and Communion services in large numbers. We come from all walks of life looking for, longing for, a sacred moment in time when things have a chance to start fresh—a new center, a new beginning; a rebirth of faith, hope, and love.

This is the culmination of a busy season of planning, decorating, gift buying, and joyous gatherings. Christmas Eve invites us to stop and be still. We linger in the sacred memory of one momentous birth that changed everything. We envision the baby Jesus, newly born, wrapped snugly, and resting in a manger. We remain in awe of the mystery of how this baby was both human and divine, God's unique gift of the new creation. Christmas Eve invites us to stop our human striving and discover ourselves again as God's blessed creatures.

We need these times of true stillness and quietness in order to hear the music of life. Music theorists say that the momentary silence between the notes is as important as the notes themselves. Choral directors instruct singers to breathe. Christmas Eve is like that: the momentary silence between the notes and a time to breathe.

The rush of the season is over, and we can rest in God's grace and renewal. We can rest in the trust that in Jesus, God gave us the gift of beginning again. Jesus! Once a babe, then a man, always the Son of God.

"Now thy manger's halo bright hallows night with newborn light; let no night this light subdue, let our faith shine ever new." Amen.

CHRISTMAS DAY

Sentinels lift your voices! Sing out together! How beautiful upon the mountains are the feet of a messenger who proclaims peace, brings good news, and proclaims salvation. This messenger has come. A son is given, a savior born. The sign is a newborn baby wrapped snugly and lying in a manger in Bethlehem of Judea.

Those around at the time could only ponder who and what he might be. We know from hindsight that the child Jesus grew up, became strong, was filled with wisdom, and God's favor was upon him. Jesus lived fully, graciously, and redemptively.

Believers beheld his glory, glory like the Father's only son, full of grace and truth. Jesus as the Word existed with God from the beginning. And this Word had now taken up residence as a human being, closing the distance between God and creation.

The transformation of life that began with the babe of Bethlehem continues to this moment. We who believe in him and follow his way can become children of God, born not just of flesh but of God, and we too can heal, forgive, reconcile, and bring good news. The very name of Jesus, his story, and his presence still release divine power to make life new. John refers to this power as "grace upon grace."

We on this journey of grace continue another season of waiting. We await the blessed hope and ultimate glorious appearance of our great God and savior Jesus Christ. Between now and then, let us live as though God has already done the saving. Let us live in grace and truth and be the presence of Jesus for everyone else so that grace upon grace will unfold.

"Finish, then, thy new creation; pure and spotless let us be. Let us see thy great salvation perfectly restored in thee." Amen.

The Lord Provides

DECEMBER 26–31, 2016 • DANNY WRIGHT

Scripture Overview: Isaiah 60:1-6 recalls the coming of God into the world as a brilliant light. That light carries with it the power to transform Israel so that those outside Israel are drawn to her light. Ephesians 3:1-12 points out God's mysterious inclusion of the Gentiles among God's people. The gift of light carries with it the obligation to accept and proclaim the inclusion of all outsiders. The psalm and Gospel passages draw on imagery of the king and his enthronement. For the psalmist, the king's power and longevity must serve the purpose of the people's good. The magi in Matthew are drawn by the light that marks the infant king's birth and thus begin the process of outsiders who see in the gospel the mystery of salvation.

Questions and Thoughts for Reflection

- Read Psalm 72:1-7; 10-14. How should we pray for our world's leaders? What is our responsibility in working for justice and righteousness in our world today?

- Read Isaiah 60:1-6. Where have you seen evidence of God's presence? How has God used you as a light to dispel darkness?

- Read Matthew 2:1-12. How do you respond when people ask you spiritual questions? In what ways have you sought the Lord and been sensitive to God's guidance?

- Read Ephesians 3:1-12. How has God blessed you beyond your perceived boundaries?

Associate minister, New Paradigm Christian Church, Broadripple area of Indianapolis, Indiana

All eyes were focused on Washington, DC. Rick Warren prayed; Aretha Franklin sang; and Barack Obama was sworn in as the forty-fourth president of the United States—an exciting and historic day for America. All manner of opinions, hopes, and dreams swirled in the echoes of a campaign that had been touted as hope personified.

The occasion does not differ that much in ancient Israel as the country crowns a new king. The event brings pomp and circumstance, parades and dancing, as well as shouts of joy and dreams of another great king like David.

The king serves as God's representative, bringing *God's* justice and righteousness to the land. The people pray for justice, righteousness, and prosperity for the land. The justice they pray for will be realized when the poor and needy receive the care that meets God's desired standards. It will be a world where everyone has enough and no one is overlooked. The righteousness that fulfills their prayers comes when the king ensures a life lived in accordance with God's will.

The psalm moves from the health of the king to the health of the community. The king, embodying God's attributes, delivers, has pity, saves, and redeems. Israel knows that leadership that honors justice and righteousness will please God and bring them peace and prosperity. The weak and needy, desperate for rescue, are seen as precious, and their ultimate king will never forget them.

Lord, may we pray for our leaders and, in so doing, become leaders ourselves. Amen.

We have to be careful with the weight of the world's burdens. They grow heavier as we watch the news, which reminds us of the world's brokenness. The bad news seems never to end, and the good news is barely sprinkled in like salt in the diet of a friend with hypertension. But more than the news drags us down. We struggle with the promises that never seem to come true. We find it hard to wait on God, while acknowledging that everything will be all right without our being in charge.

I cannot imagine what it would have been like to return from exile and find my home city in ruins and the people who had remained there destitute and hopeless. Darkness and gloom surround Jerusalem and the chosen people of God. But, into that darkness, the word of God erupts through the prophet: "Arise, shine, for your light has come, and the glory of the LORD rises upon you. See, darkness covers the earth and thick darkness is over the peoples, but the LORD rises upon you and his glory appears over you" (NIV).

The "glory of the LORD" refers to God's very presence. It has burst on the scene, and everything is changing. The people of the world will take notice, and God will provide for the chosen people through their own hands. God will bring their long-lost and loved exiles back home while providing for their needs and conveying restoration from the farthest reaches of the world. Cue the magi from stage right. As the necessities for the fulfillment of prophecies arrive, we watch in amazement while our hearts thrill and swell with joy.

Help us, Lord, to rise and shine and never stop looking for your provision as it approaches—and to become that provision for others. Amen.

Centuries before the writing of this Gospel, Jerusalem fell to the Babylonians and the Israelites found themselves exiled in a land far from home. As the faithful Israelites recounted God's faithfulness to their ancestors, their captors could not help but take notice. Traces of their faith remained in the East. Indeed, some interpreters have stated that Judaism's impact on the East was significant enough to color today's narrative. The magi would have seen the star in the sky, recalled the ancient Hebrew prophecies of a future king, and set out toward Jerusalem, gifts in tow—contributing characters on the eternal stage.

The star disappears as the wise men arrive in Jerusalem. Perhaps to them it seems that divine providence has run out. They come to Jerusalem to inquire, "Where is the one who has been born king of the Jews?" Their inquiry makes King Herod raise the same question: "Where" will the Christ child be born? His religious leaders rattle off the prophecy from Micah and return to their day jobs. King Herod is simply rattled.

Prophecy in mind, the wise men, with the gift of the distance of perspective, journey on to the little town of Bethlehem. The star reappears as the heavens bear witness that God never falls short on guidance. It stops over the place where Jesus lies.

When the magi arrive and see Jesus, they have no choice but to worship. They offer gifts that seem less fitting for a child. Those gifts, however, give a different type of provision. The child and his family will require rescue from King Herod who has given only lip service and will eventually kill all male children age two and under in an attempt to remove the disturbance of a God who keeps age-old promises. Herod tries to stop God's promise; the religious leaders ignore it; but the faithful from the past, present, and future know that God always provides.

Lord, help us always keep our hearts tuned to an eternal perspective. Amen.

We live a storied existence but often forget how God weaves those stories together. Jesus' birth fleshes out biblical prophecies, and history forever changes. Jewish people were storytellers who passed on oral traditions. They knew their prophets; they anticipated messiah. But some Jewish leaders had failed to connect the plot points between prophetic utterance and the birth of the Christ.

The magi, however, seem more in tune with events and are heavily invested in the acts of the present moment. They seek an answer with head and heart. They ask the questions that need to be asked and listen intently to the answers as well as to their dreams. They respond to God's invitation to follow. With sincerity they persist in their search, guided by God. I have always been fascinated by the word *overjoyed* (NIV) and how it describes their emotions at the star's reappearance.

When the wise men see Mary and Jesus, they fall down and worship, even though they do not fully understand the event. They offer their expensive gifts, probably never realizing anything beyond the fact that gold is a fitting gift for a king. Do they know that the priests used frankincense in Temple worship, thus signifying Jesus' priesthood? And might they have fathomed that priests employed myrrh in anointing oil and for burials?

The wise men follow a mystery to its conclusion, going home by another way. Do they hear the walls of division crumbling as they return home?

May we be overjoyed and lost in the story, worshiping the Author who still writes the greatest stories ever told. May we patiently await their resolutions.

All creation has gifts to offer when it comes to beauty and wonder, but I believe the American West has a unique beauty. I can ride through the expanses of Kansas and head out toward the high deserts of Nevada or New Mexico, and the boundless nature of the space that unfolds before me invites my wondering and dreaming. It calls me to broader thinking and beckons my spirit to soar and my mind to create. The stories almost write themselves as the pictures shift endlessly with the sunlight that invades and fades on the canyon walls.

The apostle Paul became a servant of the gospel by God's grace that was given to him in power. It would have been hard to forget the bright light, the voice, being blind for three days, and not eating while being set straight on Straight Street. He never forgot how far he had come—from breathing murderous threats against the Lord's disciples to preaching the boundless riches of Christ that includes the Gentiles.

Paul speaks of the present revelation of God's mystery, which addresses the expansive nature of God's gift in Jesus Christ: "The Gentiles have become fellow heirs, members of the same body, and sharers in the promise in Christ Jesus." This revelation has broadened Paul's mind, enabling a spiritual soaring that goes far beyond the early church's understanding of the gospel message!

Perhaps we too have experienced the boundless riches of Christ that are now apparent in our lives. We affirm that God's provision is always more than, greater than, and beyond. All— Gentiles and Jews alike—share in the extravagant, endless inheritance of the saints.

Gracious God, may we ever search the boundless riches of Christ. Amen.

My youth minister strummed his guitar and sang his own lyrics, "The sun burst orange-yellow-red, lighting caverns in my head." When I watch sunrises and sunsets those words often slip into my mind and aid my wonder. They have also snuck up on me today as I have meditated on the "manifold wisdom" (v. 10, NIV) of God. The word translated "manifold" is used only here in the Greek New Testament and can be defined as variegated or many-colored.

Paul notes that "the mystery" revealed to him is now revealed to holy apostles and prophets—those who proclaim God's word. So let the word go forth: In God's wisdom, Jews and Gentiles are now unified in one body with Christ. The church in its proclamation makes God's wisdom known. We become part of a local, global, and even cosmic witness to God's glory.

As we find ourselves forgiven through Christ, we receive free and confident access to God here—now and forever. Through Jesus Christ, we "have access to God in boldness and confidence through faith in him." In boldness we speak without regard to consequences, and we draw near to God through Jesus Christ. We become God's wisdom for those whom we can see, as well as for those whom we will never see on this side of the veil. Our relationship with God through Christ rearranges and recreates our world. As we live out God's message, the sun bursts orange-yellow-red while the blues, greens, indigos, and violets dance on the universal stage through our witness and reveal God's wisdom for all creation.

May we both *be* and *see* the provision of God's manifold wisdom.

How has God used you to show divine wisdom to others?

The Revised Common Lectionary* for 2016
Year C – Advent / Christmas Year A
(Disciplines Edition)

January 1–3
NEW YEAR'S DAY
Ecclesiastes 3:1-13
Psalm 8
Revelation 21:1-6a
Matthew 25:31-46

January 6
EPIPHANY
Isaiah 60:1-6
Psalm 72:1-7, 10-14
Ephesians 3:1-12
Matthew 2:1-12

January 4–10
BAPTISM OF THE LORD
Isaiah 43:1-7
Psalm 29
Acts 8:14-17
Luke 3:15-17, 21-22

January 11–17
Isaiah 62:1-5
Psalm 36:5-10
1 Corinthians 12:1-11
John 2:1-11

January 18–24
Nehemiah 8:1-3, 5-6, 8-10
Psalm 19
1 Corinthians 12:12-31
Luke 4:14-21

January 25–31
Jeremiah 1:4-10
Psalm 71:1-6
1 Corinthians 13
Luke 4:21-30

February 1–7
TRANSFIGURATION
Exodus 34:29-35
Psalm 99
2 Corinthians 3:12–4:2
Luke 9:28-43

February 10
ASH WEDNESDAY
Joel 2:1-2, 12-17 or
  Isaiah 58:1-12
Psalm 51:1-17
2 Corinthians 5:20b–6:10
Matthew 6:1-6, 16-21

February 8–14
FIRST SUNDAY IN LENT
Deuteronomy 26:1-11
Psalm 91:2, 9-16
Romans 10:8b-13
Luke 4:1-13

February 15–21
SECOND SUNDAY IN LENT
Genesis 15:1-12, 17-18
Psalm 27
Philippians 3:17–4:1
Luke 13:31-35

February 22–28
THIRD SUNDAY IN LENT
Isaiah 55:1-9
Psalm 63:1-8
1 Corinthians 10:1-13
Luke 13:1-9

February 29–March 6
FOURTH SUNDAY IN LENT
Joshua 5:9-12
Psalm 32
2 Corinthians 5:16-21
Luke 15:1-3, 11b-32

March 7–13
FIFTH SUNDAY IN LENT
Isaiah 43:16-21
Psalm 126
Philippians 3:4b-14
John 12:1-8

March 14–20
PALM/PASSION SUNDAY

Liturgy of the Palms
Psalm 118:1-2, 19-29
Luke 19:28-40

Liturgy of the Passion
Isaiah 50:4-9a
Psalm 31:9-16
Philippians 2:5-11
Luke 22:14–23:56

March 21–27
HOLY WEEK

Monday
Isaiah 42:1-9
Psalm 36:5-11
Hebrews 9:11-15
John 12:1-11

Tuesday
Isaiah 49:1-7
Psalm 71:1-14
1 Corinthians 1:18-31
John 12:20-36

Wednesday
Isaiah 50:4-9a
Psalm 70
Hebrews 12:1-3
John 13:21-32

Maundy Thursday
Exodus 12:1-14
Psalm 116:1-4, 12-19
1 Corinthians 11:23-26
John 13:1-17, 31b-35

Good Friday
Isaiah 52:13–53:12
Psalm 22
Hebrews 4:14-16; 5:7-9
John 18:1–19:42

Holy Saturday
Job 14:1-14
Psalm 31:1-4, 15-16
1 Peter 4:1-8
Matthew 27:57-66

Easter
Acts 10:34-43
Psalm 118:1-2, 14-24
1 Corinthians 15:19-26
John 20:1-18
Luke 24:1-12

March 28–April 3
Acts 5:27-32
Psalm 150
Revelation 1:4-8
John 20:19-31

April 4–10
Acts 9:1-6, 7-20
Psalm 30
Revelation 5:11-14
John 21:1-19

April 11–17
Acts 9:36-43
Psalm 23
Revelation 7:9-17
John 10:22-30

April 18–24
Acts 11:1-18
Psalm 148
Revelation 21:1-6
John 13:31-35

April 25–May 1
Acts 16:9-15
Psalm 67
Revelation 21:10, 22–22:5
John 14:23-29

May 2–8
Acts 16:16-34
Psalm 97
Revelation 22:12-14, 16-17, 20-21
John 17:20-26

> **May 5**
> ASCENSION DAY
> Acts 1:1-11
> Psalm 47
> Ephesians 1:15-23
> Luke 24:44-53

May 9–15
PENTECOST
Acts 2:1-21
Psalm 104:24-34, 35b
Romans 8:14-17
John 14:8-17, 25-27

May 16–22
TRINITY SUNDAY
Proverbs 8:1-4, 22-31
Psalm 8
Romans 5:1-5
John 16:12-15

May 23–29
1 Kings 18:20-39
Psalm 96
Galatians 1:1-12
Luke 7:1-10

May 30–June 5
1 Kings 17:8-24
Psalm 146
Galatians 1:11-24
Luke 7:11-17

June 6–12
1 Kings 21:1-21a
Psalm 5:1-8
Galatians 2:15-21
Luke 7:36–8:3

June 13–19
1 Kings 19:1-15a
Psalm 42
Galatians 3:23-29
Luke 8:26-39

June 20–26
2 Kings 2:1-2, 6-14
Psalm 77:1-2, 11-20
Galatians 5:1, 13-25
Luke 9:51-62

June 27–July 3
2 Kings 5:1-14
Psalm 30
Galatians 6:1-16
Luke 10:1-11, 16-20

July 4–10
Amos 7:7-17
Psalm 82
Colossians 1:1-14
Luke 10:25-37

July 11–17
Amos 8:1-12
Psalm 52 *or* Psalm 82
Colossians 1:15-28
Luke 10:38-42

July 18–24
Hosea 1:2-10
Psalm 85
Colossians 2:6-19
Luke 11:1-13

July 25–31
Hosea 11:1-11
Psalm 107:1-9, 43
Colossians 3:1-11
Luke 12:13-21

August 1–7
Isaiah 1:1, 10-20
Psalm 50:1-8, 22-23
Hebrews 11:1-3, 8-16
Luke 12:32-40

August 8–14
Isaiah 5:1-7
Psalm 80:1-2, 8-19
Hebrews 11:29–12:2
Luke 12:49-56

August 15–21
Jeremiah 1:4-10
Psalm 71:1-6
Hebrews 12:18-29
Luke 13:10-17

August 22–28
Jeremiah 2:4-13
Psalm 81:1, 10-16
Hebrews 13:1-8, 15-16
Luke 14:1, 7-14

August 29–September 4
Jeremiah 18:1-11
Psalm 139:1-6, 13-18
Philemon 1-21
Luke 14:25-33

September 5–11
Jeremiah 4:11-12, 22-28
Psalm 14
1 Timothy 1:12-17
Luke 15:1-10

September 12–18
Jeremiah 8:18–9:1
Psalm 79:1-9 *or* Psalm 4
1 Timothy 2:1-7
Luke 16:1-13

September 19–25
Jeremiah 32:1-3*a*, 6-15
Psalm 91:1-6, 14-16
1 Timothy 6:6-19
Luke 16:19-31

September 26–October 2
Lamentations 1:1-6
Psalm 137
2 Timothy 1:1-14
Luke 17:5-10

October 3–9
Jeremiah 29:1, 4-7
Psalm 66:1-12
2 Timothy 2:8-15
Luke 17:11-19

October 10
THANKSGIVING DAY CANADA
Deuteronomy 26:1-11
Psalm 100
Philippians 4:4-9
John 6:25-35

October 10–16
Jeremiah 31:27-34
Psalm 119:97-104 *or* Psalm 19
2 Timothy 3:14–4:5
Luke 18:1-8

October 17–23
Joel 2:23-32
Psalm 65
2 Timothy 4:6-8, 16-18
Luke 18:9-14

October 24–30
Habakkuk 1:1-4; 2:1-4
Psalm 119:137-144
2 Thessalonians 1:1-4, 11-12
Luke 19:1-10

November 1
ALL SAINTS DAY
Daniel 7:1-3, 15-18
Psalm 149 *or* Psalm 150
Ephesians 1:11-23
Luke 6:20-31

October 31–November 6
Haggai 1:15b–2:9
Psalm 145:1-5, 17-21
2 Thessalonians 2:1-5, 13-17
Luke 20:27-38

November 7–13
Isaiah 65:17-25
Isaiah 12 *or* Psalm 118
2 Thessalonians 3:6-13
Luke 21:5-19

November 14–20
THE REIGN OF CHRIST
Jeremiah 23:1-6
Luke 1:68-79
Colossians 1:11-20
Luke 23:33-43

November 21–27
FIRST SUNDAY OF ADVENT
Isaiah 2:1-5
Psalm 122
Romans 13:11-14
Matthew 24:36-44

November 24
THANKSGIVING DAY, USA
Deuteronomy 26:1-11
Psalm 100
Philippians 4:4-9
John 6:25-35

November 28–December 4
SECOND SUNDAY OF ADVENT
Isaiah 11:1-10
Psalm 72:1-7, 18-19
Romans 15:4-13
Matthew 3:1-12

December 5–11
THIRD SUNDAY OF ADVENT
Isaiah 35:1-10
Luke 1:47-55
Psalm 146:5-10
James 5:7-10
Matthew 11:2-11

December 12–18
FOURTH SUNDAY OF ADVENT
Isaiah 7:10-16
Psalm 80:1-7, 17-19
Romans 1:1-7
Matthew 1:18-25

December 19–25
Isaiah 52:7-10
Psalm 98
Hebrews 1:1-12
John 1:1-14

> **December 24**
> CHRISTMAS EVE
> Isaiah 9:2-7
> Psalm 96
> Titus 2:11-14
> Luke 2:1-20

December 26–31
Isaiah 60:1-6
Psalm 72:1-7, 10-14
Ephesians 3:1-12
Matthew 2:1-12

A Guide to Daily Prayer

These prayers imply worship time with a group; feel free to adapt the plural pronouns for personal use.

MORNING PRAYER

"In the morning, O LORD, you hear my voice;
　　in the morning I lay my requests before you
　　and wait in expectation."
—Psalm 5:3

Gathering and Silence

Call to Praise and Prayer
God said: Let there be light; and there was light.
And God saw that the light was good.

Psalm 63:2-6

God, my God, you I crave;
my soul thirsts for you,
my body aches for you
like a dry and weary land.
　　Let me gaze on you in your temple:
　　a Vision of strength and glory
　　Your love is better than life,
　　my speech is full of praise.
　　I give you a lifetime of worship,
　　my hands raised in your name.
　　I feast at a rich table
　　my lips sing of your glory.

Prayer of Thanksgiving

We praise you with joy, loving God, for your grace is better than life itself. You have sustained us through the darkness: and you bless us with life in this new day. In the shadow of your wings we sing for joy and bless your holy name. Amen.

Scripture Reading

Silence

Prayers of the People

The Lord's Prayer (see Midday Prayer for text)

Blessing

May the light of your mercy shine brightly on all who walk in your presence today, O Lord.

"I will extol the LORD at all times;
 God's praise will always be on my lips."
—Psalm 34:1

Gathering and Silence

Call to Praise and Prayer

O LORD, my Savior, teach me your ways.
 My hope is in you all day long.

Prayer of Thanksgiving

God of mercy, we acknowledge this midday pause
of refreshment as one of your many generous gifts.
Look kindly upon our work this day; may it be made
perfect in your time. May our purpose and prayers
be pleasing to you. This we ask through Christ our
Lord. Amen.

Scripture Reading

Silence

Prayers of the People

The Lord's Prayer (ecumenical text)

Our Father in heaven,
 hallowed be your name,
 your kingdom come,
 your will be done,
 on earth as in heaven.
Give us today our daily bread.
Forgive us our sins as we forgive
 those who sin against us.

Save us from the time of trial,
and deliver us from evil.
For the kingdom, the power, and the glory
are yours, now and forever. Amen.

Blessing

Strong is the love embracing us, faithful the Lord from morning to night.

"My soul finds rest in God alone;
my salvation comes from God."
—Psalm 62:1

Gathering and Silence

Call to Praise and Prayer

From the rising of the sun to its setting,
let the name of the LORD be praised.

Psalm 134

Bless the Lord,
all who serve in God's house,
who stand watch
throughout the night.

Lift up your hands
in the holy place
and bless the Lord.

And may God,
the maker of earth and sky,
bless you from Zion.

Prayer of Thanksgiving

Sovereign God, You have been our help during the day and you promise to be with us at night. Receive this prayer as a sign of our trust in you. Save us from all evil, keep us from all harm, and guide us in your way. We belong to you, Lord. Protect us by the power of your name, in Jesus Christ we pray. Amen.

Scripture Reading

Silence

Prayers of the People

The Lord's Prayer (see Midday Prayer for text)

Blessing

> May your unfailing love rest upon us, O LORD,
> even as we hope in you.

This Guide to Prayer was compiled from scripture and other resources by Rueben P. Job and then adapted by the Pathways Center for Spiritual Leadership while under the direction of Marjorie J. Thompson.

CPSIA information can be obtained at www.ICGtesting.com
Printed in the USA
LVOW10s0836151215

466674LV00001B/1/P